great dishes

from New Jersey's Favorite Restaurants

rutgers university press

NEW BRUNSWICK, NEW JERSEY

great dishes

from New Jersey's
Favorite Restaurants

vicki j. caparulo
photography by steve caparulo

FOREWORD BY ARTHUR SCHWARTZ

LIBRARY OF CONGRESS CATOLOGUING-IN-PUBLICATION DATA

Caparulo, Vicki J., 1949–

Great dishes from New Jersey's favorite restaurants / Vicki J.
Caparulo ; with photography by Steve Caparulo.

    p. cm.

Includes index.

  ISBN 0-8135-3311-2 (hardcover : alk. paper)

1. Cookery—New Jersey. 2. Restaurants—New Jersey—Guidebooks. I.
Title.

  TX714.C367 2003

  641.59749—dc21   2003005941

British Cataloging-in-Publication data for this book is available from the British Library

Designed and composed by Kevin Hanek
Set in FF Scala

Manufactured in China

The publication program of Rutgers University is supported by the Board of Governors
of Rutgers, the State University of New Jersey.

When the time came to consider the dedication of this book, we each privately wrote something and then shared what we'd written with the other. They were nearly identical. So we decided to combine and share with you our "love notes" and dedicate this book to each other.

To my partner, in life and in love . . .

"It just keeps getting better.

"We've worked side by side for all of our lives together, in one way or another, in one pursuit or another. You learn a lot about someone when you're not only married but also spend 7 days a week and most of the 24 hours in a day together.

"This book, one thing in a long list of things we have done together, was started as a new adventure. It has been an amazing and incredible journey, peppered with steep learning curves and new plateaus, but I have really enjoyed the ride and have been rewarded with another accomplishment of which I am very proud.

"I am endlessly awed by your ability to continually grow, attempt and conquer something new, and excel at it. To my biggest cheerleader, I love you.

And I love you, too."

contents

restaurant guide by region

NORTH

Il Villaggio
651 Route 17 North
Carlstadt, NJ 07072
201/935-7733

Il Tulipano
1131 Pompton Avenue
Cedar Grove, NJ 07009
973/256-9300

Scalini Fedeli
63 Main Street
Chatham, NJ 07928
973/701-9200

A Taste of Asia
245 Main Street
Chatham, NJ 07928
973/701-8821

Amanda's
908 Washington Street
Hoboken, NJ 07030
201/798-0101

Jocelyne's
168 Maplewood Avenue
Maplewood, NJ 07040
973/763-4460

The Grand Café
42 Washington Street
Morristown, NJ 07960
973/540-9444

Pierre's Bistro Restaurant
995 Mount Kemble Avenue
Morristown, NJ 07960
973/425-1212

Esty Street
86 Spring Valley Road
Park Ridge, NJ 07656
201/307-1515

Café Panache
130 East Main Street
Ramsey, NJ 07446
201/934-0030

An American Grill
246 Route 10 West
Randolph, NJ 07869
973/442-9311

Café Matisse
167 Park Avenue
Rutherford, NJ 07070
201/935-2995

The Dining Room at
  the Short Hills Hilton
Hilton at Short Hills
41 JFK Parkway
Short Hills, NJ 07078
973/379-0100

Arthur's Landing at Port Imperial
Pershing Road
Weehawken, NJ 07086
201/867-4567

Highlawn Pavilion
Eagle Rock Reservation
Eagle Rock Avenue
West Orange, NJ 07052
973/731-3463

The Manor
111 Prospect Avenue
West Orange, NJ 07052
973/731-2360

Il Capriccio
633 Route 10 East
Whippany, NJ 07981
973/884-9175

great
dishes

x

CENTRAL

The Bernards Inn
27 Mine Brook Road
Bernardsville, NJ 07924
908/766-0002

Le Petit Chateau
121 Claremont Road
Bernardsville, NJ 07924
908/766-4544

Royal Thai
1700 Oaktree Road
Edison, NJ 08820
732/767-1263

The Frenchtown Inn
7 Bridge Street
Frenchtown, NJ 08825
908/996-3300

Rat's
Grounds for Sculpture
16 Fairgrounds Road
Hamilton, NJ 08619
609/584-7800

Old Man Rafferty's
284 Route 206
Hillsborough, NJ 08844
908/904-9731

Le Rendez-vous Bistro
520 Boulevard
Kenilworth, NJ 07033
908/931-0888

Anton's at the Swan
43 South Main Street
Lambertville, NJ 08530
609/397-1960

The Columbia Inn
29 Main Road (Route 202)
Montville, NJ 07045
973/263-1300

The Frog and the Peach
29 Dennis Street
New Brunswick, NJ 08901
732/846-3216

Old Man Rafferty's
106 Albany Street
New Brunswick, NJ 08901
732/846-6153

Panico's
103 Church Street
New Brunswick, NJ 08901
732/545-6100

SoHo on George
335 George Street
New Brunswick, NJ 08901
732/296-0533

The Perryville Inn
167 Perryville Road
Perryville, NJ 08827
908/730-9500

Nicholas
160 Highway 35
Red Bank, NJ 07701
732/345-9977

Harvest Moon Inn
1039 Old York Road
Ringoes, NJ 08551
908/806-6020

Fromagerie
26 Ridge Road
Rumson, NJ 07760
732/842-8088

Stage House Inn
366 Park Avenue
Scotch Plains, NJ 07076
908/322-4224

Black Forest Inn
249 Route 206 North
Stanhope, NJ 07874
973/347-3344

The Ryland Inn
Route 22 West
Whitehouse, NJ 08888
908/534-4011

SOUTH

Ram's Head Inn
9 West White Horse Pike
Absecon, NJ 08201
609/652-1700

Tre Figlio
500 West White Horse Pike
Egg Harbor City, NJ 08215
609/965-3303

Tre Piani
120 Rockingham Row
Princeton, NJ 08540
609/452-1515

Jeffrey's
73 Main Street
Toms River, NJ 08753
732/914-9544

Giumarello's
329 Haddon Avenue
Westmont, NJ 08108
856/858-9400

SHORE

Moonstruck
517 Lake Avenue
Asbury Park, NJ 07712
732/988-0123

The Ebbit Room
  at the Virginia Hotel
25 Jackson Street
Cape May, NJ 08204
609/884-5310

Mad Batter
Carroll Villa Hotel
19 Jackson Street
Cape May, NJ 08204
609/884-5970

Washington Inn
801 Washington Street
Cape May, NJ 08204
609/884-5697

Waters Edge
1317 Beach Drive
Cape May, NJ 08204
609/884-1717

Doris & Ed's
348 Shore Drive
Highlands, NJ 07732
732/872-1565

Casa Comida
336 Branchport Avenue
Long Branch, NJ 07740
732/229-7774

Joe & Maggie's Bistro on Broadway
591 Broadway
Long Branch, NJ 07740
732/571-8848

Kuishimbo
330 Ninety-sixth Street
Stone Harbor, NJ 08247
609/967-7007

Daniel's on Broadway
416 South Broadway
West Cape May, NJ 08204
609/898-8770

foreword by
arthur schwartz

I USED TO BE ONE OF those snobby, provincial New Yorkers who called my neighboring state *Joyzee*. My sister cringed when I did. And she would scold me. She moved to the Garden State more than twenty-five years ago, and although she had to admit that our . . . let me call it our "regional accent" was as prevalent on the other side of the Hudson as it was back in Brooklyn, she insisted that New Jersey was a decidedly different sort of place that deserved my respect and interest.

Now, after twelve years as a talk show host on WOR, the New York City radio station that New Jersey considers its own, I more than agree. In fact, I'll go further. I have become a New Jersey booster. It may be the most industrialized state in the union, but it is called the Garden State for a reason. Besides its verdant hills, meadows, and residential communities, it has great agriculture, which is the first requirement for good food, my special passion. Gastronomically it is a stellar state. It has everything that students of food culture consider requirements for great cuisine. Aside from wonderful locally grown ingredients—asparagus, tomatoes, corn, peaches, to name just the most obvious—it has an affluent, well-traveled, and well-educated populace that demands quality. It has incredible ethnic diversity, which guarantees variety and cosmopolitan flavor. And most of its people come from traditions that honor the kitchen and the culture of the table. New Jersey truly has everything: the stuff that great home cooking is made of, and restaurants ranging from beachside hot dog stands, through ethnic restaurants of every persuasion, and, as this book beautifully exemplifies, world-class dining rooms with kitchens manned by awesomely talented and accomplished chefs.

New Jersey is so impressive that I have taken it upon myself to start a campaign to have it recognized, culinarily speaking, as one of the fifty states of the nation and not just a suburb of New York City. Unfortunately, when it comes to food, the national press treats it as merely as an adjunct to the Big Apple. They'll extol the gastronomic glories of Minnesota, which has exactly seven good restaurants, but skip over the Garden State, which must have seventy.

Vicki and Steve Caparulo have captured the best of the best in New Jersey, with, respectively, recipes that exemplify the particular style of the state's most impressive restaurants, and photographs that will make you want to run into the kitchen and prepare them—or, at least, get on the phone and make a reservation.

The Caparulos are uniquely suited to the task they've taken on for themselves. Vicki is an accomplished cooking teacher (a former president of the New York Association of Culinary Professionals) and, from my long experience as a cookbook critic, I can tell you that cooking teachers write the best recipes. As a relative newcomer to the teaching field, I've learned why: it's the students. They ask questions, they demand to know details of technique, specifics of preparation that no chef in a restaurant is even aware that he does. Hold your thumb this way when you peel. Grasp the knife like this. Look for this signpost—the foam will disappear on the top of a stove-top custard—or that the meat will take on the color of well-worn Coach wallet. Okay, so I exaggerate.

It's true, however, that a cooking teacher can go into a kitchen with a chef (not to mention a grandma who has never measured anything in her life) and come out with a recipe that anyone can make at home. A cooking teacher also knows which restaurant recipes are achievable by an amateur or basic home cook. This book is all about them.

Vicki and Steve are, I think, the only married couple in America who teach together. Certainly they are the only one in New Jersey. As a team—in the kitchen and out—they compliment each other. Vicki talks. Steve is the strong, silent type without whose support and talent for keen observation (not to mention the more than occasional interjection) Vicki couldn't explain things as well as she does. In this book, he turns his great "eye" into a reality we can all see. His pictures of those finished plates of food are absolutely gorgeous.

Here's hoping this book of great food, delicious food, beautiful food, from New Jersey's favorite restaurants will give you, your family and friends much pleasure, but I also hope it establishes the Garden State as one of the best places to eat in the world. California Here I Come? Nah. New York State of Mind? There was a time I thought of New Jersey as the sixth borough. But no more.

Arthur Schwartz
Host, "Food Talk with Arthur Schwartz"
WOR-Radio, New York City

a word about the recipes . . .

RECIPES ARE MEANT to be guidelines—that's all—although admittedly, a guideline for someone who speaks kitchen shorthand will be significantly different than for one whose level of comfort is established by being able to find the cooking time on a pasta box.

Case in point:To communicate to a fellow pro last night's great treatment of something neat and seasonal that we found at the market, we might say, "I just cut it into a small dice, blanched it, browned off a mirepoix, deglazed with chix stock to sec, threw it in and slow braised it with resinous herbs. Good. Nice mouth feel." The chef would know exactly what we did, how we did it and for how long, and would also likely have a vision of the end result in his or her head, complete with smell, taste, and texture. Maybe you can see the pattern here—it's really all technique-driven.

But most people need more info—and because we're teachers, we know that. When we're working with something entirely new to us, we need more information too. So we hope we asked the right questions, those questions you would ask, maybe even some you might not think to ask, and answered them in recipe form before you had to wonder about them. We've tried to include multiple markers—what to look for, listen for, smell—as well as an idea of how long it will take to get there.

But again, it's important to keep in mind that recipes are only guidelines, an architecture, if you will. A good cook will use all five senses and then apply the sixth—common sense.

Linear thinking is not always the best way to go in the kitchen. If a recipe instructs to roast something in the oven for 20 minutes and it's on fire after 10, it is presumed that we do not stand facing the oven and count down the remaining time before making a move with a fire extinguisher to remove the incinerated carcass from the oven. Conversely, if after 20 minutes the food is ice cold and inedibly raw, we do not serve it. We use our sixth sense when it's called for and certainly when we're in doubt.

Bear in mind that the type and size of the cookware, the type of heat or cooking surface, the temperature of the food, the freshness of the food, and the size and consistency of the cuts all have a direct bearing on the length of time anything will take to cook. But the one thing that will always serve the cook well is to operate by using all five senses. If it smells burned, it probably is. If it's hot on the outside and ice cold when you cut into it, it probably needs further attention.

One of the first things we ask our students when we try to convey this concept and then see panic in their eyes is, "If you follow the instruction to 'add liquid and scrape up the browned bits' and you do so but DON'T hear 'szzzsszzzs,' what's wrong?" Inevitably, to a person, they all speak up: "The pan's not hot enough." And they smile, relax, and realize what we knew before we asked the question—you really KNOW much of this stuff. It's usually just a matter of paying attention to it.

Another pitfall you'll want to avoid is what we call "cooking by the paragraph." We've all done it. You begin a recipe and along about the third or fourth paragraph you get to the part where it says "Chill for twenty-four hours" and your guests are arriving in twenty minutes. Plan ahead, think ahead, and do ahead. It takes only a few minutes at a time. That's the way it's done in the restaurant.

Having said that, we should also note that restaurant food has several characteristics that define it as restaurant food versus typical home cooking—like high-end, hard-to-find, or unusual ingredients, extensive preparation before you even begin to "cook" it, equipment or technique that requires some knowledge or skill you didn't learn in HomeEc, when there *was* HomeEc, a walk-in refrigerator or limitless freezer space, endless time, more than the usual allotment of two hands, and so on. That's why you go out to eat it—if it was easy to do at home, if it required no unusual effort or had no unusual or focal point of interest, it wouldn't be special.

Some of these dishes will be easy and some will require concentrated effort, but whatever your approach, we've taken care to write each recipe in this book in a highly informational format so that just about anyone who is willing to attempt them can be successful.

We decided to develop all the recipes to serve two—for no other reason than it was one of the thrilling little decisions we two authors got to make, and we wanted you to be able to enjoy them as we did. All will scale up to serve more if that's your game plan—it's always nice to share.

And one last thought—with all due respect to the artists who use food as their medium, us included, in the end it's only food. Of all the kitchens we've worked in, we've never seen one without a garbage can. If you mess up, you have options—purée it, dump it onto pasta, add it to rice or top a toasted baguette with it and call it something else, or simply toss it. Pour yourself some cereal (and a glass of wine) or call out for pizza. It's only food—this isn't rocket science or neurosurgery, and it's not the end of the world. Everyone started at the beginning.

Keep in mind that tomorrow is a new day, and with it comes the promise of three more meals.

Vicki J. Caparulo, CCP
Food Writer, Recipe Developer,
Culinary Educator
Beauty and the Feast, Inc.

a word about the photography . . .

GIVEN THE NATURE of the project and the particular and individual characteristics of the locations involved, we felt it would have been an additional and burdensome imposition to invade the restaurants and kitchens with lights and other lighting equipment.

The photographs throughout this book were taken on location with only the use of a digital camera. No artificial or enhanced lighting was used; nor were the photographs manipulated with sophisticated software.

No food-styling techniques were employed, and, other than positioning items on a plate and without exception, the food was photographed exactly as it came off the line.

The food you see pictured here is simply the gorgeously edible artwork of the generous chefs of New Jersey's favorite restaurants. We hope it makes your mouth water.

Steve Caparulo, CCP
Food Photographer, Culinary Educator
Beauty and the Feast, Inc.

acknowledgments

OURS MAY BE the names on the cover, but we did not create this book alone—far from it. We have so many people to thank, people who have contributed to us personally, professionally, privately, and publicly in so many ways, people who contributed to our ability to take on and complete this project, people who have helped us along our career paths, knowingly or not.

We know this is only a partial list and a token attempt to thank:

The owners, chefs, staff, and families of New Jersey's favorite restaurants

We have long felt that New Jersey deserves to be recognized as home to some of the finest chefs and restaurants on the East Coast and not just as a "side dish" of the Big Apple.

Our toques are off to you, the wonderful people who make New Jersey the outstanding culinary resource it is, and to those who enjoy and appreciate its good food and good service.

Arthur Schwartz

. . . for his friendship and support of us personally and professionally, his culinary wisdom and skill as an educator, and his dedication to the mission of showcasing the culinary resources of the great state of New Jersey. *Mille grazie, Turo!*

Joanne Szibdat

. . . New Jersey's best restaurant and chef marketing and promotion pro, to whom we're eternally grateful for the "royal flush!"

Marlie Wasserman

. . . our gifted editor, for her vision, faith, flexibility, and patience, for exercising her sense of adventure, and for her contagious excitement. We hope your nails have grown back!

The Publication Staff at Rutgers University Press

Nicole Manganaro, Anne Hegeman, Michele Gisbert, Jessica Pellien, Lisa Gillard Hanson— How did we get this lucky? If we set out to gather up a great group of literary foodies, all with a sense of humor and a willingness to work outside the lunchbox, we couldn't have come up with a better, more collaborative group. You guys are the "A" team!

David Martone

. . . for sending Marlie Wasserman, our beloved editor (and therefore the idea for this book), in our direction.

The Culinary Schools throughout the United States

. . . in which we are proud to teach, because every time we teach we learn.

Anita and Karsten Dierk

. . . twice . . . for the condensed but colorful course on who's who and what's what in Cape May and for your gracious hospitality in allowing us to share and enjoy your beautiful home and B&B, The Manse.

And an extra special thanks because they're extra special people in our lives . . .

Our Children

Kerry, Eric and Celeste, Sena and Joe, Sasha and Jeremy, Tara and Jake, for their understanding and patience when we were not so readily available (or not too much fun when we were) during the time it took to put this project together, and for their help and support in the many ways they so generously gave it. Kids don't come better than you; nor could they possibly be loved more.

Our Sibs

. . . the one who taught us less is more (sorry the understanding of the "garlic" part of that was so unfortunately extended), the one who taught us to practice economy of motion, the ones who think we walk on water (at least in the kitchen), the ones who allowed us to experiment on them, their friends, their kids, their friends' kids, and their kids' friends. We love you guys. Really.

. . . and to the mothers who inspired us, one way or the other, whether that was the plan or not—we're grateful because we otherwise wouldn't be doing what we love.

Chuck Zoccola

. . . our dear and longtime friend and the most selflessly giving and generous human being on the planet. Thanks for all the encouragement and assistance with this project, for lending us your experience and expertise in the fields of art and imagery and for your sound, honest advice—and for loving us as much as we love you. It is inconceivable that any three people can eat so much fat in one sitting and laugh so hard, so continually, and not die from doing it.

introduction

To invite a person to your house is to take charge of his happiness as long as he is under your roof.

— BRILLAT-SAVARIN

WITH ALL DUE RESPECT and an affectionate nod to our colleagues in the many fine restaurants of nearby New York City and Philadelphia, in our opinion there's no reason to ever leave New Jersey. And that's why we wrote this book.

We should begin by stressing that we are not restaurant reviewers. Those hardworking journalists who dedicate their lives and waistlines in service of the restaurant-going public, attending to the painful and exhaustive job of eating their way through three meals a day and then writing about it, have our greatest respect. It's a dirty job, but someone's got to do it. In truth, it's a huge responsibility and one we don't envy.

First and foremost, we should establish that we've never met a food group we didn't like, and we adore all foods in most of their permutations.

I'm a recipe developer, but Steve and I both love to play with our food, and it just gets better for us when we can share that, which is why we're also cooking teachers, traveling and teaching in dozens of great cooking schools throughout the country.

As a food photographer, Steve's found yet another way to share the fun and beauty of great food, and together we hope you will keep picking up this book, using, reading, and enjoying it, again and again.

The idea here is not to attempt to replicate the restaurant experience at home. That's simply not possible—nor should it be. A restaurant is the sum of its parts. The restaurant dining experience is a treat, a full-body, five-senses experience when it's done right. Leave it to the experts to do what they do best, and you do your part and enjoy it for what it's meant to be.

Chef, service, cuisine, decor, ambience—they all come together (or they don't) to make the whole experience. Take away one component and the whole changes—sometimes for better, sometimes not. But one truth we hold to be self-evident is that no one sets out to make a bad meal or cause a bad experience.

And that's what this book is about. It's a love letter to the amazing chefs, restaurateurs, and culinary resources of the great state of New Jersey first—but it's also a cookbook with recipes for great dishes from New Jersey's favorite restaurants deconstructed and reconstructed so that you can prepare them successfully at home.

THE RESTAURANTS

The restaurants that are featured in this book were actually chosen by YOU. They are those that year after year win accolades for being the best at what they do from those who know best—the discerning, restaurant-going public.

There were many times when we asked ourselves why we agreed to do this book, but in the end we're very glad we did. Along the way we met an amazing breed of people, in some cases entire families, and received a most profound education in what it means to own, run, and work in a successful restaurant—the business of hospitality.

Here's something to think about: If you were offered two careers—one reasonably secure with a comfortable working environment, in which you'd have nights, weekends, and holidays to yourself and time to spend with your family, control over things like career growth, and the potential to earn better income; or one in which you're working in frenzied, tight quarters in temperatures over a hundred degrees for twelve to sixteen hours a day, six days a week, including nights, weekends, and holidays when other people are not, and your job easily could be here today and, at the whim of its public, a down-turned economy, or an order of bad or spoiled food, gone tomorrow—which would you choose?

For some, it's no contest—it's the restaurant industry because it's their passion and there's just no other place they'd want to be.

How do they do it and maintain their quality of life at the same time? That was a question we asked everyone we worked with on this project. The answers varied slightly but pretty much boiled down to balance and the concentrated, conscious effort to achieve it with the help of supportive and understanding spouses and children, as well as inviolable time off—not much time off, but whatever it is, it's set in stone.

The restaurant business attracts a certain kind of person, a creative and giving person who thrives on sharing, who derives inspiration, pleasure, and rewards from food service and hospitality. If those people are lucky, they attract a like person, one who understands their motivation and builds the rest of his or her world around it. It's a tough business and one that requires the innate passion that fuels it.

This is a special breed of people, supported and loved by a special breed of people. We give them our absolute admiration and respect for their ability to do what they do and to do it so well at such great personal sacrifice.

An interesting note—we would have been happy to find a girl in the group, but all we came across were boys named "Sous." Food for thought . . .

HOW IT WORKS IN RESTAURANTS . . . AND WHY IT DOESN'T AT HOME

It's the BIG things that count—huge ovens, multiple burners with major firepower, a limitless selection of pans, endless freezer space, speed racks to hold equipment and plated salads and desserts and walk-in refrigerators large enough to wheel them into and still have room left for a table for pastry work.

It's also the LITTLE things that count—mandolines, squirt bottles filled with all kinds of neat sauces and oil infusions, ring molds, pasta pentolas, an eclectic variety of herbs and spices at your fingertips and a limitless supply of kitchen towels.

It also doesn't hurt to be able to pick up the phone, spit out a wish list of great ingredients, and have it delivered to your kitchen door.

But it's not the kitchen that makes the cook. You DO need good-quality, well-maintained equipment, even though we've taught bread baking in a hotel conference room with no running water and also turned out some great food on a portable burner in the middle of a bookstore.

One of our acid tests of whether cooks are worth their salt is when they step into our forty-five-square-foot, two-tushy kitchen. We know they know what they're doing when, instead of remarking on its diminutive size, the first thing they notice is how clean, well equipped, and well laid out it is, with everything within easy reaching distance.

SET YOURSELF UP FOR SUCCESS

If there's any one thing that sets professional cooking apart from home cooking, it's probably the support work that is done before the first burner gets lit—the *mise en place*. This is the prep, the chef's palette, the stash of already cleaned, trimmed, chopped-up ingredients that allows a chef to grab a pinch of this or a handful of that and create fabulous food on the fly.

The mise en place isn't effortless and doesn't appear magically—someone has to do it. At home, that someone is likely you. That's okay—if you plan ahead and do a little bit here and a little bit there, it becomes manageable. Some jobs, like washing greens, squeezing lemon juice, or measuring out flour or sugar or all the ingredients for baking, can be done days in advance as time allows.

Chaos promotes anxiety, and cooking creatively is supposed to be fun. Having our *mise en place* complete before we begin—and that includes the pots, pans, their lids, the utensils, platters, and anything else we think we'll need—keeps the anxiety level down and the enjoyment level where it should be. It's not fun to smell the garlic burning while you're rooting around beneath the sink looking for the lid to the pan.

And this brings us to the why and wherefore of how we have formatted the recipes. When we cook at home, we bridge the gap between preparing these dishes in a restaurant kitchen and preparing them in a home kitchen by organizing and prioritizing—the tasks, the ingredients, and the timing—and this is the way we've set it up for you.

Beginning with the mise en place, the ingredients are grouped and titled in accordance with the specific component of the dish in which they're used. If special or particular equipment is needed, that list follows the ingredients list. The recipes are sectioned by task—each one is titled and the instruction relative to it follows—and we hope you'll be pleased by the many do-ahead tips that appear interspersed throughout.

Sometimes the recipe will be preceded by a chef's *truc*. A *truc* is culinary lingo for "kitchen trick," and we hope they educate you and delight you as well as make your work in the kitchen more fun and easier.

Like you, we don't have a kitchen staff of dishwashers, either. So we keep a hefty supply of sealable freezer bags and disposable cups into which we place chopped-up, measured-out ingredients. Once we have our mise en place complete, we clean the kitchen—no one ever looks forward to leaving the table after a great meal to wash dishes. We pour a glass of great wine and only then do we begin to cook. We're calm, organized, and in the moment. That's when we're our most creative and have our most enjoyable kitchen experiences.

And one last bit of advice before you move on . . .

Don't allow yourself to be roadblocked by what you don't know! Life is (or should be) about reaching beyond your grasp. If there's a term you aren't familiar with or a task you've never done before, peruse "The Tools, the Terms, the Ingredients, and When to Use Them" and the "Procedures and Techniques" chapters. We ARE, after all, teachers . . .

ONE MORE WORD ABOUT RESTAURANTS

The great James Beard once said that his favorite restaurant is the one where they know him.

Considering that we were working with your favorite restaurants, we thought it might be interesting to ask the chefs where they go when they go out to eat. Their replies were:

"Where . . .

. . .I can be anonymous"
. . .they know me"
. . .my kids can be comfortable"
. . .I can feel comfortable bringing my kids"
. . .I can learn something"
. . .it's family-owned and hands-on"
. . .they really care"
. . .I get treated well"

Ditto, to all of the above, especially if it's in New Jersey!

great dishes
from New Jersey's Favorite Restaurants

restaurants and recipes

amanda's

908 Washington Street
Hoboken 07030
201/798-0101

HOBOKEN IS PRETTY FUNKY, with great browsing and terrifically interesting nooks and crannies to explore, and Amanda's is a reflection of its hometown. There are intimate little sitting areas throughout, beginning at the entrance, which houses the beautiful bar and through which you'll pass on your way to the charming outdoor garden. Upstairs and adjacent to a central sunny

window room are several smaller dining areas, each with its own personality and all designed to backdrop giddy romance. Downstairs is a wine-cellar-style private dining area that reminded us of Italy, perfect for a small celebration or to host a private wining and dining experience exploring Amanda's outstanding wine list.

But in whichever room you dine, once you've met Joyce and Eugene Flinn (and if you're lucky, Sam and Celia, their gorgeous, bright, and personable children), it will be evident that the personalities reflected in the whimsical, romantic design are completely theirs. They're a beautiful couple, both with sparkling personalities and long, impressive restaurant and hospitality credentials. Keying into the hospitality, they also have plans to develop the residential upper floors into a bed and breakfast, and, with typical Flinn whimsy, they plan to call it the Little Inn on Washington Street.

Their treasured chef, Rodney Petersen, is a California find, motivated by the seasons and his own personal flavor logic. He excels at successfully incorporating interesting ingredients into cross-cultural renditions, as in the phyllo-wrapped Asian-style shrimp (recipe follows). General Manager Doug Yacka, aka the Cheese Whiz, has jumped onto the *fromagaissance*—the recently renewed interest in cheese—of America by offering a seasonally selected, European-style cheese service that we think pairs perfectly with his creatively infused spirits, like the tequila-pear or vodka-apple. They're tasty—have two—you can count them toward your five-a-day plan for fruits and vegetables.

Take note of Joyce's collection of unmatched "lay" plates at each place setting—they make for a great ice-breaker, and Amanda's makes for a great first-date place with someone you really want to get to know.

Phyllo-Wrapped Shrimp
WITH THAI SLAW AND SOY VINAIGRETTE

Kataiffi is phyllo dough that has been shredded into thin long strands, available frozen in Greek and Mediterranean markets (see the chapter "Resources"). A small amount of kataiffi can be cut away and thawed just for this recipe, but any extra can be pulled apart, tossed with clarified butter and sugar and finely chopped nuts, and baked into delicious crisps to top ice cream or garnish a custard. Thawed kataiffi can also be refrozen.

Mise en Place:

FOR THE SOY VINAIGRETTE:

1 tsp. finely grated ginger

Juice of 2 whole limes

2 T. rice wine vinegar

1 tsp. dark sesame oil

3 T. soy sauce

$^1/_2$ cup grapeseed oil

$1^1/_2$ T. light brown sugar

FOR THE SHRIMP:

About 2 ozs. kataiffi (shredded phyllo dough)

6 U-12 shrimp, shelled and deveined

Canola oil for deep-frying

FOR THE SLAW:

$^2/_3$ cup shredded Napa cabbage (Chinese cabbage)

$^1/_2$ cup fine julienne of carrots

2 T. fine julienne of red bell pepper

1 T. red onion cut paper-thin (use a mandoline)

1 T. chiffonade of cilantro (see the chapter "Procedures and Techniques")

1 T. thinly sliced scallion, cut diagonally, green and white part

1 tsp. minced jalapeño pepper

FOR GARNISH:

12 paper-thin slices English cucumber (use a mandoline)

Whole cilantro leaves and whole chives

Equipment:

Mandoline

Deep-fry thermometer

Prepare the Soy Vinaigrette: In a small bowl, whisk together the dressing ingredients. Set aside for 10 minutes for the flavors to develop and blend.

Prepare the Shrimp: Place a deep medium saucepan over medium-high heat and add canola oil for deep-frying to a depth of 3 inches, making sure the oil fills the pan by no more than half.

Pull apart the kataiffi and "comb" out the strands in one direction. Pinch off enough kataiffi to wrap a $^1/_2$-inch "band," like a cummerbund, around the middle of each shrimp.

When the oil reaches 375°F on a deep-fry thermometer, add the shrimp pieces, two or three at a time, and cook just until they turn pink and opaque and the kataiffi is golden, about 1 to 2 minutes. Set aside to drain on a cooling rack.

To Finish the Dish: In a medium bowl, toss the cabbage, carrots, bell pepper, red onions, cilantro, scallions, and jalapeño with the dressing.

To Plate: Place a circle of 6 overlapping cucumber slices on each of two plates.

Divide the slaw in half and mound it on top of the circles of cucumber. Place a shrimp on its side on top of the slaw and stand two shrimp, tails up, on top. Garnish with a couple of cilantro leaves and whole chives.

an american grill

246 Route 10 West

Randolph 07869

973/442-9311

CHEF-OWNER LOU REDA has lineage and experience, and it shows at An American Grill. The son of Frank Reda, owner of Il Villaggio and the Italian Chalet, Lou was busing tables at 14, serving at 18, bartending at 19, and managing the restaurants by the time he was 23. We were embryos at 23.

He's now not much older (or at least he doesn't look like it), and with the help of his extremely talented chef de cuisine, Fernando Corrente, whom Lou kidnapped from Il Villaggio, An American Grill is one of our favorite places to spend an evening eating great food paired with great wines. We also look forward to Lou's weekly TV show, *Classic Cooking*, which airs locally on Friday evenings.

The menu is eclectic, the specials are always innovative, and whether we're in the mood for interesting twists on chops, fish, or pasta or just for grazing and sampling a few of their vast selection of brews, it's guaranteed that each dish will have its own great personality. In fact, the specials are so distinct in their individual identity that each arrives on a unique plate!

Veal Chop

IN JACK DANIEL'S SAUCE

WITH WILD MUSHROOM RAVIOLI

Wild or porcini mushroom ravioli are widely available these days and work just fine for this dish, as does frozen commercial veal stock. Just be sure to slightly undercook and then shock the ravioli in ice water so they will be perfectly cooked when they're finished in the sauce.

On the addition of the Jack Daniel's, two things are extremely important—the liquor should be added to a hot pan, which, if you follow the instructions, will happen. (Alcohol ignites better when warmed.) However, be sure that the burner is TURNED OFF until AFTER the addition of the liquor. This is important because it is actually the fumes from the liquor that ignite, so despite careful aim and a good pouring arm, an open flame can ignite the whole mess in an uncontrollable way and long before you're ready for it!

And you have our permission to carefully measure out Jack Daniel's twice—the second one is for the cook.

Mise en Place:

FOR THE RAVIOLI:

12 prepared wild mushroom ravioli

Kosher salt for the pasta water

FOR THE VEAL CHOPS:

2 center-cut veal rib chops, 12 ozs. each

$1/4$ cup cracked black peppercorns

Salt

Flour for dusting chops

2 T. olive oil

FOR THE JACK DANIEL'S SAUCE:

2 peeled shallot lobes

$1/2$ tsp. salt

3 T. unsalted butter

$1/3$ cup Jack Daniel's whiskey

$1/3$ cup veal stock

Prepare the Ravioli: Prepare a large bowl of ice and water to shock the ravioli after cooking.

Bring a medium pot of cold water to a boil for the ravioli and add kosher salt. Add the ravioli to the boiling salted water and cook according to the package directions until almost tender. Scoop the ravioli into the ice bath to shock and stop the cooking process. Drain the ravioli well and set aside.

Prepare the Veal Chops: Preheat the oven to 425°F.

Place a dry heavy ovenproof skillet large enough to hold both chops without crowding over high heat. Press the black peppercorns onto one side of each chop, lightly salt and dust both sides with flour.

Add 2 tablespoons of olive oil to the hot pan, swirl to coat, and add the veal chops, peppercorn side down. Press the chops into the pan and place the pan into the hot oven to roast for 5 minutes. Turn the chops and continue to roast until they are cooked through to medium rare, about 6 to 8 minutes more. Remove the chops to a plate; season lightly with salt and pepper and lightly tent with foil to keep warm.

Prepare the Jack Daniel's Sauce: Pour off the oil and place the hot skillet on the stovetop; DO NOT IGNITE THE BURNER. Add the shallot lobes, salt, butter, and Jack Daniel's to the hot skillet and use a long match to carefully light the contents of the pan. Allow the flames to subside, ignite the burner and set to medium-high, and cook until the liquids are reduced by about half. Add the veal stock and continue to cook until the liquids are again reduced by about one-third.

Add the ravioli to the pan and toss in the sauce until heated through.

To Plate: Place a veal chop on each of two warmed plates, top with ravioli and sauce, and serve immediately.

anton's at the swan

43 South Main Street

Lambertville 08530

609/397-1960

www.antonsattheswan.com

DESPITE THE FACT that Anton's is situated in a historic building in a historic town, chef-owner Chris Connors's food is distinctly *real* today food—interestingly uncomplicated and well-executed combos that work perfectly by an unfussy guy with his feet on the ground.

Named for its founder, Anton Dodel, but defined by Chris Connors's straightforward and natural style, the restaurant has a great and loyal audience, maybe because it has something for everyone—outdoor dining in summer, rooms upstairs for private functions, and a lively and busy bar with a great grazing menu of its own, including the famous and fabulous Mashed Potato Pizza.

Chris trained in some of the best restaurants in the country and in many New Jersey hall-of-famers included in this book, which might be what has given him the confidence to remain true to his minimalist sensibilities. He buys as much as possible locally, cooks seasonally, and has moved away from ring molds, towering food, and up-ended ramekins in favor of natural presentations. Quite refreshing, we think!

Go antiquing in Lambertville or goofing around in New Hope, finish the day at Anton's—spend some quality time in the funky rest rooms—and don't miss the "gentlemen's bar" upstairs!

Soft-Shell Crab BLT Salad

Chef-owner Chris Connors uses freshly killed soft-shell crabs and good-quality applewood-smoked bacon for this salad; the clean flavors really shine through and make all the difference.

For the practical and intrepid, instructions on preparing the crabs can be found in the chapter "Procedures and Techniques." Just be sure to puncture the air bubble located behind the eyes and under the carapace—if you miss it, you'll know it when the bubble expands, pops in the pan, and sends a spray of hot fat flying.

If, however, you are uncomfortable murdering defenseless little sea creatures (despite your plan to later devour them), have your fishmonger do it for you—but be sure to keep them on ice and use them within a few hours.

Mise en Place:

FOR THE ROASTED TOMATOES:

4 whole plum tomatoes

2 whole sprigs of fresh thyme

3 T. olive oil

Salt and freshly ground black pepper

FOR THE SALAD DRESSING:

3 T. extra virgin olive oil

Salt and freshly ground black pepper

1½ T. freshly squeezed lemon juice

FOR THE CRABS:

4 slices applewood-smoked bacon,
each cut in half crosswise (see the
chapter "Resources")

2 jumbo freshly killed, dressed
soft-shell crabs (see the chapter
"Procedures and Techniques")

Salt and freshly ground black pepper

1 T. olive oil

FOR THE PLATE:

1 large bunch arugula, trimmed,
cleaned, and spun very dry

Prepared pesto

Roast the Tomatoes: Preheat the oven to 375°F.

Place the tomatoes and thyme sprigs in a small baking dish, drizzle with olive oil, and season with salt and pepper. Roast the tomatoes, stirring occasionally, just until they are tender and the skin has a few brown spots. Remove the tomatoes and cool. The tomatoes can be stored in a covered container, refrigerated, with the oil they were cooked in for up to 4 days. When you are ready to use them, warm the tomatoes slightly with a little of their oil in a sauté pan.

Prepare the Dressing: Pour the olive oil into a small bowl and season to taste with salt and pepper. Add the lemon juice slowly, whisking constantly to form an emulsion. Set aside.

Finish the Dish: In a medium skillet large enough to hold the crabs, sauté the bacon slices until crisp. Remove the bacon with tongs, leaving the fat in the skillet, and set the bacon aside on paper towels to drain.

Season the crabs with salt and pepper. Add 1 tablespoon of olive oil to the hot skillet the bacon was cooked in and sauté the crabs over high heat, turning once, until well browned and crispy, about 4 minutes per side.

Place the arugula in a medium bowl and toss with just enough dressing to lightly coat the leaves.

To Plate: Mound the dressed arugula on two individual plates. Cut the crabs into halves and position them, cut sides down, on top of the arugula. Place 4 pieces of bacon on the salad greens and garnish with a few pieces of cut roasted tomato. Drop spoonfuls of pesto around the edge of the plate.

arthur's landing at port imperial

Pershing Road

Weehawken 07086

201/867-4567

www.arthurslanding.com

*T*HE NIGHT LIGHTS and skyline of Manhattan are certainly magnificent when reflected off the river, but have you realized that the only way to actually experience that is to be on the New Jersey side?

Sorry, should have known how smart you are—so you probably also know that Arthur's Landing is the place from which to do it.

Visionary owner Arthur Imperatore has created every reason to make Arthur's Landing the first stop for citygoers, and it's not just the spectacular view. The innovative and creative New American–style food is reason enough, but when packaged together with a ferry ride to and from Manhattan, it becomes a pretheater deal that rivals any Manhattan has to offer.

However, there's much more to Arthur's Landing than a stop on the way to Manhattan. The fabulous lunch menu makes it a perfect place to conduct midday business, the Sunday brunch menu is outstanding and gets washed down with a complimentary mimosa, screwdriver, or other breakfast drink, and if you like your jazz served up with a backdrop of the city, Friday night on the veranda is definitely where you want to be.

Pan-Seared Red Snapper
WITH ROASTED JERSEY CORN HASH AND SMOKED YELLOW TOMATO COULIS

If the process of smoking the yellow tomato coulis is intimidating you, get over it! It's incredibly simple and highly flavorful kitchen magic and can be done 1 to 2 days ahead. Chef E. J. Laguerra uses a regular stovetop smoker, which can be easily found just about anywhere that cooking gadgets are sold—and once you try it, a whole world of smokily delicious possibilities will open up!

Mise en Place:

FOR THE YELLOW TOMATO COULIS:

4 whole yellow beefsteak tomatoes

1 T. canola or vegetable oil

1 cup chopped yellow onion

$^3/_4$ cup chicken or vegetable stock

Pinch salt

FOR THE ROASTED JERSEY CORN HASH:

2 T. unsalted butter

$1^1/_2$ cups freshly shucked Jersey corn kernels

1 cup $^1/_2$-inch diced red bliss potatoes

$^3/_4$ cup chopped yellow onion

2 tsp. finely chopped fresh Italian parsley leaves

2 tsp. finely chopped fresh tarragon leaves

2 tsp. finely chopped fresh chervil leaves

2 tsp. finely chopped fresh chives

Salt and pepper

FOR THE SNAPPER:

2 red snapper filets, 8 ozs. each, skin on, each cut into two pieces

Salt and freshly ground black pepper

2 T. canola or vegetable oil

FOR THE GARNISH:

Parsley sprigs

Chive oil (see the chapter "Procedures and Techniques")

Equipment:

Stovetop smoker

Hickory chips

Traditional or immersion blender

3-inch ring mold

Prepare the Smoked Tomato Coulis: Place a handful of hickory chips in the bottom of the stovetop smoker and position the perforated metal plate on top of the chips. Place the whole tomatoes on the plate, close the smoker, and place it over medium-high heat until it begins to smoke. Shut off the heat and let the smoker sit for 5 to 7 minutes.

In a medium skillet over low heat, sweat 1 cup of chopped onions in 1 tablespoon of canola or vegetable oil until tender, stirring occasionally, without allowing them to color.

Remove the tomatoes from the smoker and add them to the pan with the softened onions. Cook the tomatoes for 1 to 2 minutes, breaking them up with the side of a wooden paddle, and then add the stock and a pinch of salt. Raise the heat to medium-high and cook for about 5

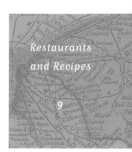

minutes more, until the liquid is reduced somewhat, the tomatoes are broken down, and it's all quite fragrant. Use an immersion blender, or transfer the contents of the pan to a traditional blender, and process to a smooth purée. Pass the sauce through a strainer and set aside. The sauce can be made 1 to 2 days ahead and refrigerated in a covered container until ready to use. Reheat very gently over low heat.

Prepare the Roasted Jersey Corn Hash: Place a medium skillet over high heat and add 1 tablespoon butter. When the butter melts, add the corn and sauté, tossing occasionally, until the corn is browned in spots. Remove the corn to a plate and set aside.

Add the remaining tablespoon of butter to the same skillet and sauté the potatoes over medium-high heat, tossing occasionally, until they are golden brown on all sides, about 5 minutes. Remove the potatoes to a plate and set aside.

Reduce the heat to medium-low and add the onions to the skillet. Cook the onions slowly, without coloring them, until they are translucent and tender, about 5 to 7 minutes.

Return the corn and the potatoes to the skillet and fold in the herbs. Season to taste with salt and pepper and remove from the heat.

To Finish the Dish: Heat a medium skillet over medium-high heat and add 2 tablespoons of canola or vegetable oil. Season the snapper on both sides with salt and pepper. When the oil is very hot, place the snapper skin side down into the pan and press down to sear the skin. Cook the fish, undisturbed, until the skin is crisp and the filets move easily in the pan, about 4 to 5 minutes. Turn and cook the other side just until the fish is opaque, about 3 to 4 minutes. Remove the pan from the heat.

To Plate: Place a 3-inch ring mold in the center of the plate and pack it with the hash. Carefully remove the ring mold and spoon a circle of the tomato coulis around the hash. Place the filets, one on top of the other, atop the hash, garnish with parsley sprigs, and dot the plate decoratively with chive oil.

the bernards inn

27 Mine Brook Road
Bernardsville 07924
908/766-0002
www.bernardsinn.com

W E H A V E A S P E C I A L place in our hearts for executive chef and managing partner Ed Stone and for the Bernards Inn, deep in the heart of New Jersey's hunt country. We first met Ed through the Dinner of Hope, a charitable event he started a decade ago and hosts annually; over the years the Dinner of Hope has raised more than $1.5 million for children in need. He is what we call a *mensch*—a special person with a strong sense of community and who is motivated by a firm commitment to give back.

A meal at this DiRōNA (Distinguished Restaurants of North America) Award winner means fine dining, as sophisticated as the setting. It's a place where we don't even mind behaving like grownups—admittedly a stretch for anyone who knows us—but it's definitely not stuffy. It's simply, quietly elegant.

Ed is also an incredibly gifted chef who looks for the finest-quality seasonal ingredients and then treats them with respect. He has a special talent with game meats and raises sauces, which he calls "liquid seasoning," to an art form. The award-winning wine list is exceptional, and there's an extensive listing of wines by the glass that either of the two sommeliers will skillfully help you to pair with your food (or simply taste for whatever reason you can think of). We've undertaken the formidable task of trying to work our way through it for nearly a decade—it's a tough job, but we figure someone's got to do it, might as well be us.

The inn really is one and feels like a small European luxury hotel. The rooms are well appointed with exquisite antiques and original oil paintings and thick, soft terrycloth robes that whisper "take me home" when you wrap yourself up in them. This is definitely the place to propose, get married, celebrate a positive pregnancy test or a special anniversary, kiss and make up, or just plain kiss. If you really want to make your visit to the Bernards Inn memorable, include an overnight stay.

Roasted Pheasant

WITH MOUSSELINE OF FOIE GRAS
AND BLACK TRUMPET MUSHROOMS WITH
A BEAUJOLAIS PEAR

Most people will take one look at the intricate preparation of this dish, work up an appetite, pour a drink, and make a reservation at the Bernards Inn, and that's okay—mention our names, you'll get a good seat.

But for the type-A, overachieving few who will actually want to see if they really can re-create it, the high-end ingredients that were at one time reserved for and available only to restaurants are now not particularly difficult to obtain, especially if you aren't averse to Web-shopping.

Pheasant and foie gras can now be found at many high-end markets and specialty shops, thanks to Griggstown Farm and D'Artagnan, and can also be ordered directly from D'Artagnan's Web site (see the chapter "Resources"). If you order the pheasant through a local market, though, you may be able to coax the butcher into boning it out for you. We suspect if you're ambitious enough to even try this dish at home, you probably won't even blink at the idea of boning it out yourself. And don't forget that the pheasant will need to luxuriate in cognac overnight—plan ahead!

Caul fat is a lacy, weblike membrane that lines the stomachs of hogs and sheep and is sometimes used to wrap forcement-filled or skinless meats such as rabbit for roasting or braising because it melts down quickly, basting as it goes.

Mise en Place:

FOR THE PHEASANT:

1 pheasant, 2 to 2^1/$_2$ lbs.

1 cup cognac

Caul fat

1 T. clarified unsalted butter (see the chapter "Procedures and Techniques")

1 T. extra virgin olive oil

1 cup chopped yellow onion

^{1}/$_2$ cup chopped celery

^{1}/$_2$ cup chopped carrot

2 tsp. fresh thyme leaves

1 cup demi-glace or veal stock (see the chapter "Resources")

Salt and freshly ground black pepper, to taste

FOR THE MOUSSELINE:

1 to 1^1/$_2$ cups meat scraps from boned pheasant

2 large egg yolks

^{1}/$_2$ cup heavy cream

1^1/$_2$ tsp. salt

Pinch freshly ground black pepper

3 T. dry sherry

^{1}/$_2$ cup finely chopped black trumpet mushrooms (see the chapter "Resources")

2 slabs foie gras, 1^1/$_2$ × 4 inches each (about 3 ozs. total)

FOR THE SAUTÉED SPINACH:

1 lb. fresh flat-leaf spinach, stemmed, cleaned, and spun very dry

Kosher salt for the blanching water

2 T. clarified unsalted butter

2 T. chicken stock or canned low-sodium, fat-free chicken broth

Salt and freshly ground black pepper, to taste

FOR THE BEAUJOLAIS PEARS:

2 Seckel pears

1^1/$_2$ cups Beaujolais

^{1}/$_4$ cup sugar

2 tsp. orange zest

^{1}/$_3$ cinnamon stick

^{1}/$_3$ vanilla bean, split lengthwise

2 black peppercorns

1 small clove

^{1}/$_4$ cup crème de cassis

Equipment:

Food processor

Sharp boning knife

Prepare the Pheasant: Use a very sharp boning knife to bone out the pheasant from the back, cutting neatly and in one line down to the joint where the thighbone meets the leg bone, removing the thigh bones but leaving the leg bones intact. Halve the pheasant at the breastbone. Carefully remove the skin from each half bird intact and in one piece.

Working with one half-bird at a time, place it skin side down on a clean cutting board. Carefully trim away all loose pieces of meat so you are left with the whole leg, bone intact and attached to it a large flap of meat in one piece, approximately 4 inches long and 4 inches wide.

You should have about 1 to 1¹/₂ cups of meat scraps for the mousseline when you're finished. If you have less than 1 cup, trim away a bit more. Transfer the meat scraps to a bowl and chill thoroughly (about 2 hours) before proceeding with the mousseline.

If it appears as though the flap of meat might be too narrow or short to contain a filling, you can place it between two layers of plastic wrap and gently pound it to achieve the size you need.

Place the trimmed birds in a sealable freezer bag, add the cognac, and refrigerate for at least 8 hours or overnight.

Prepare the Mousseline: In the work bowl of a food processor, pulse the chilled meat scraps until finely ground, scraping down the sides of the work bowl as necessary. Add the egg yolks, cream, salt, and pepper and process to a coarse purée. Add the sherry and continue to process to a smooth purée. Transfer the mousseline to a

mixing bowl and fold in the chopped mushrooms. Cover with plastic wrap and keep the mousseline chilled until ready to use.

Prepare the Spinach: Bring a large pot of cold water to a boil for blanching the spinach and add 1 tablespoon of kosher salt. Prepare a bowl of ice and water to shock the spinach after blanching.

Add the spinach to the boiling water, in batches if necessary, and stir just until the leaves wilt, about 20 seconds. Scoop out the spinach and plunge it into the ice bath to stop the cooking. Swirl the spinach around a bit to be sure it's completely cooled, drain, and use your hands to squeeze out as much water as possible. Transfer the spinach to a clean kitchen towel and squeeze out as much additional water as possible. Set aside. The spinach can be prepared ahead to this point and kept, refrigerated in a covered bowl (not a plastic bag), for up to 2 days.

Prepare the Beaujolais Pears: Peel the pears carefully, leaving the stems intact. In a saucepan just large enough to hold the pears, mix together the wine, sugar, orange zest, cinnamon stick, and vanilla bean. Add the peppercorns and clove bring to a boil; boil for 5 minutes. Place the pears in the wine and let cook at a gentle simmer for 20 minutes, turning frequently.

Remove the pan from the heat and let the pears cool in the wine, turning them occasionally. Place the pears in a shallow serving dish. Stir the crème de cassis into the cooled wine syrup and pour over the pears. The pears can be served at this point or kept, refrigerated in a covered container, for up to 3 days. Bring the pears and the sauce to room temperature or warm slightly before serving.

To Finish the Dish: Heat a small dry black steel or other good heat-conducting pan over high heat until very hot.

With a sharp knife, score the foie gras in a shallow crosshatch pattern. Add the foie gras slabs to the hot pan and sear quickly, turning once, on both sides. Remove the foie gras from the pan immediately and set aside.

Remove the pheasant from the cognac bath and pat dry with paper towels. Reserve 1/2 cup of the cognac.

Working with one half-bird at a time, place the pheasant skin side down and spread with an even layer of just a bit less than half of the mousseline. Place one piece of the seared foie gras on top of the mousseline and cover the foie gras with a bit more mousseline.

Spread out the reserved skin on the work surface, place the half-bird on top, and use the skin to roll up the meat so the foie gras is centered.

Stretch out a length of caul fat and wrap each stuffed pheasant half completely but not too tightly, until it is fully enclosed in 1 1/2 to 2 thicknesses of the caul fat, twisting the ends and tucking them underneath. Repeat with the remaining half-bird.

Preheat the oven to 425°F.

In a large ovenproof skillet over medium-high heat, melt the clarified butter and oil and brown the pheasant on all sides. Transfer to a platter.

Add the onions, celery, and carrots to the hot pan and sauté, stirring occasionally, until they are tender and beginning to color, about 3 minutes. SHUT OFF THE HEAT and add the reserved 1/2 cup of cognac. Relight the burner and cook until the cognac is reduced by half, about 1 minute. Stir in 1/2 cup of the demi-glace and cook until the liquid is reduced again by half, about 1 to 2 minutes more.

Spread the vegetables out in an even layer and sprinkle with the thyme leaves. Position the pheasant on top of the vegetables and transfer the skillet to the oven. Roast for 15 minutes.

Remove the pan from the oven and turn the pheasant. Add the remaining 1/2 cup of demi-glace to the skillet, using a wooden paddle to scrape the bottom of the skillet, and return the skillet to the oven to finish roasting, about 10 minutes more.

Remove the skillet from the oven and transfer the pheasant to a cutting board. Strain the contents of the skillet into a measuring glass with a pouring lip, pressing on the vegetables to extract all the juices. Discard the solids.

Meanwhile, in a large skillet over medium-low heat, melt the clarified butter in the chicken broth. Add the spinach and cook until tender and heated through, tossing to coat the leaves in the sauce, about 2 minutes. Season to taste with salt and pepper.

To Plate: Place a bed of spinach on each warmed plate.

Spoon a bit of the Beaujolais sauce over the pears just before placing one alongside the spinach.

Use a sharp carving knife to separate the whole leg in one piece. Slice the stuffed portion of the pheasant crosswise into 1-inch-thick pieces. Arrange the meat on top of the spinach and spoon the sauce on top.

black forest inn

249 Route 206 North

Stanhope 07874

973/347-3344

www.blackforestinn.com

W E A R R I V E D beer steins in hand and decked out in lederhosen, all set for a major taste of Bavaria—we were looking for real, true German food like schnitzels, sauerbraten, and the best of the wursts, and if that's your game plan, you'll be happily satisfied that you've found the best place in New Jersey to get it.

But that's just a sampling of what these guys can do—if you love real, true Continental cuisine, classics with a gentle tweak, game menus, and surprisingly fabulous ways with fresh fish such as this creative dish semiretired chef-owner Heinz Aichem and his son, executive chef-owner Heiner, created for us when we visited, you'll find yourself in the right place when you visit the Black Forest Inn. This recently renovated family-run restaurant (daughter Barbara manages the restaurant and the wine list with Heiner) has been a favorite and a Stanhope institution for almost twenty-five years.

The extensive menu, stained glass walls, huge center-stage bar, and comfy leather banquettes are a great combination for a business lunch or dinner or a good old-fashioned weekend dining experience. And make it a habit to log onto their Web site to keep up with special events like their multicourse, wine-paired German Game Night.

Oh and you might want to skip the lederhosen—they just rolled their eyes and mumbled something that sounded suspiciously like "knobby knees."

Salmon Filet in Phyllo

WITH MAINE LOBSTER CLAWS

ON CHIVE BEURRE BLANC

This stunningly elegant dish presents beautifully! It requires a bit of effort, but each component is very simple and can be done in advance. The salmon roll can also be assembled ahead and held for up to 2 hours before baking, making this perfect to serve for a special occasion.

Mise en Place:

6 Maine lobster claws

FOR THE CODFISH MOUSSE:

1 T. unsalted butter

$1/4$ cup chopped shallots

2 T. finely chopped celery

2 T. finely chopped red bell pepper

2 T. finely chopped yellow bell pepper

2 T. chopped shiitake mushrooms

$1/4$ lb. boned codfish

1 large egg white, lightly beaten

6 T. chilled heavy cream

1 lb. whole skinless salmon filet, cut from the wide end

Salt and freshly ground white pepper, to taste

3 sheets thawed phyllo dough

4 tsp. fresh unflavored breadcrumbs

$1/2$ cup melted unsalted butter

4 T. ($\frac{1}{2}$ stick) unsalted butter

$\frac{1}{4}$ cup chopped shallots

2 cloves garlic, finely chopped and mashed with 1/2 tsp. kosher salt

1 sprig fresh thyme

$\frac{1}{2}$ cup Reisling wine

$\frac{1}{8}$ tsp. freshly ground white pepper

1 T. champagne vinegar

Freshly squeezed juice of $\frac{1}{2}$ lemon (about 2 T.)

1 cup heavy cream

1 T. cornstarch mixed with 2 T. Reisling wine

3 T. snipped fresh chives

1 T. unsalted butter

1 T. brandy

1 T. dry white wine

Equipment:

Parchment paper

Food processor

Prepare the Lobster: Bring a large pot of water to a boil. Have ready a bowl filled with ice cubes and cold water for shocking the lobster.

Wrap each lobster claw tightly in three layers of plastic wrap. When the water is at a rolling boil, add the wrapped lobster claws all at once and cook for exactly 8 minutes. Remove and plunge the claws into the ice water to stop the cooking process. When the lobster is cool, remove the plastic wrap. Use a very sharp kitchen scissor to cut all the way through the claws at two or three points so the meat can be removed intact. Rinse the meat lightly and pat dry with paper towels. Reserve the four nicest claws and refrigerate, covered, in a small bowl. Dice the remaining clawmeat into $\frac{1}{2}$-inch pieces and set aside.

Prepare the Codfish Mousse: In a small skillet over medium heat, gently sauté the shallots, celery, and bell pepper in the tablespoon of butter just until tender, stirring occasionally, without allowing the vegetables to

color. Add the mushrooms and cook for a minute or two until they're tender. Remove from the heat and set aside to cool.

Cut the codfish into small chunks, place them in the work bowl of a food processor, and pulse a few times to chop them up a bit. Add the egg white and heavy cream and process the mixture to a very smooth mousse, stopping to scrape down the sides of the work bowl as needed. Transfer the mousse to a mixing bowl and fold in the lobster meat and sautéed vegetables. The mousse can be made ahead and held, refrigerated, in a covered container, for up to 1 day.

Prepare the Salmon Roll: Line a baking sheet with parchment paper and spray lightly with vegetable oil spray.

Place 3 sheets of phyllo on a clean work surface with the long edge nearest you. Position the salmon with its length parallel to the long edge of the phyllo and use a sharp knife to trim the phyllo sheets about 2 inches longer than the salmon at each side edge. Remove the salmon to a plate. Beginning about 2 inches above the edge of the phyllo and working on the lower $\frac{1}{3}$ of the phyllo, spread about a $\frac{1}{2}$-inch-thick layer of the codfish mousse about as long and as wide as the salmon filet.

Season the salmon filet with salt and pepper and place it on top of the mousse. Brush the top $\frac{2}{3}$ of the phyllo with a light coating of the melted butter. Lift the edge nearest you and bring it up and over the salmon filet to securely enclose it. Fold each side up and over the salmon and then tightly roll up the salmon bundle, brushing the last 2 inches of phyllo with melted butter to seal. Carefully transfer the roll to the prepared baking sheet, brush the top and sides with melted butter, and dust the top with breadcrumbs. The salmon roll can be prepared up to this point and held, lightly covered with plastic wrap and refrigerated, for up to 4 hours.

Prepare the Chive Beurre Blanc: In a medium saucepan over medium-low heat, gently sauté the shallots in the butter, without allowing them to color, just

until transparent. Add the mashed garlic and thyme and continue to gently cook until tender.

Add ¹/₂ cup of Reisling, white pepper, champagne vinegar, and the lemon juice and raise the heat to high. Bring the sauce to a boil and cook until it is reduced by half. Add the cup of heavy cream and continue to boil until the sauce is reduced again by half. The sauce may be prepared to this point and then held in a covered container, refrigerated, for up to 2 days. Reheat gently before continuing. Stir in the cornstarch and Reisling mixture and cook until the sauce has thickened. Remove from the heat and strain. Stir in the chives and keep warm.

Finish the Dish: Preheat the oven to 350°F.

When ready to bake, place the uncovered salmon in the preheated oven and bake for 20 to 25 minutes until golden brown. Remove the roll from the oven and let rest for 10 minutes before cutting.

Melt the 1 T. of butter in a small skillet over medium-low heat. Add the brandy and white wine and heat through. Add the reserved lobster claws and gently heat through, turning occasionally to coat them with the sauce.

To Plate: Spoon about 3 T. of the beurre blanc onto each plate. Slice off a ¹/₂-inch piece of the salmon roll from each end and discard (or taste-test!) and cut the remaining roll crosswise into two pieces. Cut each piece crosswise into three pieces, making a total of six slices. Place 3 slices of salmon roll in the center of the plate on top of the sauce. Place 2 lobster claws alongside the salmon roll and spoon a bit of beurre blanc on top of the salmon, if desired.

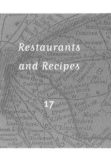

café matisse

167 Park Avenue
Rutherford 07070
201/935-2995
www.cafematisse.com

THEY SAY YOU can tell a lot about people from a visit to their bathroom . . . but more on that later.

Chef-owners Peter Loria and Paula Hayward characterize their food as artful cuisine. We agree—there's

definitely artwork taking place here, no doubt about it, and it's the kind that touches all five senses. Peter's menu and Paula's desserts are at once textural, colorful, and subtly complex, the chefs mirroring and complementing each other in food as they do in their lives and creating a truly great big picture.

The Café Matisse part comes from their love of the artist, and we give it the design award for creative attention to detail. The cozy restaurant honors its namesake—every square inch of the restaurant is a delight of original artwork, from the ceilings to the doorjambs, the fixtures to the cushions . . . and the bathrooms.

The creativity doesn't stop there, either—although the restaurant is a BYO, their solution to the lack of a liquor license was pretty creative, too. Peter and Paula co-opted a small adjacent space and turned it into a retail wine boutique. In typical fashion, they've sought out and sell some of the best, most interesting, and most unusual wines we've enjoyed anywhere, and they knowledgeably assist in pairing wine and menu selections.

Heads up: Peter likes "small plates" and is a real a*fish*ianado, probably a result from a "stage" at Le Bernardin. Choose to go with the grazing menu and you won't be disappointed.

Dusted and Glazed Scallops

WITH POTATO PANCAKE, SEARED FOIE GRAS, AND VANILLA-ALMOND VINAIGRETTE

Although chef-owner Peter Loria serves this spectacular dish as an appetizer, we'd happily consider it an entrée and stop there to wonder if we'd died and gone to heaven yet.

Once nearly impossible to get for home use, foie gras is no longer only available to restaurants and can now be found as vacuum-sealed "slabs" at many specialty stores and better supermarkets (see the chapter "Resources"). Buy it. Eat it. You deserve it.

Mise en Place:

FOR THE BROWN SUGAR DUST:

$1/_4$ cup light brown sugar

2 tsp. dried orange peel

FOR THE SWEET VINEGAR GLAZE:

$1/_2$ cup mirin (Japanese rice wine or cooking sake)

2 T. rice wine vinegar

$1/_2$ tsp. sugar

FOR THE VANILLA-ALMOND VINAIGRETTE:

1 cup mirin

$^{1}/_{4}$ cup rice wine vinegar

1 vanilla bean

$^{1}/_{4}$ tsp. almond extract

FOR THE POTATO PANCAKE:

1 cup peeled and shredded
   Yukon Gold potato

Salt and freshly ground white pepper,
   to taste

2 tsp. canola or vegetable oil

FOR THE FOIE GRAS AND SCALLOPS:

2 slabs of fresh foie gras, 4 ozs. each

Salt and freshly ground black pepper

1 tsp. canola or vegetable oil

6 dry U-12 scallops, tough side muscle
   removed

2 T. canola or vegetable oil

Pinch brown sugar dust

1 tsp. unsalted butter

FOR THE GARNISH:

2 T. sliced almonds, lightly toasted for 5 minutes in
   a preheated 350°F oven

2 tsp. finely chopped fresh Italian parsley leaves

Prepare the Brown Sugar Dust: Sprinkle the brown sugar onto a parchment-lined baking pan and set aside at room temperature overnight to dry out.

Mix together the brown sugar and dried orange peel. Use a handheld nutmeg grater to finely grate the mixture. Set aside. The mixture can be made ahead and kept in an airtight container at room temperature for up to 5 days.

Prepare the Sweet Vinegar Glaze: Place a small saucepan over high heat and add the mirin, rice wine vinegar, and sugar. Bring to a boil and cook until the liquid is reduced by half. Remove from heat and set aside. The mixture can be made ahead and kept in an airtight container at room temperature for up to 5 days.

Prepare the Vanilla-Almond Vinaigrette: Place a small saucepan over high heat and add the mirin and rice wine vinegar. Cut the vanilla bean lengthwise to open and use a sharp paring knife to scrape the seeds and pulp into the pan. Bring to a boil and cook until the liquid is reduced by half. Remove from heat, stir in the almond extract, and set aside. The mixture can be made ahead and kept in an airtight container at room temperature for up to 5 days.

Prepare the Potato Pancakes: Preheat the oven to 200°F. Set a cooling rack onto a baking sheet and place in the oven.

Pile the shredded potato onto a double thickness of paper toweling, wrap up, and squeeze out the excess moisture. Season the potato shreds with salt and pepper.

Heat the canola or vegetable oil in a medium skillet over medium-high heat until hot. Divide the shredded potato into two patties and add them to the hot pan, pressing down with a spatula to flatten into pancakes.

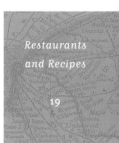

Cook the pancakes, turning once, until golden brown and crispy on both sides, about 6 minutes. Remove the pancakes to the cooling rack in the oven to keep warm for up to 20 minutes.

To Finish the Dish: Season the foie gras with salt and pepper.

Heat a medium dry black steel or other good heat-conducting ovenproof pan over high heat until very hot. Add a teaspoon of canola or vegetable oil and the foie gras and quickly sear the foie gras on both sides. Immediately transfer the foie gras to a plate.

Dust the tops of the scallops lightly with the brown sugar dust.

Add the 2 tablespoons of oil to the hot pan, add the scallops, sugar-dusted side down, and sear. Turn the scallops when they move easily and place the hot pan in the oven for about 5 minutes to finish them. Remove the pan from the oven and add the 1 tsp. of butter to the hot pan along with a pinch of the brown sugar dust and 1 tsp. of the sweet vinegar glaze. Toss gently to coat the scallops.

To Plate: Place 3 scallops in the center of each of two plates. Top the scallops with a potato pancake and sprinkle the toasted almonds on top. Place the seared foie gras on top of the pancake, drizzle the whole with the vanilla-almond vinaigrette, and sprinkle with the chopped parsley.

café panache

130 East Main Street
Ramsey 07446
201/934-0030

I T ' S   N O   W O N D E R so many other chefs in the area call chef-owner Kevin Kohler brilliant. It's not easy to stay fresh and at the top of your game for nearly twenty years, let alone live up to the reputation that you just keep getting better, but Kevin has succeeded in doing so quietly and casually and says his winning formula is to not take himself too seriously. One way he does that is to make sure he keeps learning, and to assure he gets the best education money can't buy, he travels beyond his ego for one "vacation" week every

year and "trails" anonymously in someone else's restaurant, sometimes here in the United States and sometimes in Europe.

We knew Kevin would have a good perspective on the evolution of American cuisine, and we agreed when he predicted that food will continue to become more basic and less fussy and that the focus will continue to move toward growing and working with the best ingredients. The chef puts his money where his mouth is—he has two farmers growing some sixty va-

rieties of herbs and vegetables in the one-acre organic garden where he and his staff get to pick the best of the season.

Kevin is a thinking man, and he intelligently captures your interest with simple, fast, technique-driven dishes—everything is familiar and recognizable, but how did he get it to taste *so* good?! Don't be surprised when you find yourself thinking about what you'll next put on your fork and into your mouth.

Fettuccine

WITH PESTO, ENGLISH PEAS, AND SUN-DRIED TOMATOES

The pasta at Café Panache is house-made, handcut, and ethereally light. What chef-owner Kevin Kohler calls fettuccine, you'd probably recognize as pappardelle—we think it's so good that Kevin can call it whatever he likes.

If you make your own pasta, don't let us stop you— by all means use it. But you can also use a good-quality artisanal pasta and achieve really great results. We think there's no substitute for homemade pesto, but we found that using frozen peas in this dish was perfectly fine.

Mise en Place:

8 ozs. fresh or 6 ozs. good-quality dried
    artisanal pappardelle or fettuccine
Kosher salt for the pasta water

FOR THE SAUCE:

1 cup basil pesto
1 cup fresh or thawed frozen peas
$^1/_2$ cup diced drained, oil-marinated
    sun-dried tomatoes

FOR GARNISH:

Sprigs of fresh mint

Chef's TRUC:

Instead of salting the finished dish, Kevin cooks down a little of the salted pasta water before adding the sauce ingredients to the pan. The result? Perfectly seasoned pasta!

Prepare the Pasta: Bring a large pot of cold water to a boil. When the water has reached a rolling boil, add enough kosher salt so that the water tastes as salty as sea water, about 4 or 5 tablespoons to 6 quarts of water.

Prepare the Sauce: Heat a medium skillet over medium-high heat and add about ¹/₂ cup of the salty pasta water. Bring the water to a boil and reduce by about half.

Meanwhile, add the pesto to the skillet and cook it down until it's thick and bubbling. Stir in the peas and sun-dried tomatoes and cook, tossing the pan contents now and then, until the peas are tender, adding a bit of water if the sauce appears too dry (don't get nervous—you can always add more water or reduce the sauce a bit if you've added too much).

Add the pasta to the pot of boiling water and cook, stirring frequently, until the pasta is almost tender but still quite firm.

To Finish the Dish: Drain the pasta and add it to the skillet. Cook the pasta and sauce together, tossing almost constantly, until the pasta is tender and well coated with the sauce, adding more water if necessary. When finished, the sauce should be thickly coating the pasta as a vegetable purée would.

To Plate: Use tongs to pick up the pasta and use a twisting motion to pile it into a high mound. Garnish with a fresh sprig of mint.

casa comida

336 Branchport Avenue

Long Branch 07740

732/229-7774

*Y*A GOTTA LOVE A PLACE that stocks forty-four different tequilas. Certainly not least for the fact that they are put to good use in what are quite possibly the best frozen *real fruit* margaritas on the planet. This would be a good thing because you'll definitely need them to wash down their over-the-top, abundant food.

Be prepared to be pleased—this is not typical one-dimensional Tex-Mex fare. No gratuitous use of heat here—the sauces and salsa are complex, beautifully blended, and balanced creations by executive chef–owner Kristin Catlett and chili maestro chef Ivan Soto. And the vegetarian menu is extensive, outstanding, and not just for herbivores.

Summer perfection could be as simple as a winning day at Monmouth Racetrack and a Casa Comida evening.

Fiery Garlic Shrimp Quesadillas

This dish exemplifies our idea of the best way to cook—just a few ingredients, a simple and easy preparation, and an absolutely addictive end result. The fiery garlic mix is now a permanent resident of our refrigerated pantry so we can whip up a platter of shrimp whenever the mood strikes—and that's often.

Chiles de arbol are small dried chiles that we easily find in most supermarkets (see the chapter "Resources"). From their leathery texture it might seem as though they won't chop up well, but carry on—they will.

Mise en Place:

FOR THE LIME-CILANTRO MAYONNAISE:

$^1/_2$ cup mayonnaise

Freshly squeezed juice of 1 lime

2 T. chopped fresh cilantro leaves

Pinch salt

FOR THE FIERY GARLIC SHRIMP:

3 large cloves peeled garlic

6 dried, stemmed chiles de arbol, torn in half

$^3/_4$ cup canola oil

Salt and freshly ground black pepper

1 lb. extra-large (26–30 count) raw shrimp, cleaned, peeled, and deveined

FOR THE QUESADILLAS:

4 flour tortillas

$^1/_2$ cup shredded jack cheese or a combination of shredded jack and cheddar cheeses

1 T. chopped fresh cilantro leaves

Prepare the Lime-Cilantro Mayonnaise: In a small bowl, whisk together the mayonnaise, cilantro, and lime juice with a pinch of salt. Transfer to a clean bowl, cover, and refrigerate. The lime-cilantro mayonnaise can be made ahead; cover and refrigerate for up to 4 days.

Prepare the Fiery Garlic Shrimp Mixture: Place the garlic and chiles in a mini-processor or blender and pulse until finely chopped, scraping down the work bowl as necessary. Add the canola oil and blend. Season to taste with salt and pepper. This mix can be made ahead and stored to use as needed, in a covered container in the refrigerator, for up to 1 week.

Prepare the Quesadillas: Preheat the oven to 375°F. Line a baking sheet with parchment paper.

Place 2 tortillas on the prepared baking sheet and sprinkle each with half of the shredded cheese and half of the chopped cilantro leaves. Place the remaining 2 tortillas on top of each and press down to flatten into quesadillas. Bake in the preheated oven until the cheese melts, about 10 minutes. Remove the quesadillas and allow them to

cool for about 2 minutes before using a pizza wheel and cutting each into 6 wedges.

Finish the Dish: In a large skillet over medium-high heat, warm the fiery garlic oil until it is very fragrant and beginning to bubble. Add the shrimp and sauté just until they are pink.

To Plate: Spoon the shrimp with some of its fiery sauce into the center of two platters. Scoop some of the lime-cilantro mayonnaise on one side and place quesadilla wedges on the other side.

the columbia inn

29 Main Road (Route 202)

Montville 07045

973/263-1300

www.thecolumbiainn.com

ACCORDING TO OWNER Ryan McDermott, chef Franco Brattoli is a natural, a guy with an innate understanding of food. Having grown up in the business and now the owner of two crowd-pleasing local restaurants, Ryan should know. It also doesn't hurt to have the dual gifts of being able to spot a talent when he sees one and to let go and give him all the freedom and support to be what he is.

Chef Franco Brattoli learned his approach to food from gardening with his mother in Italy, and his understanding of food is from the ground up. Gifted with the ability to pair without thinking, and knowing innately that what grows together goes together, chef Franco uses seasonal ingredients and designs his food in a way that reflects his conviction that you have to be able to taste each ingredient.

The Columbia Inn is a family restaurant—it's comfortable, casual, and a favorite with families with kids whether they come for the best cracker-thin pizzas in New Jersey or Franco's sophisticated creations, which are often entries from the latest competitions he's won. For us, it's a place we choose to meet up with friends who really know food and wine and know how to comfortably enjoy them.

Artichoke Three Ways
(Carciofi—Assaggi di Punta)
STUFFED, FLASH-FRIED, AND A SALAD

We're artichoke nuts and are absolutely ecstatic that fresh baby artichokes are now available here on the "right" coast! These little guys are really easy to work with because they haven't yet developed their "choke," the fuzzy thistle that fills the interior of the bigger guys and needs to be removed. And just when we thought we were running out of new ideas for these babies, chef Franco Brattoli came up with this terrific and diverse "flight."

Mise en Place:

> 6 baby artichokes
>
> $^1/_2$ lemon
>
> Kosher salt for the blanching water
>
> About 1 cup all-purpose flour
>
> 1 cup cold water
>
> Canola oil for deep-frying

FOR THE FRESH TOMATO SAUCE:

> 1 T. extra virgin olive oil
>
> 1 tsp. finely minced fresh garlic
>
> 2 fresh basil leaves, torn into small pieces
>
> 1 cup peeled, seeded, chopped fresh ripe tomato
>
> Salt and freshly ground black pepper, to taste

FOR THE STUFFING:

1 T. extra virgin olive oil

1 T. chopped scallion, white and green parts

1 tsp. minced shallot

1/3 cup chopped fresh, raw shrimp

Salt and freshly ground black pepper, to taste

1 T. roughly torn crustless, firm white bread

1 large egg white, lightly beaten

FOR THE LEMON VINAIGRETTE:

3 T. extra virgin olive oil

Pinch salt

Pinch freshly ground black pepper

1 1/2 T. freshly squeezed lemon juice

FOR THE FRESH PEA PURÉE:

2 T. extra virgin olive oil

1 tsp. finely minced garlic

1/3 cup fresh or thawed frozen peas

Pinch salt

Pinch freshly ground white pepper

2 T. hot water

FOR THE GARNISHES:

4 slices fresh, ripe plum tomato, each 1/4 inch thick

2 fresh sprigs of basil

Shavings of Parmigiano-Reggiano cheese

Equipment:

Mini-processor

Deep-fry thermometer

Prepare the Artichokes: Fill a medium bowl with cold water. Squeeze the juice of half a lemon into the bowl, followed by the lemon shell.

Trim the artichokes by pulling off the tough outer leaves until only light green leaves remain that snap easily when folded in half. Trim about 1/2 inch off the top of the artichokes and, taking care to leave as much of the base and stem as possible, carefully pare away the fibrous outside of the base and stems. Drop the pared artichokes into the

bowl of lemon water as you finish them to keep them from browning.

Place 4 tablespoons of all-purpose flour in a small bowl and gradually whisk in 1 cup of cold water to form a slurry.

Bring a large pot of cold water to a boil. When the water comes to a rolling boil, stir in 1 tablespoon of kosher salt and the flour slurry.

Drop the artichokes into the boiling water and cook just until tender, about 12 to 15 minutes.

Prepare a bowl of ice and water to shock the artichokes after blanching.

Scoop out the artichokes and drop them into the ice bath to stop the cooking process. Set the cooled artichokes aside on paper towels to drain. The artichokes may be prepared up to this point and held in a dry bowl, refrigerated, for up to 4 hours.

Prepare the Tomato Sauce: In a small skillet over medium-high heat, sauté the garlic and basil in 1 tablespoon of olive oil just until soft and fragrant. Add the chopped tomato, salt, and pepper and cook for 1 to 2 minutes, just until fragrant. Remove from the heat, allow to cool for a minute or two, and then process to a smooth purée in a mini-processor or simply mash through a strainer with a wooden spoon. The sauce may be prepared up to this point and held, refrigerated, in a covered container for up to 3 days. Rewarm the sauce when ready to use.

Prepare the Stuffing: In a small skillet over medium-high heat, sauté the scallion and shallot in the olive oil until soft and fragrant. Add the shrimp to the pan and cook, stirring almost constantly, until the shrimp is cooked through, about 1 minute. Season with salt and pepper and mix in the bread. Transfer the mixture to a small bowl and allow it to cool. Once it's cool, fold in the egg white to bind it all together.

Prepare the Lemon Vinaigrette: Pour the olive oil into a small bowl and add the salt and pepper. Whisking constantly, gradually add the lemon juice to form an emulsion.

Chef's TRUC:

To keep the artichokes from turning an unappealing grey-green, Franco adds a flour "slurry" to the water in which they are cooked

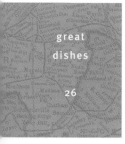

The vinaigrette may be prepared up to this point and held, refrigerated, in a covered container for up to 3 days. Bring to room temperature and rewhisk when ready to use.

Prepare the Pea Purée: In a small skillet over medium heat, sauté the garlic in the olive oil just until fragrant. Add the peas and cook just until they are tender, about 3 minutes. Add 2 tablespoons of hot water to the pan and season with salt and pepper. Transfer the contents of the pan to a bowl to cool. When the peas are cool, purée them in a mini-processor until smooth and then strain the purée. The sauce may be prepared up to this point and held, refrigerated, in a covered container for up to 3 days. Rewarm the sauce when ready to use.

To Finish the Dish: Preheat the oven to 400°F.

Cut 2 of the artichokes in half lengthwise and pull out a few of the center leaves and any thistle to create a depression for the stuffing. Divide the shrimp stuffing into 4 equal parts and press a mound of stuffing into the depression. Drizzle with a tiny bit of olive oil and place the stuffed artichokes on a baking sheet and bake until golden brown, about 8 to 10 minutes

Fill a small saucepan with canola oil to a depth of 2 inches and place over medium-high heat. When the oil reaches 375°F on a deep-fry thermometer, dredge 2 artichokes in flour and flash-fry until golden brown. Remove the artichokes to a plate lined with paper towels to drain.

Use a sharp paring knife to cut the 2 remaining artichokes lengthwise into thirds.

To Plate: For each plate, spoon a small puddle of tomato sauce on the plate and place the stuffed artichoke halves on top.

Spoon a small puddle of the pea purée on the plate and place the fried artichoke, stem up, on top. Garnish with a piece of shaved Parmigiano.

Spoon a small puddle of the lemon vinaigrette on the plate and place a slice of artichoke cut side up on top. Place a tomato slice on the artichoke, followed by a slice of artichoke, another slice of tomato, and top with the remaining slice of artichoke. Spoon a bit more vinaigrette on top and garnish with a sprig of fresh basil.

daniel's on broadway

416 South Broadway

West Cape May 08204

609/898-8770

www.danielscapemay.com

I N OUR OPINION, Cape May might well be the greatest square mile of food in New Jersey, and Daniel's on Broadway, housed in one of the lovely historical Cape May Victorians, is at the top of the list of the greatest restaurants there.

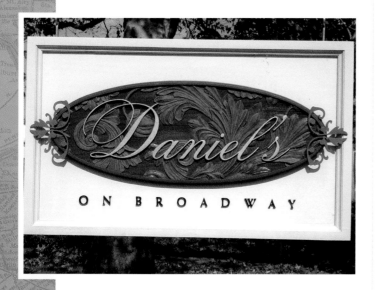

Named after chef-owner Harry Gleason's father-in-law, Daniel's is a family affair—the rooms were beautifully decorated by Harry's mother-in-law, and, until recently, the front of the house was managed by his wife, Kristin. Each of the three dining rooms has its own charm, and, yes, those French posters are original canvases.

Despite the insanity of "the season," when he can work ninety days straight, chef-owner Harry Gleason manages to hit the mark every time with his original and imaginative New American renditions. Daniel's is

a romantic place, with intimate seating spaces throughout, and, true to that theme, it opens its season on Valentine's Day, when, despite the unseasonal weather, the restaurant is inevitably packed.

What really impressed us, besides the consistently amazing food that just seems to flow from his mind to his plates, was that Harry pretty much does it all with just the help of his sous chef and his longtime pastry chef, Lynne Armstrong, and not only barely breaks a sweat but actually runs his kitchen with a contagiously happy energy that flows through to the staff and the dining rooms.

His mom was a chef, and Harry is self-taught, lending credence to our suspicion that sometimes the ability to create magic with food might be genetic, which we'll keep an eye on—one of his two sons is paying the same close attention to Harry that the chef paid to his mom. The kid's got some mighty big clogs to fill, but he definitely bears watching.

Lobster, Leek, and Mascarpone Dumplings

WITH LOBSTER-BRANDY SAUCE

If this is fusion food, then we're all for it—the rich filling of mascarpone and lobster in a potsticker-style dumpling is sophisticated and sexy! It takes just a few seconds to form these dumplings using an Asian dumpling press, which is available at any decent cookware store for about a dollar—think about making up a large batch, since they can be frozen for up to a month and steamed directly from a frozen state before pan-frying to crisp up the outside. For the shellfish stock, we used More Than Gourmet's Fruits de Mer, which is available at many better supermarkets and specialty stores and uncomfortably close to our own homemade!

Mise en Place:

FOR THE LOBSTER-MASCARPONE DUMPLINGS:

2 T. clarified butter (see the chapter "Procedures and Techniques")

2 T. $1/8$-inch crosswise half-round slices of leek, white part only

1 tsp. finely minced garlic

Salt and freshly ground white pepper, to taste

3 T. mascarpone cheese, room temperature

1 tsp. finely chopped fresh tarragon

$1/2$ cup finely chopped cooked lobster meat

Dumpling wrappers (round gyoza or wonton skins)

1 T. cornstarch mixed with 3 T. cold water for sealing the dumplings

FOR THE LOBSTER-BRANDY SAUCE:

2 tsp. clarified butter

2 tsp. finely chopped shallots

$1/2$ cup brandy

$1/2$ cup dry white wine

$1/2$ cup shellfish stock (see the chapter "Resources")

1 tsp. Dijon mustard

2 tsp. Worcestershire sauce

$1/2$ cup heavy cream

2 T. finely chopped cooked lobster meat

Salt and freshly ground white pepper, to taste

Nonstick vegetable spray

3 T. water

2 T. clarified butter

FOR THE GARNISH:

Chive oil (see "Procedures and Techniques")

Sprigs of fresh watercress or tarragon

Equipment:

Asian dumpling press

Parchment paper

Prepare the Lobster-Mascarpone Filling: In a small skillet over medium-low heat, cook the leeks in 2 tablespoons of clarified butter until soft, stirring often, and not allowing the leeks to brown, about 5 minutes. Add the garlic and cook for a minute more, until soft and fragrant. Remove the pan from the heat, season with salt and pepper, and allow the contents to cool.

In a medium mixing bowl, using a rubber spatula, mix together the mascarpone, tarragon, and the softened leek mixture. Gently fold in the lobster meat.

Prepare the Dumplings: Line a sheet pan with parchment paper.

Place a dumpling wrapper onto the open dumpling press with 1 teaspoon of lobster-mascarpone filling in the center of the wrapper. Brush the edges of the wrapper with the cornstarch mixture and close the press to seal. Place the dumpling on the prepared sheet pan. Repeat with the remaining filling. The dumplings can be prepared up to this point and frozen—place the sheet pan in the freezer, and when

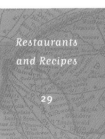

Restaurants and Recipes

29

the dumplings are frozen solid, they can be placed in a sealable freezer bag and frozen for up to 1 month. The dumplings can be steamed from a frozen state before pan-frying to crisp.

Prepare the Lobster-Brandy Sauce: In a medium skillet over medium-high heat, sauté the shallots in 2 teaspoons of clarified butter until soft and fragrant.

SHUT OFF THE HEAT, add the brandy, and ignite the contents of the pan. When the flames die out, relight the burner and cook until the liquids are almost gone.

Again, SHUT OFF THE HEAT and add the wine. Relight the burner and cook, scraping the bottom of the pan with a paddle, until the liquid is reduced by half.

Whisk in the shellfish stock, mustard, and Worcestershire sauce and continue to cook until the liquids are reduced by about $1/3$, about 2 minutes.

Add the heavy cream and bring to a boil. Cook until reduced by about half and then add the lobster meat. Season with salt and pepper, remove the pan from the heat, and, if not using immediately, keep the sauce warm.

To Finish the Dish: Spray a medium skillet with non-stick vegetable spray and place 6 dumplings in the pan. Add 3 tablespoons of water to the pan and cover. Place the pan over medium-low heat and cook until the wrappers are translucent, about 4 minutes. Remove the dumplings to a plate and wipe out the pan.

Place the skillet over medium-high heat until very hot and add 2 tablespoons of clarified butter. When the butter is melted and foamy, add the dumplings and crisp them until golden brown on both sides, about 1 to 2 minutes total cooking time.

To Plate: Spoon a puddle of sauce into the middle of each plate, place 3 dumplings on top of the puddle, and garnish with a sprig of watercress or tarragon. Drizzle chive oil around the edge of the plate.

the dining room at the short hills hilton

Hilton at Short Hills
41 JFK Parkway
Short Hills 07078
973/379-0100
www.hiltonatshorthills.com

OUR PLAY DATE with executive chef Walter Leffler was one of the highlights of doing this book. We're privileged to call this multitalented man our friend and one of our most respected colleagues, and the time we spent in his vast and busy kitchens at the Hilton at Short Hills was among the most enjoyable and educational time we spent all year.

Walter is a born and enthusiastic teacher who also recognizes that the best teachers are those who never stop learning. This from a guy who had such terrible food allergies as a kid that at thirteen he had to endure a summer of ten allergy shots a week and three bowls of liver purée each day. Some people would give up food altogether—Walter thinks his experience is the reason he became interested and pursued a career in food.

His skills seem limitless—not only does he teach and practice *garde-manger* as an art form, but he does it ambidexterously! And he is possessed of an unerring taste for pairing flavors and the sensibility to observe and respect the core beliefs that make up the architecture of his work. He's a chef who begins with the rule "If it looks like a duck, walks like a duck, and quacks like a duck, it should taste like a duck."

He has amassed a stunning array of awards, including twelve years worth of 5-Diamond awards for the dining room, several Wine Spectator Awards of Excellence, and five years' worth of the distinguished DiRō NA (Distinguished Restaurants of North America) Awards. He has also trained many of the excellent chefs throughout the Hilton empire, worked on the 1988 Food Olympics NY team, and cooked throughout Europe on the Orient Express. And despite his monumental achievements in our world, this is a man who checks his ego at the door. He is a truly nice guy.

We could go on and on, but we'll share one last fact that should tell you all you need to know. When we were privileged to be visited by Julia Child, it was to chef Walter Leffler's private dining room that we took her for what was one of the most outstanding meals of our lives and, according to him, one of the highlights of his.

Pan-Seared Venison Loin
WITH CHANTERELLES AND ARTICHOKES
WITH LINGONBERRY SAUCE

Every now and then, a cook needs to step up to the plate, reach beyond his or her grasp, and accept the challenge to attempt something new. This dish may seem complex or even difficult—certainly it's something to reserve for a special menu—but it is really just a series of simple procedures, and the reward is an exquisite dish, well worth the investment!

Fennel pollen is one of the new and unusual (and admittedly exciting) "spice darlings" in the chefs' pantry of late that, in our Web-shrunk world, is actually fairly easy to get hold of (see the chapter "Resources")—and definitely a worthwhile addition to your own pantry.

Mise en Place:

FOR THE CRANBERRY SPAETZLE:

1 quart cranberry juice cocktail

2 eggs

2 cups milk

2 to 3 cups all-purpose flour

$^1/_2$ tsp. salt

$^1/_4$ tsp. freshly ground white pepper

Kosher salt for the pasta water

FOR THE SAUCE:

1 lb. rack of venison

3 ozs. venison scraps and bones

Salt and freshly ground black pepper, to taste

1 whole shallot, sliced

4 thyme sprigs

2 parsley sprigs

2 T. unsalted butter

1 T. olive oil

1 cup dry red wine

2 cups veal demi-glace

$^3/_4$ cup chicken stock

2 T. lingonberry jam

FOR THE ARTICHOKES:

3 cups vegetable stock

1 cup dry white wine

6 garlic cloves

1 carrot, peeled and cut into several large pieces

2 artichokes

2 T. olive oil

FOR THE VENISON:

Fennel pollen (see the chapter "Resources")—
    OR $^1/_2$ tsp. fennel seeds, lightly toasted in a preheated
    350°F oven just until fragrant

Salt and freshly ground black pepper, to taste

2 T. unsalted butter

1 shallot lobe, halved

1 large branch of fresh thyme

FOR THE CHANTERELLES:

1 T. unsalted butter

1 T. minced shallots

4 medium halved chanterelle mushrooms

Salt and freshly ground black pepper, to taste

$^1/_4$ cup dry white wine

2 T. unsalted butter for sautéing spaetzle

FOR THE GARNISH:

Sprigs of chervil or parsley

Equipment:

Spaetzle maker or colander

Prepare the Spaetzle: In a medium saucepan over high heat, bring the cranberry juice cocktail to a boil and cook until the liquid is syrupy and reduced to about $^1/_4$ cup. Transfer to a small bowl and allow to cool—it will be almost like jello.

In a medium bowl, whisk together the eggs and reduced cranberry syrup. Add the milk and whisk to blend well.

In a separate large bowl, whisk together 2 cups of the flour, salt, and pepper. Slowly whisk in the egg mixture to create a smooth batter. Cover with plastic wrap and refrigerate for at least 30 minutes. The batter can be prepared up to this point and held, refrigerated, for up to 1 day.

Bring a large pot of cold water to a boil and add the kosher salt. Prepare a large bowl of ice and water to shock the spaetzle after boiling.

When the water returns to a full boil, reduce the heat until it is only gently boiling.

great
dishes

32

Scrape the spaetzle dough into the reservoir of a spaetzle maker and work the dough through the holes and into the water. Alternatively, use a colander and push the dough through the colander holes with a spatula. The spaetzle are done when they float to the top of the water.

Scoop out the spaetzle and drop them immediately into the ice bath to stop the cooking. The spaetzle are ready to use or can be well drained and held, refrigerated, in an airtight covered container for up to 2 days.

Prepare the Sauce: Carve the rib bones from the meat of the venison rack. Trim away any fat, sinew, or silverskin and discard. Season the venison scraps and bones with salt and pepper.

In a shallow saucepan over medium heat, sauté the shallot, thyme sprigs, parsley sprigs, venison bones, and scraps in the butter and oil, stirring occasionally, until the meat is well browned and the bottom of the pan is well glazed.

SHUT THE HEAT OFF and add the red wine to deglaze the pan. Turn the heat back on to medium-high, and cook until the wine is reduced by about two-thirds.

Add the veal demi-glace and chicken stock and continue to cook until the sauce is reduced again by about three-quarters and very thick.

Strain the sauce and return it to the pan. Stir in the lingonberry jam. Set aside. The sauce can be prepared up to this point and held, refrigerated, in an airtight covered container for up to 2 days.

Prepare the Artichokes: Place the medium saucepan over medium-high heat, add the vegetable stock, dry white wine, garlic cloves, and carrot and bring to a boil.

Meanwhile, trim away the tough outer leaves from the artichokes and pare the base and stem with a vegetable peeler. Slice off about a $1/2$ to $3/4$ inch from the top to remove any remaining thorny tips. Then use a sharp knife to cut the artichoke in half lengthwise and carve out the fuzzy thistle in the center along with any prickly leaves surrounding it.

Add the artichokes to the pan and cook at a simmer until the artichokes are tender but still somewhat firm, about 15 minutes. Drain, transfer the artichokes to a bowl, and drizzle with olive oil.

For the Venison: Season the venison roast with salt and pepper and sprinkle with the fennel pollen or lightly toasted fennel seeds.

Place a medium skillet over high heat and melt the butter. When the butter is hot and foaming, add the shallot, thyme, and the venison. Brown the venison well on all

sides. Transfer the venison to a plate, lightly tent with aluminum foil, and let the roast rest for 10 minutes.

For the Chanterelles: In a medium skillet over medium-high heat, sauté the chanterelles with the shallots in the butter until the mushrooms are just tender and the shallots are "toasted" but not too brown. Add the wine to deglaze the pan and cook until it evaporates. Add the artichokes and cook, tossing occasionally, until everything is golden brown.

To Finish the Dish: Warm the sauce.

In a medium skillet, sauté 1¹/₂ cups of the spaetzle in 2 tablespoons unsalted butter until very fragrant and barely browned. Season to taste with salt and pepper.

Slice the venison into ¹/₂-inch thick steaks and sprinkle with fennel pollen.

Pour a puddle of sauce off center on each plate. Place the venison steaks on top of the sauce. Spoon the spaetzle next to the venison and top with the artichokes and chanterelles. Garnish with parsley or thyme.

doris & ed's

348 Shore Drive
Highlands 07732

732/872-1565

www.dorisandeds.com

W E   C A L L   H I M Gentleman Jim, and he's alive, well, and charming guests nightly at his mostly seafood restaurant overlooking Sandy Hook Bay. Doris & Ed's is a consistent award winner and listed by *Gourmet* magazine as one of America's Top Tables. But it might be the *Wine Spectator* Award of Excellence that the restaurant has won for almost two decades straight that illuminates the key to what makes self-taught wine connoisseur and award-winning restaurateur Jim Filip tick. Jim simply and completely dedicates himself to excellence by learning about, seeking out, and then acquiring the best of whatever it is he plans to offer his customers—from fresh wasabi root from Oregon to oysters from Nova Scotia to Royal Doulton bone china and Riedl stemware on which his loyal patrons dine and wine.

Lest you think otherwise, we should tell you that Doris & Ed's is not a fussy place—we don't do fussy. It's more about careful and thoughtful attention to the tiniest detail, and that was but one of the delightful characteristics of Doris & Ed's that rang our chimes. Another was that it's done in a relaxed atmosphere and with an easy, natural style that may go unobserved by some, but to those with like sensibilities, it makes Doris & Ed's a complete dining experience.

As for the food, it's prepared expertly by James Beard Award winner chef Russell Dare, who works with skilled confidence to highlight as simply as possible the high-quality ingredients that are always available, and there was not a dish (or even an ingredient) that we tasted that was less than simply outstanding. To this day, we compare all sashimi tuna with the one we tasted there, which, with your eyes closed, you'd think was filet mignon.

Two tips: Don't wait for fair weather to visit Doris & Ed's or you might miss a rare opportunity to enjoy a great New Jersey seafood experience off-season. And don't leave without a slice of Dot's pie.

PEI Mussels and Linguine
WITH CHORIZO, TOMATOES, AND SCALLIONS AND PERNOD

PEI (Prince Edward Isle) mussels are large, deliciously sweet mussels harvested from the waters off Canada's Prince Edward Island in the Gulf of St. Lawrence. We've also made this dish with local mussels with great results. But whichever you use, be sure to buy from a reliable fishmonger and choose the freshest, most uniformly large mussels you can.

Chorizo is a garlicky spiced sausage made from smoked pork and is available in Latin markets and better supermarkets. Pernod is a French anise-flavored liqueur . . . and that's one of the ingredients that makes this dish happen.

It's always a good idea to familiarize yourself with

Chef's TRUC:

The pasta is pre- but under-cooked, until the outside is tender but the inner core is still quite firm. It's immediately plunged into an ice bath to stop the cooking and drained very well. At service, the pasta is plunged once again into boiling, salted water and then drained and finished in the sauce. The result is perfectly *al dente* pasta with a velvety exterior that has absorbed and taken on the full flavors of the sauce.

new ingredients, so if you're not familiar with Pernod, pour yourself a shot and taste it. No, you're probably not having a stroke—it's likely the Pernod that's numbed your tongue. For the serious forensic, pour yourself a "flight" of Pernod, Sambucca, anisette, Galliano, Absinthe . . . and then take the phone off the hook, sit down someplace where you can also fall asleep, and do a "scientific" comparison of licorice transcendent.

Mise en Place:

    12 ozs. linguine

    Kosher salt for the pasta water

    FOR THE SAUCE:

      2 T. unsalted butter

      $1/_4$ cup minced shallots

      2 tsp. minced garlic

8 ozs. chorizo, quartered lengthwise, then cut across into $3/_4$-inch lengths

$2/_3$ cup Pernod

$1/_2$ cup chopped scallions

Salt and freshly ground black pepper

Pinch crushed red pepper flakes

1 cup peeled, seeded, and diced tomato

1 cup heavy cream

20 fresh PEI mussels

Prepare the Pasta: Bring a large pot of cold water to a boil for pasta. Prepare bowl of ice and water to shock the pasta and stop the cooking process.

When the pasta water has reached a full, rolling boil, add 2 tablespoons of kosher salt. When the water returns to a boil, add the pasta all at once and cook, stirring frequently, until the pasta is almost al dente but still quite firm in the center. Drain and shock the pasta in cold water, swishing it around to cool it quickly. Drain well and set aside in a dry bowl. The pasta can be prepared to this point, covered, and held at room temperature for up to 2 hours or refrigerated overnight. It will stick together in a mass but will readily come apart on its own when refreshed prior to finishing.

Prepare the Sauce: Have a large platter ready to receive the mussels as they open.

In a large heavy skillet over medium-high heat, sauté the shallots and garlic in the butter until softened. Add the chorizo and cook until it is fragrant and begins to render its fat.

SHUT OFF THE HEAT and add the Pernod. Relight the burner and cook over high heat until the liquid is reduced by about half.

Add the scallions, salt and pepper to taste, crushed red pepper, and diced tomatoes and cook for about 30 seconds, just to take the raw edge off.

Stir in the cream and then add the mussels and cook, stirring occasionally, until the mussels open.

Remove the mussels to the platter as they open and set aside.

To Finish the Dish: Add the linguine to the pan and cook for about 1 minute, using tongs to toss and coat the pasta with the sauce.

To Plate: Use tongs to pick up the pasta and use a twisting motion to pile it into a high mound on each plate. Spoon the chorizo and any residual sauce over the pasta and arrange the mussels on top.

the ebbitt room
at the virginia

Virginia Hotel
25 Jackson Street
Cape May 08204
609/884-5310
www.virginiahotel.com

NOT TOO LONG AGO you'd have been hard pressed to get great food at a hotel restaurant, but in the past several years that's changed dramatically, and chef Andrew Carthy is at the forefront of that effort.

The perfectly prepared, gorgeously presented food at the Ebbitt Room reflects the influence of the flavor principles and simplicity of Mediterranean cuisine

that shapes Andrew's menus. And the out-of-context accents he subtly and expertly uses to "cross-pollinate" his creations have kept his food so interesting that on any given night you'll find as many or more locals dining there as out-of-towners or hotel guests.

Interestingly, Andrew began his career at the Virginia Hotel during a summer visit from his native Ireland. He first fell in love with Cape May and in the fall moved into the kitchen as a line cook and then spent the next several years working his way up to executive chef. He next fell in love with the waitress who became his wife, and we thank her profusely for keeping this handsome guy right where he was. Yup, handsome, too—it should be criminal both to be this talented and have that killer smile and the blue eyes and dimples to go with it, but this guy is changing the face of hotel dining, and as long as *his* face remains the same, we're all for it.

Heirloom Tomato Salad

Here's a chance to make a deceptively simple but sophisticated salad look professionally done. We found ring molds difficult to find and cost-prohibitive, so we perused our grocery store aisles for a can of just the right size and removed both the top and bottom to make our own ring mold. Works great!

Fennel is the secret ingredient here, and an Asian mandoline is key to shaving the fennel to just the right paper-thinness, as well as for cutting the cucumber base for this salad. Check out the "Resources" chapter for where to get this inexpensive but can't-do-without kitchen tool.

Mise en Place:

FOR THE WHITE BALSAMIC REDUCTION:

1 cup white balsamic vinegar

3 to 4 large red and yellow ripe
   Jersey heirloom tomatoes,
   cut into $3/4$-inch wedges

$1/2$ bulb fennel, shaved paper-thin
   (use a mandoline)

$1/2$ medium red onion, cut into
   $1/8$-inch wedges

Sea salt and freshly ground
   black pepper, to taste

3 T. good-quality lemon-flavored
   olive oil

1 cup $1/2$-inch cubed ricotta
   salata cheese

2 T. fine chiffonade of fresh basil
   leaves (see the chapter
   "Procedures and Techniques")

$1/4$ hothouse or English seedless
   cucumber, sliced paper-thin
   (use a mandoline)

1 cup mesclun greens

1 T. lemon-flavored olive oil

Salt and pepper, to taste

Equipment:

Mandoline

3-inch-diameter, $2^1/2$-inch deep
   ring molds (see Headnote)

Prepare the White Balsamic Reduction: Pour the white balsamic vinegar into a small saucepan and place over high heat. Bring the vinegar to a boil and cook until the it's reduced to about $1/3$ cup. Remove the pan from the heat and set aside to cool.

Prepare the Salad: Place the tomatoes, fennel, and red onion in a medium bowl and season to taste with salt and pepper. Drizzle with the 3 tablespoons of lemon oil and $1^1/2$ tablespoons of white balsamic reduction and toss gently. Add the ricotta salata cubes and basil chiffonade and gently toss again.

Decoratively arrange the cucumber slices in a circle about 4 inches in diameter on each plate. Position a ring mold on the cucumber circle, adjusting the cucumbers so as to create a border exceeding the diameter of the ring mold.

Mound the tomato salad into the ring mold, pressing down to compact it. Carefully remove the ring mold.

Toss the mesclun greens with the remaining tablespoon of lemon-flavored oil, salt, and pepper and mound the greens on top of the tomato salad.

esty street

86 Spring Valley Road

Park Ridge 07656

201/307-1515

www.estystreet.com

You'd expect nothing less than the popularity of Esty Street from owner Scott Tremble—it was his parents who owned the Iron Horse restaurant of the stuffed cheeseburger fame. Admittedly a tough act to follow, but probably not for a guy who, with roomie Drew Nieporent, graduated from Cornell's hospitality school, where they lived on the original and inspirational Esty Street for which the restaurant was named.

Still, the only guarantee of success is getting it right, and after many years in upscale catering, Scott has proved he knows how to make it work—he sets the parameters and then has the security and wisdom to turn it over to executive chef Jack Mistretta, who takes the lead and goes to town with it.

Of course, in Park Ridge, "town" often refers to Manhattan, a short ride for sophisticated locals. Yet mention Esty Street to people from the tony towns around, and those "you know our secret!" or "have you been there?" smiles creep across their faces, and its clear these guys can hold their own alongside the best Manhattan eateries.

Jack says he feels the weather, and his produce-driven menu, which naturally changes seasonally, is peppered with lots of vegetable-based sauces—his sweet corn-chipotle sauce this summer knocked our socks off.

Pick a season, any season, and go eat the best of it.

Arugula Salad

WITH SHAVED PECORINO ROMANO, OVEN-DRIED TOMATOES, AND RED ONION IN A LEMON VINAIGRETTE

Oven-dried is the creative chef's answer to how to enjoy tomatoes year-round, and this salad is a perfect application for them. These tomatoes can turn the "off" season back on, and chef Jack Mistretta prepares them in quantity and keeps them refrigerated and submerged in fruity olive oil for up to a week so they're available throughout the non-tomato-friendly seasons. Once you fall in love with them, chop them with some of their oil and freshly chopped herbs of choice and toss with hot pasta and a handful of Parmigiano-Reggiano.

Mise en Place:

FOR THE OVEN-DRIED TOMATOES:

12 large plum tomatoes

4 cloves garlic, peeled and lightly smashed

2 tsp. chopped fresh Italian flat-leaf parsley

2 tsp. chopped fresh basil

2 tsp. chopped fresh oregano

2 tsp. chopped fresh chives

$1/4$ cup extra virgin olive oil

Salt and freshly ground black pepper, to taste

FOR THE LEMON VINAIGRETTE:

3 T. canola oil

1 T. extra virgin olive oil

1 tsp. Dijon mustard

2 tsp. finely minced shallot

Salt and freshly ground black pepper, to taste

$1^1/2$ T. freshly squeezed lemon juice

FOR THE SALAD:

1 large bunch arugula, tough stems trimmed, cleaned and spun very dry

$1/2$ small red onion, cut into $1/8$-inch wedges

Shavings of Pecorino-Romano cheese, shaved with a vegetable peeler

Prepare the Oven-Dried Tomatoes: Preheat the oven to 200°F. Line a baking sheet with parchment paper and set a cooling rack on top.

Slice the tomatoes into ¹/₂-inch-thick lengthwise wedges and place them in a large bowl. Add the garlic cloves, herbs, olive oil, salt, and pepper and gently toss everything together.

Spoon the tomatoes onto the rack and bake until the tomatoes are dehydrated but not leathery, about 6 to 8 hours. The tomatoes can be prepared up to this point, transferred to an airtight container filled with extra virgin olive oil to cover, and held, refrigerated, for up to 1 week.

Prepare the Lemon Vinaigrette: Pour the oils into a medium mixing bowl and whisk in the mustard, shallot, salt, and pepper. Slowly add the lemon juice, whisking constantly to form an emulsion.

To Plate: Place the arugula in a large mixing bowl and toss with just enough lemon vinaigrette to coat the leaves. Mound the arugula onto chilled salad plates and top with several tomato slices. Garnish with shavings of Pecorino-Romano and red onion wedges.

the frenchtown inn

7 Bridge Street
Frenchtown 08825
908/996-3300
www.frenchtowninn.com

W E M I G H T H A V E M E T chef-owner Andrew Tomko and his wife, Colleen, many years ago when they both worked at the Frenchtown Inn, which was a favorite place for us to treat ourselves after a day in New Hope. But cut to the present and this hand-

some couple have come full circle—they now own this historic building and live on one of the spacious upstairs floors with their two gorgeous kids and a spectacular view of the Delaware River.

Andrew grew up in nearby Alexandria, one of New Jersey's thriving farm communities, and this is likely the reason he's so in tune with the seasons and with keeping things natural and simplistic. He waits to change his menu until the season totally kicks in, and it pretty much builds itself based on what he's hungry for. Hey—if it's good enough for Andy, it's good enough for us!

Colleen, who grew up just across the river, is the restaurant's skilled sommelier, and Andy's brother is hands on in the kitchen, working garde-manger and on the line with him. Together they perform to a packed house with lunch and dinner six days a week as well as a Sunday brunch they're famous for. And with all this on their plate, this young family still manages to regularly make time to support and participate in more than a few fund-raising efforts each year to benefit people in need.

More to come—they are continuing and have expanded the renovation that began before their time in 1985, and it won't be long before the Frenchtown Inn is more than just one of the top-rated restaurants in New Jersey.

Rack of Lamb

OVER STILTON-POTATO GENOISE CAKE
WITH APRICOT-PISTACHIO CHUTNEY

Chef Andrew Tomko's uniquely delicious Stilton-Potato Genoise Cakes are the savory treasure that literally elevates this beautifully presented dish beyond just a great rack of lamb. We used English muffin rings, available at most kitchenware stores, to punch out the cakes after baking.

Mise en Place:

An 8-rib rack of American lamb, bones frenched
(see the chapter "The Tools, the Terms, the Ingredients, and When to Use Them")

2 tsp. canola oil

Salt and freshly ground black pepper

FOR THE APRICOT-PISTACHIO CHUTNEY:

4 ozs. dried apricots, chopped

$1/4$ cup shelled and chopped unsalted pistachio nuts, toasted for 5 minutes in a preheated 350°F oven

¹/₄ cup apricot brandy

1 T. sugar

1 T. rice wine vinegar

3 T. water

FOR THE STILTON-POTATO GENOISE CAKES:

1 lb. red bliss or Yukon Gold potatoes, peeled and cut
   into 1-inch dice

1 T. salt

¹/₄ cup all-purpose flour

¹/₄ cup crumbled Stilton blue cheese

2 T. whole milk

1 whole large egg

Salt and freshly ground white pepper, to taste

Nonstick vegetable spray

FOR THE RED-WINE REDUCTION SAUCE:

2 tsp. unsalted butter

2 T. finely chopped yellow onion

1 T. finely chopped carrot

1 T. finely chopped celery

1 small shallot lobe, finely chopped

1 clove garlic, peeled and smashed

Sprig of fresh thyme

1 bay leaf

1 tsp. chopped fresh tarragon

¹/₂ tsp. fresh chopped rosemary

1 cup port wine

¹/₄ cup red burgundy wine

¹/₄ cup veal demi-glace (see the chapter "Resources")

Salt and freshly ground black pepper, to taste

FOR GARNISH:

6 haricots verts or thin, tender green beans

Broccoli florets

2 tsp. unsalted butter

Equipment:

3-inch ring molds, or English muffin rings

Potato ricer or food mill

Prepare the Apricot-Pistachio Chutney: In a small saucepan over medium heat, bring all the ingredients to a boil, reduce the heat, and cook gently for 15 to 20 minutes, adding water 1 tablespoon at a time if the mixture gets too dry. The chutney can be prepared ahead to this point and refrigerated in a covered container for up to 1 week. Bring to room temperature or gently warm just slightly before serving.

Prepare the Stilton-Potato Genoise Cakes: Preheat the oven to 350°F.

Place the potatoes in a medium saucepan and add cold water to cover the potatoes by 2 inches. Add 1 tablespoon of salt and bring to a boil. Reduce the heat to a gentle boil and cook until the potatoes are tender when pierced with the tip of a paring knife, about 10 to 12 minutes.

Drain the potatoes and push them through a ricer or food mill into the work bowl of a stand mixer or a mixing bowl. Add the flour, Stilton cheese, milk, and egg and whip to blend the ingredients well. Season to taste with salt and pepper.

Line an 8-inch square baking pan with parchment paper and spray with nonstick vegetable spray. Spread the potato mixture in the pan in an even layer and bake until lightly golden brown, about 15 minutes.

Cool and cut out rounds with a 3-inch cookie cutter or English muffin mold. The potato cakes can be prepared ahead and kept, refrigerated and covered, for up to 2 days. Reheat on a baking sheet in a preheated 300°F oven until warm throughout, about 10 minutes.

Prepare the Red-Wine Reduction Sauce: Melt the butter in a medium saucepan over medium-low heat and add the onion, carrot, celery, shallot, and garlic and cook gently, without browning, until the vegetables are tender, about 5 minutes.

Add the thyme, bay leaf, tarragon, and rosemary and cook for 1 minute more, until the herbs are fragrant. Add the wines, raise the heat to medium-high, and bring to a

Chef's TRUC:

To create the fluffiest potatoes, Andrew pushes the cooked potato through a ricer or a foodmill before mixing in the remaining ingredients.

sides, about 8 minutes total, finishing with bones down and the meatiest side up.

Transfer the skillet to the oven to finish the lamb, about 10 to 12 minutes to medium rare.

Remove the skillet from the oven, loosely tent with foil, and let rest for 5 minutes.

To Finish the Dish: Bring a medium pot filled with cold water to a boil and add 1 tablespoon of salt. Drop in the haricots verts and cook until the beans brighten and are crisp-tender, about 3 minutes. Use a slotted spoon to transfer the haricots verts to a bowl and toss with 1 teaspoon of the butter.

Drop the broccoli into the boiling water and cook until the broccoli brightens and is crisp-tender, about 3 minutes. Use a slotted spoon to transfer the broccoli to a bowl and toss with the remaining teaspoon of butter.

boil. Boil the sauce until it is reduced to about a quarter of the original volume.

Add the veal demi-glace and heat through. Season to taste with salt and pepper. Strain the sauce through a fine sieve and keep warm.

Prepare the Lamb: Preheat the oven to 425°F.

Divide the rack into 2 equal halves. Remove 3 of the 4 bones on each half rack, leaving 1 end bone. Smear the meat with canola oil and season liberally with salt and freshly ground pepper.

Preheat an ovenproof skillet over medium-high heat and add the lamb, meaty side down. Brown the lamb on all

Heat the potato cakes.

Warm the sauce.

To Plate: Spoon a puddle of sauce into the center of each plate and place a potato cake on top. Place the haricots verts to the side of the potato cake and place the broccoli on top.

Carve the meat into 4 "steaks," leaving the end piece as a bone-in chop. Position the 3 "steaks" at the edge of the potato cake and the chop on top. Finish with a spoonful of chutney on the chop.

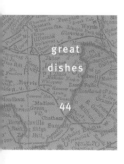

the frog and the peach

29 Dennis Street

New Brunswick 08901

732/846-3216

www.frogandpeach.com

OPENED TO ALMOST instant success in 1983, The Frog and the Peach was one of the first New American restaurants in New Jersey, and it wasn't long into our conversation with owner Betsy Alger before it became apparent why the restaurant has maintained its position on the landscape and continues to lead the pack with the fresh, clean, and straightforward character of its food.

Chatting with Betsy was like playing New Jersey chef geography—the alumni list of chefs who have gone on to open many of our (and your) favorite New Jersey restaurants is really impressive, and Betsy and her partner-husband, Jim Black, recognize that their support of professional development for the staff is the win-win that sparks creativity and promotes a sense of ownership their patrons can feel.

Jim, the official space creator and designer of the partnership, is a landscape architect in real life and according to Betsy has a great "eye." He must have, because the former industrial space that now houses The Frog and the Peach was, in its last incarnation, a factory where leather handles for suitcases were made, and when they bought the building there was glue everywhere. They gutted it but retained the character of the building by leaving exposed brick and ductwork and taking advantage of the vaulted ceiling and lofting a second-floor dining area. The patio dining area was added later, and recently that space was heated so "outdoor" dining can be almost year round.

Betsy and Jim call their food New American with World Influences—we call it happily eclectic and exciting and definitely not to be mistaken for fusion food.

The ingredients are intelligently paired and juxtaposed, the flavors come through clearly, and the attention to presentation makes the dishes look as good as they taste. This dessert clearly illustrates the point.

Napoleon

OF POACHED PEARS, PASSION FRUIT-SCENTED DATES, AND CINNAMON PHYLLO CRISPS

Pastry chef Louis Vasquez's dessert is a minimally fussy and masterful creation of simple and vibrant flavors and colors.

There are four components to this dish, but each takes only a few minutes, and all can be done well ahead. The dish is plated cold, *à la minute* (at the last minute), making it a perfect do-ahead dessert for a guest menu.

We tried several variations of passion fruit nectar, but the only brand that gave us the color, clarity, and texture of the sauce that matched chef Louis's was Looza.

Mise en Place:

FOR THE POACHED PEARS:

16 ozs. white wine

1-inch piece of ginger, peeled and sliced

2 star anise

1 cinnamon stick

6 T. sugar

1 Anjou pear, peeled, cored, and sliced crosswise about $1/8$ inch thick (use a mandoline)

FOR THE PASSION FRUIT–SCENTED DATES:

16 ozs. passion fruit nectar (see the chapter "Resources")

4 T. sugar

1 vanilla bean

1 lb. seeded, dried Medjool dates, sliced $1/4$ inch thick crosswise

FOR THE CINNAMON-PHYLLO CRISPS:

$1/2$ cup granulated sugar

$1^1/2$ tsp. ground cinnamon

3 sheets phyllo dough

Clarified butter for brushing phyllo (see the chapter "Procedures and Techniques")

FOR THE SWEETENED CRÈME FRAÎCHE:

1 T. confectioners' sugar whisked into 3 ozs. crème fraîche

Confectioners' sugar for garnishing

Equipment:

Mandoline

Parchment paper

Prepare the Poached Pears: In a medium saucepan over high heat, bring the wine, ginger, star anise, cinnamon stick, and sugar to a boil. Add the pear slices, reduce the heat to a gentle boil, and cook just until the pears are tender, about 10 minutes. Chill the pears in the poaching liquid until ready to use. The pears can be prepared up to this point and held, refrigerated in a covered container, for up to 5 days.

Prepare the Passion Fruit-Scented Dates: Place the sliced dates in a bowl.

Mix together the passion fruit nectar and sugar in a medium saucepan. Slit the vanilla bean in half lengthwise and scrape the seeds into the nectar. Bring the mixture to a boil and cook until the liquid is reduced by about a third, about 5 minutes. Pour the hot sauce over the dates and set aside to cool. The dates and sauce can be prepared up to this point and held, refrigerated in a covered container, for up to 2 days.

Prepare the Cinnamon-Phyllo Crisps: Preheat the oven to 350°F. Line a baking sheet with parchment paper.

Combine the the sugar and cinnamon. Position a sheet of phyllo on the parchment-lined sheet pan. Brush the dough all over with clarified butter and cover the dough with a light sprinkling of cinnamon sugar. Place a second sheet on top of the first, brush with butter, and sprinkle with cinnamon sugar. Repeat with the third sheet of phyllo.

Using a very sharp knife or pizza wheel, trim off messy edges and cut the phyllo in a grid pattern to make 2^1/$_2$-inch squares.

Place a sheet of parchment directly on the phyllo and fit a second baking sheet snugly on top.

Bake until the phyllo is crisp and the sugar is caramelized, about 12 to 15 minutes. Cool slightly and then transfer the phyllo squares to a fresh piece of parchment. The phyllo squares can be prepared up to this point and kept at room temperature in an airtight covered container for up to 1 week.

To Plate: Dust 6 phyllo squares heavily with confectioners' sugar.

Place several dates in the center of each cold dessert plate. Place a few slices of poached pear on top, followed by a sugar-dusted phyllo square. Top the phyllo with a few more pear slices, another sugar-dusted phyllo square, and a few more pear slices and finish with a third sugar-dusted phyllo square.

Surround the pastry with some of the reduced passion fruit nectar and a drizzle of sweetened crème fraîche.

fromagerie

26 Ridge Road

Rumson 07760

732/842-8088

www.fromagerierestaurant.com

WE'LL NEVER FORGET the first time we celebrated with friends at Fromagerie—classic, classy, and steeped in thirty years worth of Old World ambience. We knew long before we spent the day with chef-owner Hubert Peter that this was a place we'd visit again and again to set the scene for our most special occasions. By the end of that memorable day, it was clear why Fromagerie is the special place it is.

The front of the house, run by owner Markus Peter, is customer-driven and geared to the consistent excellence upon which Fromagerie has built its reputation.

The kitchen at Fromagerie is run by Hubert in the European way—like a Swiss clock, by an Austrian master, with classic French frugality and technique, and all its "musicians" working in concert to create the symphony it is. The back of the house is food-driven, and everything the kitchen produces reflects its no-shortcut, everything-done-from-scratch and in-house standard. We don't expect to ever see the level of skill and craftsmanship we witnessed in the four minutes it took Hubert to expertly fabricate (butcher) a duck, with the clear intent of using every single perfectly cut part, and still take the time and care to arrange the finished pieces as though they were the subject of an oil painting. The man is a master.

The menu changes minimally, although the award-winning wine list changes in accordance with the finest selections available from Markus's frequent buying trips to Europe and California. This is the philosophy at Fromagerie—it's a warm and well-appointed place where the classics are celebrated, perfectly executed, enhanced by excellent wines, and presented with service that sets the standard. Celebrate something special in your life at Fromagerie.

Lobster Sausage

We're well known for our homemade sausage, but despite its position on our endless to-do list, we'd never ventured into the realm of seafood sausage until we had the supreme pleasure of spending a day with a true master sausage maker, chef-owner Hubert Peter.

Filling the sausage can be intimidating, especially after witnessing Hubert do it without any high-tech equipment, using only three fingers of one hand to hold the casing open and shooting the stuffing (or *farcie*) into the casing with the fist of the other! Don't let

that scare you—we accomplished the same (or a reasonable facsimile thereof) easily with a pastry bag and a 5/8-inch plain tip.

As for the par-cooked lobster claw meat, a good fishmonger will graciously estimate how much he has to lightly steam for you to yield 2 pounds. And play it safe—make sure your ingredients are kept ice cold!

Mise en Place:

FOR THE SAUSAGE:

2 T. chopped shallots

1 tsp. unsalted butter

1 lb. ice-cold raw perch OR ¹/₂ lb. perch
and ¹/₂ lb. pike

1 lb. ice-cold raw scallops, muscle removed

4 large egg whites

3 cups ice-cold heavy cream

2 lbs. ice-cold lobster claw meat, par-cooked
and chopped

2 T. fresh chopped tarragon leaves

2 T. fresh chopped dill

Salt and freshly ground white pepper, to taste

Hog casings, well rinsed, soaked in cold water

FOR THE LEEKS:

2 T. unsalted butter

2 cups coarsely chopped white part of leeks

¹/₂ cup water

Salt and freshly ground white pepper, to taste

FOR GARNISH:

¹/₂ cup finely diced, seeded tomato

Sprig of fresh chervil

Equipment:

Food processor

Pastry bag fitted with a ⁵/₈-inch plain tip

Instant-read thermometer

Prepare the Farci (Stuffing): In a small skillet over
medium heat, gently sauté the shallots in 1 teaspoon of

butter, without browning, until soft and tender. Transfer to a bowl and chill well.

In a food processor, grind the perch (and pike, if using) and scallops, along with the egg whites and shallots, to a paste. With the machine running, add half of the cream and continue to process to a smooth purée. Keep the machine running and add the remainder of the cream—the mixture will thicken. Transfer the mixture to a large bowl and fold in the lobster meat, tarragon, and dill and season with salt and pepper. Refrigerate until well chilled.

Prepare the Melted Leeks: In a medium saucepan over medium heat, melt the butter and add the leeks, tossing to coat the leeks with the melted butter. Add $1/2$ cup water and slowly cook the leeks, stirring occasionally, without browning, until the leeks are meltingly tender. Season to taste with salt and pepper. Keep warm.

Finish the Sausage: Fit a pastry bag with a $5/8$-inch plain tip and fill the bag with the seafood mixture. Tie a knot in the end of the hog casing, gather the casing onto the tip, and squeeze in the farci, filling the casing until it is firm but still flexible and twisting at 4-inch intervals to create individual links.

Bring a large pot of cold water to a temperature of 175°F and add the sausages. The temperature will drop—use a thermometer and adjust the heat as necessary to assure that the temperature is maintained at 165 to 170°F (too high and the sausages will burst open when the egg white cooks and expands!). Drop a clean kitchen towel on top to keep the sausages submerged and poach just until cooked through, about 10 minutes.

To Plate: Spoon a mound of melted leeks in the center of each plate. Slit the sausage casing with a sharp knife and slip the poached filling out onto the bed of leeks. Garnish the plate with the diced tomato and top with a sprig of chervil.

giumarello's

329 Haddon Avenue

Westmont 08108

856/858-9400

*I*F YOU'RE GOING to own a restaurant this close to Philadelphia, you'd better be really good and stay that way, which is likely why there are so few in the Cherry Hill area. And therefore likely the reason Giumarello's has succeeded so well and for so long.

It's a family affair at Giumarello's, with chef-owner Sam in the kitchen, brother and co-owner Gian doing double duty as pastry chef and mixologist, and mom

(who looks more like sister) Rosemary hostessing now and again. And not only are they breaking those close-to-the-big-city rules, but they're also breaking the records—so much so that *Philadelphia* magazine reached across the border and named Gian's thirty-two-concoction (and still growing) martini menu Best of Philly. The bar offers more than thirty wines by the glass, and the wine list is impressive and likely to grow more so as Gian pursues his education in that area with the same focus with which he seems to do anything he undertakes.

But we were here for the food, and it turned out to be food that spoke to us. Homestyle Italian originals, many from Rosemary's home kitchen, are upskilled by Sam to a level of sophistication that can hold its own and then some with any high-end Italian restaurant we've experienced—sans the pretension, thank you very much—and without sacrificing the warmth a family-owned and -run operation brings to the table. Our new favorite fried calamari variation is the Spicy Shrimp and Calamari Salad, tossed hot from the fryer with chopped-up vinegar peppers and served on a bed of greens.

Don't even think about skipping dessert—this would definitely not be the place to do it. Did we mention that the Giumarello's also owned a bakery at one time? Yup. The desserts are all based on family recipes and made in-house, including the gelato.

Fried Chesapeake Bay Oysters
WITH SUN-DRIED TOMATO AIOLI

We must confess—oysters were never something we went out of our way to order. And at this point in our lives, we really didn't think that was because we'd never tasted them prepared so deliciously as to be irresistible. It hurts to be wrong, but in this case we'll live with the pain.

Mise en Place:

FOR THE ROASTED SHALLOT–MUSTARD VINAIGRETTE:

2 large shallot lobes, peeled and halved

$1/2$ tsp. olive oil

Pinch salt

3 T. extra virgin olive oil

$1/2$ tsp. Dijon mustard

Salt and freshly ground black pepper, to taste

2 tsp. balsamic vinegar

FOR THE SUN-DRIED TOMATO AIOLI:

$^1/_4$ cup squeezed, drained, and finely chopped oil-marinated sun-dried tomatoes

$^1/_2$ cup mayonnaise

2 tsp. freshly squeezed lemon juice

Salt and freshly ground black pepper, to taste

FOR THE CHESAPEAKE BAY OYSTERS:

8 large fresh Chesapeake Bay oysters, shelled, rinsed, and patted very dry

Salt and freshly ground black pepper, to taste

About 1 cup all-purpose flour for coating oysters

2 large eggs, beaten

1 tsp. Dijon mustard

About $1^1/_2$ cups panko (Japanese breadcrumbs; see the chapter "The Tools, the Terms, the Ingredients, and When to Use Them")

$^1/_2$ cup freshly grated Parmigiano cheese

2 T. finely chopped fresh Italian parsley leaves

Freshly ground black pepper

Canola oil for deep frying

Mesclun salad greens

Prepare the Roasted Shallot-Mustard Vinaigrette:
Preheat the oven to 350°F.

Toss the shallots with the olive oil, sprinkle with salt, and place in a small dish. Roast the shallots until tender and browned, about 45 minutes. Set the shallots and any juices they accumulate aside to cool and then mince.

In a small bowl, whisk together the olive oil, shallots, mustard, salt, and pepper. Slowly add the vinegar, whisking constantly to form an emulsion. Set aside at room temperature. The vinaigrette can be prepared ahead and kept, refrigerated in a covered container, for up to 3 days. Bring to room temperature when ready to use.

Prepare the Sun-Dried Tomato Aioli: In a small bowl, whisk together the sun-dried tomatoes and mayonnaise, then whisk in the lemon juice. Season to taste with salt and pepper.

Prepare the Oysters: Put the flour in a medium bowl and season with salt and pepper.

In a separate bowl, whisk the eggs and mustard together.

In a third bowl, mix together the panko, Parmigiano cheese, parsley, and black pepper.

To Finish the Dish: Fill a large, deep pot with 4 inches of canola oil for deep-frying, making sure the pot is deep enough so that the oil reaches a level of no more than one-third the total depth of the pot. Place the pot over high heat and heat until the oil reaches 375°F.

When the oil is ready, dredge the oysters in the flour and shake off the excess. Swish the oysters in the egg mixture and allow the excess to drip off. Then coat the oysters with the panko mixture, making sure the coating covers the oysters completely and there are no bare spots.

Lower half the oysters into the hot oil and fry until they're cooked through and the centers are just firm, about 2 minutes. Scoop them out onto the paper-towel-lined plate. Repeat with the remaining oysters.

To Plate: In a medium bowl, toss the salad greens with just enough vinaigrette to coat the leaves and place a mound of dressed greens off-center on each plate. Spoon a crescent-shaped puddle of aioli on the other half of the plate. Place the oysters on top of the aioli and serve immediately.

the grand café

42 Washington Street

Morristown 07960

973/540-9444

www.thegrandcafe.com

ONCE UPON A TIME Cadillacs had fins and gentlemen opened the doors to them for their ladies. In fact, the phrase "gentlemen and their ladies" was considered complimentary and could be freely uttered without getting socked in the face.

In those olden days, a Saturday night out to dinner was special. Gentlemen wore suits and topcoats, ladies wore dresses and furs, people drank cocktails before dinner that didn't have X-rated names and sat on upholstered chairs at elegantly appointed candlelit tables, and a good time was had by all. Welcome to Desmond and Alice Lloyd's Grand Café.

We have a special place in our hearts for the Grand Café—part nostalgic and part simply because it's one of our hometown icons and a place where we can always be assured of a great meal with great service and the great possibility that we'll run into several people we know because it's a place people come back to regularly.

The decor is classically elegant, and so is the menu. Years ago, the menu was called Continental—now we call it classic (not to be confused with unexciting) because it has stood the test of time. Chef Paul Bogardus has freshened the classics with his own talented fingerprint but not so much that they need to be recategorized. And both the decor and the menu add to the ambience that has been bringing loyal patrons back to the Grand Café for more than twenty award-winning years. If you have a Grand Café kind of place that brings back memories, you'll love a dining experience here. And if you don't, this is the place where you'll create them.

Baked Alaska

If Baked Alaska isn't THE ultimate retro dessert, we don't know what is—it makes Steve want to dig out a clip-on tie and brings back 1950s memories of acute crinoline rash of the waistline to me! Old-fogey jokes aside, this is also one dessert that has stood the test of time and still brings a special end to a celebratory meal.

Contrary to its regal appearance, Baked Alaska is not a particularly difficult dessert to execute—but it does require some last-minute attention, and it helps to have a good freezer with available space if you want to buy yourself a little time and flexibility when it comes to finishing the dish. This cake recipe will make 12 cake bases for the Baked Alaska, the extras of which can be frozen. But the cake is also delicious uncut and on its own, simply dusted with confectioners' sugar or used in any recipe that calls for a sponge or genoise cake.

Pastry chef Kristine Kaufman pipes the meringue in a beehive design because she can. We mere mortals spooned on a thick coating and swirled up a few peaks for comic relief. Hers is gorgeous—ours sort of had "character" like Marge Simpson's hair. Both were delicious.

Mise en Place:

FOR THE ALMOND CAKE:

3 cups sifted cake flour

1 T. baking powder

$1/2$ tsp. salt

$1^1/_2$ cups whole milk

$1^1/_2$ T. unsalted butter

$1/4$ cup almond extract

6 large eggs

$2^1/_2$ cups superfine sugar

FOR THE MERINGUE:

3 large egg whites, room temperature

Pinch salt

$^1/_8$ tsp. cream of tartar

$^1/_2$ cup plus 1 T. superfine sugar

Ice cream, flavor of choice, to finish the dish

Fresh berries or fruit for garnish

Sauce, either prepared chocolate sauce or defrosted sweetened frozen fruit, whizzed in a blender to a smooth purée.

Equipment:

Parchment paper

Stand mixer or electric handheld mixer

$2^1/_2$-inch round cookie cutter

Pastry bag fitted with a $^5/_8$-inch plain tip (optional)

Propane torch (optional)

Prepare the Almond Cake: Preheat the oven to 350°F. Line a buttered 12" × 18" sheet pan with parchment paper.

Sift together the flour, baking powder, and salt. Set aside.

In a medium pan over medium heat, heat together the milk and butter until the butter is melted. Remove the pan from the heat and stir in the almond extract.

In the work bowl of a stand mixer or in a clean mixing bowl using a handheld electric mixer, whip the eggs together with the sugar until thick and pale in color. Slowly add the warm milk mixture, whisking constantly.

Use a large rubber spatula to fold the dry ingredients into the egg mixture and pour the batter into the prepared sheetpan.

Bake until the cake is golden brown, springs back when

touched, and a toothpick inserted into the center comes out clean, about 15 to 20 minutes. Cool completely.

Invert the sheet pan onto a work surface or another sheet pan lined with fresh parchment paper. Peel off the exposed parchment from the bottom of the cake.

Use a 2¹/₂-inch round cookie cutter to cut out as many circles from the cake as you wish. You will use only 2 for this recipe—the remainder of the cake can be frozen. The cake can be prepared ahead and kept, wrapped in waxed paper and then aluminum foil, at room temperature for up to 4 days, or wrapped and frozen for up to 1 month. In either case, the rounds can be cut out before storage for ease of use.

Place the cake rounds on an aluminum-foil-lined sheet pan or on flat ovenproof serving dishes and top each with a well-rounded scoop of ice cream. Place the ice cream–topped cakes in the freezer while you prepare the meringue topping.

Prepare the Meringue: In the work bowl of a stand mixer fitted with the whisk attachment or with an electric handheld mixer, whip the egg whites until they look "sudsy" and then whip in the salt and the cream of tartar. Continue whipping until the mixture begins to whiten and thicken, and then, whipping constantly, slowly and steadily add the sugar. Your goal is to incorporate and have dissolved all the sugar by the time the meringue holds a stiff peak—one that, except for a tiny "flopover" at the very top, stands firm and tall right where you lifted it.

To Finish the Dish: Preheat the oven to 450°F or plan to use a propane torch to "toast" the meringue topping.

Either pipe the meringue over the ice cream and cake with a plain tip to create a beehive pattern or mound and spread a thick coating of meringue over all, swirling the meringue in a few spots to create some design and texture to its appearance. In either case, be sure to completely encase the cake and ice cream with a thick layer of meringue.

Carefully brown the meringue by using a propane torch

as for crème brûlée or by placing the sheet pan in the preheated oven for about 6 minutes and then using a metal spatula to transfer the browned desserts to individual plates.

To Plate: Garnish the plate with fresh fruit or berries and your choice of sauce and serve immediately.

harvest moon inn

1039 Old York Road

Ringoes 08551

908/806-6020

www.harvestmooninn.com

MENTION THE TOWN of Ringoes to most people and the initial response is, "Where?" And let's face it—it's not exactly a busy crossroads. But chef-owner Stanley Novak and his partner-wife, Teresa, have proved the axiom "if you build it, they will come."

OK, so they didn't build it. It had been there for a while (c. 1811) and is considered to be one of the finest examples of Federalist architecture in New Jersey. And the fans didn't *come* so much as *follow* Stan and his exceptional New American cuisine, Steve and I among them. But the awards did come, from the very first year the Harvest Moon Inn opened, and they're still coming, including five years' worth of Wine Excellence awards from the Wine Spectator and the prestigious American Academy of Hospitality Sciences Five-Star Diamond Award, which is held by fewer than one hundred hotels and resorts internationally.

Stan has a mantra—utilization—and he applies it with innovative creativity. You have only to taste his sausage, for example, to get the idea. With very little exception, everything at the Harvest Moon Inn is made in-house and all by Stan himself. He's a man of few words but not because he's shy; beneath his calm, quiet exterior is an intensely focused Renaissance man, a multitalented guy who is so creative that everything he sees morphs into something terrific—an idea, a concept, a dish, another page on his Web site.

Stan Novak is a thinking chef, enamored of learning, observant of how and why things happen in the kitchen, and if you're lucky enough to spend some time with him in his inner sanctum, he's a font of interesting information. His food is generous with big flavors, and he often gets there by breaking the rules in pursuit of one of the endless cutting-edge ideas rattling around in his amazing brain. And sometimes it's just Stanley's ability to cross-think and the application of his talent for using usual ingredients in unusual ways.

But what pulls it all together is the partnership of Stanley and Teresa. They met in kindergarten, his first job was as a teenage dishwasher at her family's restaurant, and they are true partners, two halves of a whole in everything they do, including raising Brianna and Alex, their similarly multitalented kids. The strong foundation of the Novaks' world is very obviously their relationship—they are best friends who have managed to have their cake and eat it, too. It just takes a little eye contact between them to evoke a smile or share a laugh, and both the family and the restaurant thrive on their synergy.

Go spend a day in Flemington, save lots of money at the outlets, and spend some of it on a remarkable dining experience at the Harvest Moon Inn.

Arugula Salad

WITH CRISPY DUCK CONFIT AND
LEMON-GARLIC VINAIGRETTE

It's confession time—we've been in love with this salad since our first visit to the Harvest Moon Inn. It's the first thing we look for when the menus are placed in our hands. We recommend it to everyone we bring there and always breathe a sigh of relief to find that in his ultimate wisdom, chef-owner Stanley Novak hasn't removed it from the menu. There hasn't been a time since that we haven't ordered it and enjoyed it as much as the first time—and even though we now have the recipe (and can actually BUY ready-made duck confit!), there's no doubt we'll continue to order and enjoy it every time we're there.

Mise en Place:

FOR THE CRISPY DUCK CONFIT:

2 T. duck fat

1 cup shredded duck confit (see the chapter "Resources")

FOR THE LEMON-GARLIC VINAIGRETTE:

1 large egg yolk

1 tsp. minced garlic

1 cup grapeseed or canola oil

Freshly squeezed juice of 1 lemon, about 3 T. juice

3 T. rice wine vinegar

Salt and freshly ground black pepper, to taste

4 cups cleaned and trimmed arugula

2 T. freshly grated Parmigiano-Reggiano cheese

1 cup of your favorite brand of garlic-herb croutons

Equipment:

Mini-processor

Prepare the Crispy Duck Confit: Line a plate with paper towels.

In a heavy skillet over medium-high heat, melt the duck fat. Add the shredded duck confit and cook, tossing occasionally, until the duck is cooked through and crisp like bacon—it should crackle and pop!

Transfer the crispy duck to the prepared plate to drain.

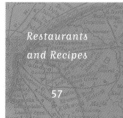

Prepare the Lemon-Garlic Vinaigrette: In a mini-processor or blender or using a whisk and a strong arm, blend together the egg yolk, garlic, and grapeseed oil. Add the lemon juice and rice wine vinegar and process (or whisk) to form an emulsion. Season to taste with salt and pepper. Set aside. The vinaigrette can be prepared up to 2 hours ahead and kept, covered and refrigerated. When ready to use, whisk again to blend and emulsify.

To Finish the Dish: Toss the arugula with just enough vinaigrette to coat the leaves. Mound the arugula onto two chilled plates.

Top the dressed arugula with the crispy duck confit. Dust the salad with the grated Parmigiano-Reggiano cheese and garnish the salad with the garlic-herb croutons.

highlawn pavilion

Eagle Rock Reservation

Eagle Rock Avenue

West Orange 07052

973/731-3463

www.highlawn.com

THE MULTIPLE-AWARD-WINNING Highlawn Pavilion, owned by the New Jersey-based Knowles family of restaurateurs, is about as spectacularly romantic as scenic dining gets. It's a place to get engaged or celebrate an anniversary because while there's much that can be put in place to enhance a dining experience, the memory-making backdrop of the breathtaking view of the Manhattan skyline can't be matched anywhere.

The restaurant could probably rest on that, but the food at the Highlawn Pavilion under the skilled direction of chef Sam Mickail is every bit the match for the view. Sam began as a pastry chef, and his creative repertoire is rooted in French and Mediterranean influences. At its core, his food is a combination of complementary flavors, but its success lies in Sam's recognition of when to stop, which results in the clear and vibrant tastes for which his food is known. And what pulls it all together is his unique presentations, such as the salad we feature here or the individual apple cobbler in its own custom-made copper pot and the spectacularly simple but sophisticated herbed smashed potato cake, ring-molded into a supporting base for a Kalamata-olive-rubbed crispy chicken leg.

But back to the scene—before Harry and Wade Knowles restored and renovated the building to its current palatial splendor, the cliffside pavilion was a crumbling remnant of a Florentine-style scenic overlook, and to locals it was either a secluded lovers' lane or a dangerous place to be after dark. Now it's once again a place for lovers and for friends, and it's a gorgeous place to be after dark—whether for fine dining in the warm ambience of the softly lit pastel dining room or for enjoying goodies from the centrally located French-style rotisserie or wood-fired brick oven in the popular and lively Piano Bar. Think of something to celebrate and make it happen at the Highlawn Pavilion.

Arugula and Grilled Portabello Salad in Endive Leaves

WITH MAYTAG BLUE-STUFFED APRICOTS

Shortly after we visited the Highlawn Pavilion, this innovative chopped salad became a staple on our entertaining menus. In fact, the idea of stuffing endive leaves with something other than fat-based dips gave birth to a whole repertoire of "pickup" salads that our entertaining menus are now never without.

Mise en Place:

FOR THE TOMATO OIL:

1 plum tomato, seeded and diced

1 tsp. tomato paste

Pinch sugar

1 cup extra virgin olive oil

Salt and freshly ground black pepper, to taste

FOR THE GRILLED PORTABELLO MUSHROOM:

2 T. extra virgin olive oil

1 tsp. finely minced or pressed garlic

1 tsp. tamari soy sauce (see the chapter "The Tools, the Terms, the Ingredients, and When to Use Them")

1 tsp. balsamic vinegar

Pinch salt and freshly ground black pepper

1 large portabello mushroom

FOR THE STUFFED APRICOTS:

6 plump dried apricots

4 to 6 tsp. Maytag blue cheese

24 cleaned and trimmed large arugula leaves

2 T. finely chopped red onion

1 ripe plum tomato, seeded and finely chopped

2 T. extra virgin olive oil

2 tsp. balsamic vinegar

Salt and freshly ground black pepper, to taste

6 large endive leaves

FOR THE GARNISH:

Balsamic reduction (see the chapter "Procedures and Techniques")

Equipment:

Mini-processor or mortar and pestle

Fine sieve

Squeeze bottle for the tomato oil

Prepare the Tomato Oil: In a mini-processor (or by hand with a mortar and pestle), process (or pound) the diced tomato with the tomato paste and sugar to a blended paste. Add the olive oil and blend (or whisk) together and season with salt and pepper.

Strain the tomato mixture through a fine sieve (the tomato oil should be almost clear).

Transfer the tomato oil to a squeeze bottle and keep refrigerated for up to 1 week.

Prepare the Mushroom: In a small bowl, whisk together the oil and garlic. Whisking constantly, add the soy sauce and balsamic vinegar to form an emulsion. Season to taste with salt and pepper.

Place the mushroom in a small sealable plastic bag and pour in the marinade. Press all the air out of the bag and seal it, manipulating the bag to completely coat the mushroom with the marinade. Set aside for at least 1 hour at room temperature. The mushroom can be prepared up to this point and held overnight, refrigerated.

Preheat a grill or seasoned grill pan to hot. Grill the mushroom, turning once, until it is cooked through and tender throughout, about 8 minutes total cooking time. Set aside to cool.

Prepare the Stuffed Apricots: Using a sharp paring knife, make a slit along one side edge of each apricot to create a pocket for stuffing and push a dab of blue cheese into the opening. Refrigerate for 10 minutes.

Prepare the Salad: Stack the arugula leaves, roll them, and cut them crosswise into thin strips to create a chiffonade. Place the chiffonade of arugula leaves in a medium bowl.

To Finish the Dish: Finely chop the mushroom and add it to the arugula along with the red onion and plum tomato. Drizzle in the olive oil and vinegar and toss to coat. Season the salad to taste with salt and pepper.

To Plate: Use tongs to fill the endive leaves with the salad and arrange 3 filled leaves on chilled salad plates.

Place 3 stuffed apricots on each plate. Drizzle the tomato oil decoratively around the perimeter of the plate and dot with balsamic vinegar reduction.

il capriccio

633 Route 10 East
Whippany 07981
973/884-9175
www.ilcapriccio.com

*I*L CAPRICCIO is the "caprice" of chef-owner Antonio Grande and his partner-wife, Clara, and the result of their not-so-capricious mission to bring fine Italian dining to New Jersey. Everything about the restaurant was carefully chosen and designed and is as authentically

Italian as Tony and Clara themselves, from the design of the building and courtyard to the frescoed walls and Italian marble inlaid bar. Comfortable and intimate seating, soft music, strategically placed spectacular floral arrangements, and the attentive tuxedo-clad wait staff all work together to create a full five senses Italian experience.

Tony began his culinary career on cruise ships, and in many ways, that experience has defined his work, not least of which is the table-side presentation of dishes like the salt-encrusted sea bass included here or the

zabaglione for two. Il Capriccio is considered one of the Top Five Italian Restaurants in New Jersey and was named one of the Best twenty-five Italian Restaurants in the U.S.A. by the Academy of Restaurant Science.

We fell in love with the whole family—easy to do if you spend more than a few hours there because, at one point or another, most of the family members will be there. Clara is a gracious hostess, assisted at the front of the house by nephew Salvatore, the restaurant's maître d', while son Natale supports his father in the kitchen. Their love for the authentic foods of Italy is contagious, and their desire to share it is what makes the experience at Il Capriccio so warmly engaging. All the desserts are made at the restaurant by the pastry chef, but we never stop there—we like to end our meal with one (or more!) of their extensive collection of imported grappas, and that's what makes the fat lady sing!

Branzino al Sale alla Erbe Aromatiche
(Sea Bass in a Salt Crust with Herbs)

Chef-owner Tony Grande's mission is to teach Americans how to enjoy whole fish—if it can't be accomplished with this dish, it can't be accomplished. Everything about it is simply spectacular—and we do mean simply. It's a simple preparation using simple ingredients—the salt crust seals in the fish's natural moisture and intensifies the flavors without making the fish salty. It's then quickly oven-baked and finished with a simple sauce with spectacular flavor.

Logic prevails here. If flavorful stocks are made from bones, it stands to reason that a fish cooked "on the bone" has a leg up. OK, maybe not a leg . . . but as Tony says, "There's more to cooking a fish whole than the drama of boning it tableside. It's more moist, more flavorful—it tastes better. Where I come from, it's the best way to cook fish."

We prepared this using small whole striped bass and red snapper with equally wonderful results. Have your fishmonger scale and "pan-dress" the fish, removing the innards, gills, and fins but leaving the head and tail intact. Make sure that the skin of the fish is intact and has no tears or cuts.

The sauce calls for fish *fumet*—if your fishmonger doesn't sell white fish stock, you can find it frozen in better supermarkets.

Mise en Place:

FOR THE FISH:

3 cloves peeled garlic, smashed with the flat side of a knife

3 sprigs fresh thyme

1 small sprig rosemary

A 2¹/₂-lb. pan-dressed whole striped bass or red snapper

FOR THE SALT CRUST:

5 large egg whites

5 cups kosher salt

FOR THE SAUCE:

3 T. extra virgin olive oil

1 clove peeled garlic, smashed with the flat side of a knife

2 fresh sage leaves, chopped

A few rosemary leaves, chopped

¹/₂ tsp. fresh thyme leaves

2 T. fish fumet

2 T. hot water

1 T. freshly squeezed lemon juice

Pinch of fresh chopped Italian flat-leaf parsley

Salt and freshly ground black pepper, to taste

Equipment:

Stand mixer or electric handheld mixer

Prepare the Fish: Preheat the oven to 500°F.

Select an ovenproof skillet or baking dish just large enough to hold the fish. Cut a piece of aluminum foil wider by about 4 inches than the body of the fish and long enough to leave a 2- to 3-inch overhang at each end. Use it to line the bottom of the skillet or baking dish.

Arrange the smashed garlic cloves and herbs in the cavity of the fish and place the fish on the foil.

In the work bowl of a stand mixer or with a handheld mixer, whip the egg whites with a pinch of salt just beyond the stiff peak stage until they begin to look dry. Use a large rubber spatula to mix in the kosher salt—the mixture should be sandy.

Use the rubber spatula to apply all the salt mixture to the fish, completely encasing the top and sides of the fish all the way to the foil, but leave enough uncovered foil at either end to use as "handles" to remove the fish from the skillet or baking dish later.

Bake the fish in the preheated oven until the salt crust is golden brown and begins to crack, about 15 minutes.

Prepare the Sauce: In a small skillet over medium heat, sauté the garlic and herbs in the olive oil until fragrant. Add the fish fumet and bring to a boil. Remove the pan from the heat and add the hot water, swirling to combine. Then whisk in the lemon juice and sprinkle in the chopped parsley. Season with salt and pepper to taste. Keep the sauce warm while you finish the dish.

To Finish the Dish: Grasp the foil overhang at either end and lift the crusted fish onto a serving platter. Use the side edge of a serving spoon to tap open a lengthwise crack down the center of the salt crust from the head to the tail. Open the crack like a book and carefully lift away and discard all the crust.

Use a small spatula along the spine or backbone of the fish to gently separate the top flesh from the skeleton, keeping the fillet intact. Place the fillet on a warmed serving plate. Remove and discard the skeleton and place the remaining fillet on a warmed serving plate.

Pour the sauce over the fish and serve immediately.

il tulipano

1131 Pompton Avenue
Cedar Grove 07009
973/256-9300
www.iltulipano.com

IF YOU TAKE your regional Italian food seriously, you owe it to yourself to dine at Il Tulipano, whose chef-owner, Gregorio Polimeni, is—and has been for the past twenty years—dedicated to authenticity. His believes that the only thing good food needs is just enough enhancement of seasoning or herbs to bring

it to its full potential but also that, in the end, food should be authentically prepared and should taste like what it is. And his food does.

Also true to Italian authenticity, the basic menu changes seasonally with dishes featuring appropriately seasonal preparations of the best and the freshest ingredients available. We visited at the end of the summer and happily devoured their signature platter of battered and fried zucchini flowers.

It's a hands-on operation at Il Tulipano, with sons Gregory and Antonio managing the front and the back of the house. The restaurant definitely holds its own as a fine-dining establishment, but the renovation eight years ago added three banquet rooms in addition to the dining room and comfortable bar, positioning Il Tulipano as an excellent choice for a catered affair, with the quality of food and service matching the elegance of the facility. Combine all that with the high priority former maître d' Gregorio places on gracious hospitality, and it's evident why Il Tulipano has remained one of New Jersey's top Italian restaurants for more than twenty years.

Involtini di Melanzane alla Siciliana
(Pasta-Stuffed Eggplant Rolls)

This unusual presentation of eggplant and pasta works equally well as a first course, a side dish to simply roasted or grilled meat, poultry, or fish, or for a light lunch accompanied by a mixed green salad. All the components can be prepared and assembled ahead and baked just before service.

When choosing eggplant, look for taut, shiny, and unbruised skin and avoid the more bulbous, heavy ones to ensure a minimum of seeds.

Mise en Place:

FOR THE TOMATO SAUCE:

1 14-oz. can whole peeled Italian tomatoes
2 tsp. extra virgin olive oil
1 tsp. minced garlic
1 T. chopped fresh basil
$^1/_4$ tsp. dried oregano
Salt and freshly ground black pepper, to taste

FOR THE PASTA:

$^1/_4$ lb. linguine or taglioni

Kosher salt for the pasta water

2 T. freshly grated Parmigiano Grana Padano cheese

2 tsp. chopped fresh basil

FOR THE EGGPLANT:

4 lengthwise slices of unpeeled eggplant, each $^1/_4$ inch thick

1 T. extra virgin olive oil

4 fresh whole basil leaves

8 slices packaged mozzarella cheese, each 1"×2"×$^1/_4$"-thick

2 T. freshly grated Parmigiano Grana Padano cheese

Fresh basil sprigs for garnish

Prepare the Tomato Sauce: Pour the tomatoes and their juices into a medium bowl and squish the tomatoes by hand to a fairly fine texture.

In a medium skillet over medium-high heat, sauté the garlic, basil, and oregano in the olive oil until fragrant without browning the garlic. Add the tomatoes and their juices all at once and mix to blend. Season with salt and pepper and allow the sauce to boil for 5 minutes, stirring frequently. Reduce the heat and simmer the sauce for 8 minutes more. The sauce can be prepared up to this point and kept, covered and refrigerated, for up to 1 week. Warm the sauce when ready to use.

Prepare the Pasta: Bring a large pot of cold water to a rolling boil for the pasta. Add the kosher salt, and when

the water returns to a boil, add the pasta and stir immediately. Cook the pasta, stirring frequently, until almost al dente—leave the pasta a little underdone, as it will be further cooked with the eggplant.

Drain the pasta, transfer it to a mixing bowl, and add just enough tomato sauce to coat it well. Toss the pasta with 2 tablespoons of the grated cheese and the 2 teaspoons of chopped basil and set aside.

Prepare the Eggplant: Add half of the olive oil to a large skillet and place over high heat. When the oil just begins to smoke, add 2 of the eggplant slices and fry quickly, turning once, until golden on both sides. Transfer the eggplant to a platter, add and heat the remaining oil, and fry the remaining 2 slices of eggplant.

To Finish the Dish: Preheat the oven to 375°F.

Mound a quarter of the pasta on the bottom end of a slice of eggplant, top with a basil leaf, roll it up, and place the roll seam side down in a small baking dish. Repeat with remaining the pasta and eggplant. Spoon tomato sauce over and around the rolls. Crisscross 2 slices of mozzarella on top of each roll and sprinkle with the remaining 2 tablespoons grated Parmigiano.

Bake the involtini until heated through and bubbling and the cheese has melted.

To Plate: Place 2 rolls on each warmed plate, spoon the pan juices around the involtini, and garnish with sprigs of basil.

il villaggio

651 Route 17 North

Carlstadt 07072

201/935-7733

If you visit at lunchtime on a weekday, you'll find Il Villaggio mobbed with business execs, many of whom lunch here up to three times a week. Visit in the evenings or on the weekend and it's mobbed with families and Meadowlands sports fans. Pretty much whenever you visit this family-run restaurant, it's mobbed because the hearty Italian food is great, abundant, and served up by friendly staff in a family atmosphere.

The menu is constant, the quality consistent, and everything is done in-house, and at any given time there's a giant vat of fresh tomato sauce cooking on the stovetop. According to Angela, who, along with sister Anna manages the restaurant, her dad, chef-owner Ralph Magliocchetti, is responsible for all the recipes and is the best cook on the line on Saturday nights. It must be hereditary because their grandmother is also a great cook and is in the restaurant every day doing the salads and the outstanding tiramisu, cannoli, ricotta cheesecakes, and other Italian desserts, often infused with a hint of her homemade vanilla.

Wear loose clothing and bring a cooler—you'll need the extra room in the waistband if you try to finish everything you order. But if you're smart, you'll quit while you're still able to get up and walk away. That's where the cooler comes in.

Chicken Scarpariello

For some unknown reason, this is a restaurant favorite that is rarely done at home—and yet this is one-dish home-style cooking at its best, warming and filling the house with the tantalizing aromas we cross-lingually call "eau d'Italian."

Although there are several steps to its preparation, none are difficult. Serve this dish with crusty Italian bread and a crisp salad—or better yet, a side of greens sautéed in garlicky oil. *Molto bene!*

Mise en Place:

FOR THE CHICKEN:

$^1/_2$ chicken, on the bone

Salt and freshly ground black pepper, to taste

2 T. extra virgin olive oil

4 cloves garlic, peeled and sliced

FOR THE POTATOES:

1 T. extra virgin olive oil

6 slices peeled Russet potatoes, each 1/4 inch thick

Salt and freshly ground black pepper, to taste

FOR THE SAUSAGE:

2 links sweet Italian sausage OR 1 link sweet and 1 link hot

2 T. water

1 T. olive oil

$^1/_2$ red bell pepper, sliced lengthwise into $^1/_2$-inch strips

$1^1/_2$ cups thickly sliced white mushrooms

4 T. red wine vinegar

1 T. dry white wine

Prepare the Chicken: Preheat the oven to 500°F with an empty metal roasting pan large enough to hold the chicken without crowding on the middle rack.

Remove the leg, thigh, and wing from the chicken. Chop off and discard the bony ankle end of the chicken leg. Chop the thigh in half. Remove and discard the wing tip and separate the wing into 2 pieces. Chop the breast into 5 or 6 small pieces.

Place the chicken pieces in a mixing bowl, season heavily with salt and pepper, and toss with the olive oil. Add the garlic and toss again.

Toss the contents of the bowl into the hot pan and roast until browned, turning once, about 10 minutes. Remove the pan from the oven, tent with aluminum foil, and set aside.

Prepare the Potatoes: Place a medium skillet over medium-high heat and add the oil. When the oil just begins to smoke, add the potato slices and sauté until golden brown on both sides. Set aside on paper towels and season to taste with salt and pepper.

Prepare the Sausage: Place the sausage in a medium skillet with a tight-fitting lid and add 2 tablespoons water. Place the covered skillet over medium-high heat, and when the water has evaporated, remove the lid. Cook the sausage, lowering the heat if necessary, until it is nicely browned on all sides. Remove the sausage to a plate to

cool. Cut the sausage diagonally into thick slices and add it to the roasting pan with the chicken.

Add 1 T. of olive oil to the hot skillet and sauté the bell pepper slices, tossing occasionally, just until crisp-tender, about 4 minutes. Transfer the peppers to the roasting pan.

Raise the heat to high, add the mushrooms to the hot skillet, and sauté, tossing occasionally, until the edges are browned, about 4 minutes. Lower the heat, add the red wine vinegar and white wine, and deglaze the skillet, scraping up the browned bits. Add the contents of the skillet to the roasting pan along with the potatoes.

To Finish the Dish: Return the roasting pan, uncovered, to the oven and heat through, about 5 minutes.

jeffrey's

73 Main Street

Toms River 08753

732/914-9544

www.jeffreysrestaurant.com

WE WERE SO GLAD that Jeffrey's came up on the list of New Jersey's favorite restaurants because we've been fans of chef-owner Jeffrey Schneekloth for many years. This may require some explanation, however, since our visit there for this book was the first time we made the trip to the restaurant.

Jeffrey is a guy who was destined to teach because Jeffrey is a guy who gets up close and personal in the very best way and is so passionate about everything he does that his gift for learning becomes a gift for teaching and his enthusiasm captures his audience. That, along with the fact that he loves exploring the whys and wherefores of what makes food work and is naturally nurturing, is probably why his school, The School at Jeffrey's, is such a success and why everyone who knows him loves him. It also probably explains why chef de cuisine Greg Manning has been a significant part of the restaurant for nearly a decade and why Jeffrey's son (Jeffrey, of course) is running The Store at Jeffrey's, which caters to a loyal clientele with its Jeffrey-esque take-out food and the very best culinary tools and equipment you can buy to get the techniques Jeffrey teaches done in the best way possible.

Jeffrey loves, bold, sharp clean flavors—and the food he designs and serves is the food he loves to eat. For years we followed his sellout classes in cooking schools throughout New Jersey and shared the same student following. And when our students talked about him, it was always with a smile and a "Wow!" about his food. He's written and published a wonderful book of his original food, *A Little Night Cooking*. We bought it—retail—need we say more?

Jeffrey "sees" things—wide screen and in techni-color. When he first stepped off the elevator at the empty space that eventually became Jeffrey's, he "saw" the restaurant. It doesn't hurt either that his wife, Barbara, has spent the past several decades whispering in his ear, "If you can picture it, you can accomplish it."

So . . . does it sound like we love and admire this guy? We hope so! And from the first bite of his food and the first megawatt smile this man will bestow upon you, we know you will, too.

Napoleon of Veal Paillards
WITH GORGONZOLA VINAIGRETTE

With an explosion of piquant flavors, a variety of textures, beautiful colors, and hot and cold ingredients all on one plate, this is one dish that has it all. It's no surprise that it's one of the most popular entrées served at Jeffrey's.

The finished dish not only presents beautifully, but just about every component can be prepared well in advance, as well as assembled and held for up to an hour before finishing, making it pretty impressive for a guest menu.

We call for superfine sugar in the vinaigrette and the marinade because it dissolves instantly. If you can't find it, dissolve the sugar in the vinegar before mixing with the rest of the ingredients. And don't get lazy and skip the pounding of the veal—it not only tenderizes the meat but also assures that it cooks quickly and uniformly and retains its shape.

Mise en Place:

FOR THE GORGONZOLA VINAIGRETTE:

1$\frac{1}{2}$ tsp. Dijon mustard

1 T. superfine sugar

1 T. white wine vinegar

$\frac{1}{2}$ cup crumbled Gorgonzola cheese

$\frac{1}{2}$ cup extra virgin olive oil

FOR THE MARINADE:

1¹/₂ tsp. Dijon mustard

¹/₂ tsp. superfine sugar

1¹/₂ tsp. olive oil

2 T. balsamic vinegar

1¹/₂ tsp. red wine

FOR THE POTATO PANCAKES:

1 lb. Idaho potatoes, peeled

2 T. beaten egg

Pinch of nutmeg

Salt and freshly ground black pepper, to taste

Vegetable oil for frying potato pancakes

4 slices veal top round, each 2 ozs.

4 slices ripe beefsteak tomato, each ¹/₂ inch thick

4 ozs. cold St. Andre cheese, cut into 4 thin slices

1 cup shredded arugula leaves or mesclun salad

Equipment:

Grill, stovetop grill, or grill pan

Prepare the Vinaigrette: Place the mustard, sugar, and vinegar in a mini-processor and pulse to blend. Add the cheese and process until smooth. Add 4 tablespoons of the olive oil and process until smooth. Add the remaining 4 tablespoons of the oil and process until the vinaigrette is completely emulsified. Refrigerate until ready to use. The vinaigrette can be prepared ahead and kept, refrigerated in a covered container, for up to 1 week.

Prepare the Marinade: In a small bowl, whisk together the mustard and sugar. Whisk in the olive oil, a little at a time, until the mixture is blended. Gradually whisk in the vinegar and the red wine to form an emulsion. The marinade can be prepared ahead and kept, refrigerated in a covered container, for up to 1 week. Whisk to blend before using.

Prepare the Potato Pancakes: Grate and rinse the potatoes and squeeze out as much liquid as possible with paper towels. Place the grated potatoes in a mixing bowl and mix in the egg, nutmeg, salt, and pepper.

Place a small skillet over medium-high heat and add oil to a depth of about ¹/₈ inch. When the oil is hot, spoon in one-quarter of the potato mixture and flatten with a spatula to form a pancake about ¹/₄ inch thick and 4–5 inches in diameter. Fry on both sides until brown and cooked through. Drain on paper towels and reserve. Repeat with remaining potato mixture, adding more oil as necessary, to make 3 more pancakes. The pancakes can be prepared ahead and kept, refrigerated on a sheet pan in a single layer,

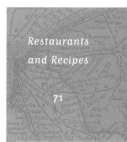

Restaurants and Recipes

71

covered with foil, for up to 1 day. Bring the pancakes to room temperature and then heat them briefly in the preheated oven to crisp them up a bit before assembling the napoleons.

Prepare the Veal and Tomatoes: Place each of the veal slices between two pieces of plastic wrap and pound to an even ¹/₄-inch thickness.

Place the veal in a small, sealable plastic freezer bag and add enough marinade to coat the veal completely. Set aside at room temperature for at least 10 to 20 minutes.

Place the tomatoes on a plate and drizzle with some of the remaining marinade. Set aside at room temperature for 10 minutes.

Preheat an oiled grill or grill pan.

Grill the tomatoes briefly (just about 30 seconds per side—they should remain firm) and remove them to a plate. Grill the meat for 1 to 2 minutes per side and remove to a plate.

To Finish the Dish: Preheat the oven to 350°F.

Place 2 potato pancakes on a baking sheet, top each with a slice of grilled veal, followed by a slice of grilled tomato, and then a slice of St. Andre cheese. Repeat again with veal, tomato, and cheese and finish with another pancake. Cover loosely with plastic wrap and set aside for up to 45 minutes.

When ready to serve, place the baking sheet in the preheated oven until the napoleons are heated through, about 8–10 minutes.

To Plate: Toss the shredded arugula or mesclun with just enough vinaigrette to coat the leaves. Place one napoleon in the center of each plate and drizzle with some of the vinaigrette and top with the salad greens.

jocelyne's

168 Maplewood Avenue

Maplewood 07040

973/763-4460

www.jocelynesrestaurant.com

SOMETIMES IN YOUR TRAVELS you meet people for the first time and you feel as though you've known them all your life. That was the case for us with chef-owner Mitchell Altholz and his partner-wife, Jocelyne. But we suspect a whole lot of people may feel that way on their very first visit to this intimate nine-table New French BYO restaurant where the menu changes daily or whenever the mood strikes and the sense is that you're a guest in Mitchell and Jocelyne's home. And essentially, you are.

We visited on a Sunday morning and crammed ourselves into the tiny kitchen where Mitchell moves in an economically choreographed ballet and makes magic to the background sounds of Edith Piaf. Jocelyne's greeting is musical, the decor is charming and romantic, and the setting is intimate and warm. Mitchell's food is fine French, and he freely laces his creations with foie gras, truffle oil, butter, and cream. Desserts are all made daily, including (of course) French vanilla ice cream. Mitchell's refrigerator pantry is a French chef's dream, with shelves of imported, exotic, and aromatic delights—brined quail, fresh herbs and house-made herb oils, fresh sorrel, escargots, truffles, vanilla beans by the bundle, French butter, and exquisite French cheeses—but his hand is deft, so the food is perfectly light, and every meal he turns out is a love letter to France and to his French-born wife, Jocelyne.

By the time we left several hours later, we were speaking French—OK, badly—but if you can experience Jocelyne's and not want to plop a beret on your head and dab truffle oil behind your ears, you won't get any closer even if you travel to Paris.

Lobster Salad with a Mango-Basil Quenelle and Truffled Vanilla Aioli
WITH MICROGREENS
IN CHAMPAGNE VINAIGRETTE

This first-course dish is so exquisite that the word *salad* doesn't do it justice. Both simple and sophisticated at once, it's a palette of colors and classic flavors that demand for it to be savored and enjoyed slowly and with someone you can communicate with using only eye contact, if you get our drift.

Perfectly representative of chef-owner Mitchell Altholz's cuisine, there are some high-end ingredients at work here, but each of the several components to the dish is simple to prepare, and all can be done ahead. It's special—send the message and prepare it for someone special . . . enjoy it with champagne (and maybe in silk pajamas).

1 dozen mussels, scrubbed and debearded

$^1/_4$ cup dry white wine

3 large egg yolks, preferably very fresh and from organic eggs

Scrapings from 1 vanilla bean

1 T. pure vanilla extract

1 generous T. Dijon mustard

Dash of Tabasco sauce

1 cup canola oil

1 T. best-quality white truffle oil

3 T. heavy cream

Salt and pepper, to taste

One fresh, live Maine lobster, 1$^1/_2$ lbs.

FOR THE CHAMPAGNE VINAIGRETTE:

$^1/_4$ tsp. Dijon mustard

Pinch *fleur du sel* (see the chapter "The Tools, the Terms, the Ingredients, and When to Use Them")

Pinch freshly ground black pepper

1$^1/_2$ tsp. finely minced shallot

2 T. good-quality extra virgin French olive oil

2 tsp. champagne vinegar

1$^1/_2$ tsp. heavy cream

$^1/_2$ tsp. best-quality white truffle oil

1 cup fine chiffonade of amaranth or microgreens, mâche, or mesclun (see the chapter "Procedures and Techniques" for how to make a chiffonade)

FOR THE GARNISH:

Saffron oil (see Procedures)

Balsamic reduction (see the chapter "Procedures and Techniques")

2 T. snipped fresh chives

Equipment:

Food processor

Sharp kitchen shears

Mise en Place:

FOR THE MANGO-BASIL QUENELLE:

$^1/_2$ ripe mango, finely diced

2 tsp. good-quality extra virgin French olive oil

Pinch finely ground black pepper

1 T. fine chiffonade of basil leaves (see the chapter "Procedures and Techniques")

great dishes

74

Prepare the Mango-Basil Quenelle: In a small bowl, mix together the mango, olive oil, and pepper. Gently fold in the basil and refrigerate for up to 4 hours.

Prepare the Truffled Vanilla Aioli: In a pot with a tight-fitting lid set over medium-high heat, cook the mussels with the wine just until they open. Remove the mussels and reserve for another use. Strain the liquid into a glass measuring cup.

In the work bowl of a food processor, place the egg yolks, vanilla bean scrapings, vanilla extract, Dijon mustard, and Tabasco and pulse to blend. With the machine running, slowly add the canola oil through the feed tube to form an emulsion. Add the white truffle oil, ¹/₂ cup of the mussel liquid, and the heavy cream and pulse until blended. Season to taste with salt and pepper. The aioli can be prepared ahead and kept, refrigerated in a covered container, for up to 1 day.

Prepare the Lobster: Bring a large pot of cold water to a boil over high heat for poaching the lobster pieces. Prepare a large bowl with ice and water to shock the lobster after blanching.

Separate the claws and the tail from the lobster body. Wrap each claw and the tail separately in several layers of plastic wrap. Reserve (freeze, if desired) the lobster body for another use such as stock.

When the water reaches a rolling boil, drop in the wrapped claws and tail and cook for 7 to 8 minutes. Scoop out the lobster pieces and plunge them into the ice bath to stop the cooking process. Drain and remove the plastic wrap. If the flesh is still translucent, rewrap the lobster and cook it for 2 or 3 minutes more, just until the flesh is opaque.

Use sharp kitchen shears to separate the claw from the jointed knuckle. Flex and bend back the small pincer and remove it from the claw. Cut the shell of the claw at the top and bottom edges, open, and remove the meat intact. Cut the knuckle shells lengthwise at the top and bottom

and remove the meat as much in one piece as possible. Cut the tail in half lengthwise and remove the meat from each piece. Place all the lobster meat on a plate and cover with a damp towel. The lobster meat can be prepared ahead and kept, refrigerated in a covered container, for up to 1 day.

Prepare the Champagne Vinaigrette: In a small bowl, whisk together the mustard, fleur du sel, pepper, and shallot. Gradually whisk in the olive oil until well blended. Add the champagne vinegar and whisk to form an emulsion. Whisk in the cream and truffle oil. The vinaigrette can be prepared ahead and kept, refrigerated in a covered container, for up to 2 days.

To Finish the Dish: Use two soup spoons to form a football-shaped quenelle with the mango-basil mixture—this is done by holding one spoon in each hand, scooping up a heaping spoonful in one spoon, and using the other spoon to scoop it out, continuing to transfer the mixture from one spoon to the other until the desired shape is obtained.

Place the greens in a small bowl and toss with just enough champagne vinaigrette to coat the leaves.

To Plate: Spoon a 3-inch-diameter pool of the truffled vanilla aioli off center on the plate. Arrange a half-tail and a claw on the aioli and sprinkle with snipped chives.

Place the mango-basil quenelle on the plate and mound dressed salad greens alongside.

Garnish the plate with dots of saffron oil with a small dot of balsamic reduction in the center of each.

Chef's TRUC:

Instead of boiling the lobster whole in an abundance of water, Mitchell captures way more intense lobster flavor by separating the claws and tail from the lobster body (which he freezes for stock) and wrapping each claw and the tail individually in several layers of plastic wrap. He then submerges the wrapped parts for 7 to 8 minutes in boiling water, where they cook in their own juices trapped inside the plastic wrap. A quick cooldown in an ice water bath and the lobster is ready for its debut!

joe & maggie's bistro on broadway

591 Broadway
Long Branch 07740
732/571-8848
www.joeandmaggiesbistro.com

WE FOUND an American bistro! Big, bold, and delicious food and lots of it is coming out of chef-owner Joe Romanowski's kitchen—he calls it home cooking with panache. He's way too modest.

Joe is happy to observe that food has "unevolved" and that chefs are shying away from making "jewelry," and his signature style shows up best with his fresh takes on classics. We were just bowled over by his country salad, a Romanowski-style remake of wilted spinach and frisée salad piled six inches high, drizzled with a warm balsamic vinaigrette, and studded with lardons of applewood-smoked bacon, gorgonzola *dolce,* and his secret spiced walnuts. The monster pork chop with clams was followed by Joe's version of peach melba—however, his was with mascarpone ice cream over shortcake, topped with a poached New Jersey peach and drowning in fresh New Jersey blueberry sauce.

This is real food with real flavor—unpretentious yet sophisticated, served in a comfortable atmosphere designed and presided over by Joe's partner-wife, Maggie Lubcke. Joe and Maggie's is exactly what you'd be rewarded with if you conjured up the quintessential American bistro.

Pan-Roasted Pork Chop

WITH LITTLENECK CLAMS, WILD MUSHROOMS, AND TOMATOES IN A SHERRY WINE SAUCE

This is chef-owner Joe Romanowski's takeoff on the classic Portuguese combination of pork and clams, and it's a winner. The dish is rounded out with mashed potatoes and steamed haricots verts and carrots tossed with a bit of butter—use your favorite recipe or substitute any vegetables you prefer.

The blackening spice is house-made at Joe & Maggie's. We tried several brands and found Paul Prudhomme's Blackening Spice to be the closest to Joe's house-made. Don't be put off by the pink interior of the finished pork—standards for doneness have relaxed since the old days, and pork is perfectly safe as long as the interior temperature of the meat reaches 140°F on an instant-read thermometer.

Mise en Place:

FOR THE BRINE:

$^1/_2$ cup granulated sugar

$^1/_2$ cup kosher salt

3 bay leaves

2 T. lightly crushed peppercorns

2 quarts cold water

4 T. (¹/₂ stick) unsalted butter, room temperature

4 T. all-purpose flour

FOR THE PORK:

2 center-cut, double-cut pork chops, each 12 ozs., bones frenched (see the chapter "The Tools, the Terms, the Ingredients, and When to Use Them")

Salt and freshly ground black pepper, to taste

Paul Prudhomme's Blackening Spice or another good-quality brand

Wondra flour for dredging

Corn oil for frying

FOR THE SHERRY WINE SAUCE:

1 clove garlic, sliced paper-thin

1 cup quartered cremini mushrooms

1 cup stemmed, thickly sliced shiitake mushroom caps

1 T. Paul Prudhomme's Blackening Spice or another good-quality brand

¹/₂ cup golden sherry or Madeira

12 fresh littleneck clams, scrubbed

1 cup chicken or vegetable stock or canned low-sodium, fat-free broth

1¹/₂ T. honey

1 cup peeled, seeded, chopped fresh tomato

Salt and freshly ground black pepper, to taste

Brine the Pork: Mix together all the ingredients in a large pot and bring to a boil, stirring to dissolve the sugar and salt. Set aside to cool.

Place the pork in an airtight container (we use jumbo sealable freezer bags and press out excess air) and add enough brine so it is completely submerged. Refrigerate for 24 hours.

Prepare the Beurre Manié: Place the butter in a small bowl and mash it with a fork. Add the flour and continue mashing until the butter and flour are well blended together. Scrape the beurre manié onto a piece of waxed paper, roll it up into a log about 2 to 3 inches long, and refrigerate. The beurre manié can be prepared ahead and kept, tightly wrapped and refrigerated, for up to 1 week.

Prepare the Pork: Preheat the oven to 350°F.

Drain the pork and pat it dry. Season with salt and pepper, dust all over with the blackening spice, and then lightly coat the pork with Wondra flour.

Place a large skillet over high heat and add a thin layer of corn oil to the pan. When the oil begins to smoke, add the pork chops and brown on all sides. Remove the chops to a baking sheet and transfer to the oven to finish, about

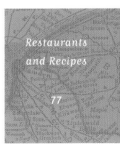

Restaurants and Recipes

77

15 to 20 minutes. The internal temperature should be at about 135°F when an instant-read thermometer is inserted into the meatiest part of the chop. Remove the pan from the oven and loosely tent the chops with aluminum foil—the temperature will then rise to between 140°F and 145°F, and the meat will be medium-rare and juicy.

Prepare the Sherry Wine Sauce: Pour out the oil, wipe the pan with paper towels, and return it to the heat. Add 1 tablespoon of fresh corn oil and toss in the garlic. Sauté the garlic for a few seconds to soften and release the fragrance, and then add the mushrooms to the pan. Cook the mushrooms, tossing occasionally, until the juices they release have cooked off.

Add the 1 tablespoon of blackening spice and toss to coat the mushrooms. SHUT THE HEAT OFF. Pour in the sherry or Madeira, turn the heat back on high, and cook until the liquid is reduced by about half.

Prepare the Clams: Add the clams to the pan along with the stock or broth and the honey. Cover and cook until the clams open, about 2 to 3 minutes. Discard any clams that don't open.

To Finish the Dish: Add the chopped tomatoes to the pan and cook, stirring occasionally, for 2 minutes.

Remove the beurre manié from the refrigerator and cut it into 3 pieces. Thicken the sauce by stirring in the beurre manié, one piece at a time, making sure it is completely incorporated before the next addition. Season to taste with salt and pepper.

To Plate: Carve the pork from the bones, slice it across the grain into 4 or 5 pieces, and arrange it on warmed plates. Spoon the clams and mushrooms around the pork slices and spoon the sauce over all.

Serve with mashed potatoes and sautéed haricots verts and carrots alongside the pork and garnish with snipped chives.

kuishimbo

330 Ninety-sixth Street
Stone Harbor 08247
609/967-7007

KUISHIMBO roughly translates as "people who love to eat." That would be us. It could also mean "you pig," applicable to us as well, especially when we're presented with dishes prepared with that elusive combination of understatement and aesthetics that defines great Japanese food.

The restaurant, owned by chef-owner Daniel Takayama and his wife, Susan Rosell, is small but airy and open. It closes for the winter season and reopens in the spring, and aficionados of great Japanese food are already lined up when it does.

Several times a week, Daniel makes an early morning trek halfway up the parkway to a meeting point where he selects the highest-quality seafood brought to him by the only fishmonger he trusts. The menu is limited and authentic—the California roll is made with real crabmeat, nothing faux going on here, and you won't find Godzilla rolls or other weird creations at Kuishimbo. But what you can depend on, always, is the finest and freshest ingredients to be found anywhere. And that (along with Susan's warm hospitality) is what has made this award-winning restaurant famous for many years and miles around. If it's not the best, Daniel doesn't buy or work with it, and late diners to the restaurant will sometimes have to deal with the disappointment that certain dishes are sold out. The upside of that is the guarantee that the food at Kuishimbo is as good and as fresh as it can get.

Tuna Tataki

If you're a true tuna aficionado, you know it's just about criminal to fool with it—the simpler the preparation, the better able you are to experience the very special delight that is great sashimi-grade tuna. A warning, though—unless you are certain you have a reliable source for best-quality sashimi-grade tuna, don't try this at home! In this preparation from chef-owner Daniel Takayama, we sear the tuna, but because the interior remains rare, we consider and treat it with utmost care.

Expect to pay what it's worth, about $25 to $30 per pound and one way to assure that it's top grade. And now that you've spent all that money and taken all that care, make sure you transport it straight home in a cooler, on ice, and serve it within twelve hours!

Chances are if you've found a good Asian market for your tuna, you'll also find the ponzu sauce there. Chef Daniel uses Miyako brand.

Mise en Place:

FOR THE TATAKI SAUCE:

2 fresh jalapeño peppers, seeds and ribs removed

2 cloves peeled garlic, smashed

15 to 20 roughly chopped whole cilantro sprigs with stems

1/4 cup ponzu sauce

1 cup mayonnaise

Salt and freshly ground black pepper, to taste

FOR THE TUNA:

2 T. extra virgin olive oil

2 tsp. toasted sesame oil

1 T. coarsely chopped fresh garlic

1 T. chopped fresh ginger

Salt and freshly ground black pepper, to taste

4 to 5 ozs. fresh sashimi-grade tuna

Equipment:

Mini-processor

Prepare the Tataki Sauce: Place the jalapeños, garlic, and cilantro in the work bowl of a mini-processor and pulse several times to chop uniformly. Add the ponzu sauce, pulse several times, and then add the mayonnaise and process to a coarse purée. Season to taste with salt and pepper. The sauce can be prepared ahead and kept, refrigerated in a covered container, for up to 2 weeks.

Prepare the Tuna: Whisk together the oils, garlic, ginger, salt, and pepper. Place the tuna on a plate, brush on all sides with the oil mixture, and place uncovered in the refrigerator to marinate for 5 to 10 minutes. Any leftover oil mixture can be kept, refrigerated in a covered container, for up to 4 days.

To Finish the Dish: Heat a medium skillet, grill, or grill pan until hot. Sear the tuna quickly on all sides.

Remove the tuna to a cutting board and carve into ¹/₄-inch-thick slices against the grain.

To Plate: Spoon the tataki sauce in a puddle on a serving plate and arrange the sliced tuna on top. Serve immediately.

le petit chateau

121 Claremont Road
Bernardsville 07924
908/766-4544

VIRTUALLY FROM the day chef-owner Scott Cutaneo took over Le Petit Chateau in 1998, this classic French restaurant has been racking up four- and five-star awards for its casual, simple elegance and culinary excellence.

Scott is a perfectionist who sets out every night to exceed his customers' expectations, starting with the best ingredients he can get his hands on and then carefully nurturing the food to be the best it can be. He has no trouble meeting his goal. He orchestrates his dishes to reflect his belief that in French cooking, the sum of the parts is greater than the whole and no one flavor should stand out. Despite that philosophy, the wine DOES stand out, but only in the excellence of the selections from Le Petit Chateau's well-stocked wine cellar. And the classic desserts are the perfect complementary components to the complete dining experience.

The restaurant is intimate and made for special occasions, and so is the absolutely exquisite food being created with one high-end ingredient after another. As the sign posted in the kitchen reads, "Every element of every plate, executed 100% every time—it's the only option."

This is what we call "moaner" food, which might predispose you to reserve the private dining area in the intimacy of the wine cellar, where you won't be embarrassed to be overheard—because no words are as appreciative as the simple moans and groans of heavenly pleasure.

Grand Marnier Soufflés

Indicative of chef-owner Scott Cutaneo's philosophy that in French cooking, the sum of the parts is greater than the whole and no one flavor should stand out, these soufflés are a perfect combination of simple ingredients that combine to transcend their individual identities.

At Le Petit Chateau, Grand Marnier Soufflés are served in custom-made sterling silver molds—the better to see your heaven-bound reflection as these exquisite soufflés melt in your mouth.

Back here on earth, we just love the fact that they can be prepared up to four hours ahead before being baked and served magnificently puffed up, straight from the oven. And should you be blessed with leftover batter, whisk in a little milk and you have a fabulously decadent dessert sauce!

Mise en Place:

FOR THE PASTRY CREAM:

¼ cup superfine sugar

3 large egg yolks

Pinch salt

3 T. all-purpose flour

1 cup whole milk

1 tsp. pure vanilla extract

FOR THE SOUFFLÉ MOLDS:

1 T. melted unsalted butter

Granulated sugar for dusting the molds

FOR THE SOUFFLÉ MIXTURE:

2 large egg whites

Pinch salt

1 T. pastry cream

1¹/₂ tsp. granulated sugar

1 large egg yolk

1 T. Grand Marnier

Equipment:

2 6-oz. ramekins

Stand mixer or electric handheld mixer

Prepare the Pastry Cream: Whisk together 2 table-spoons of the sugar with the egg yolks and a pinch of salt. Sift the flour over the egg mixture and whisk to blend well. Whisking constantly, drizzle in ¹/₂ cup of the milk until the mixture is smooth.

Heat the remaining ¹/₂ cup of milk with the remaining 2 tablespoons of sugar in a medium saucepan over medium heat, stirring to dissolve the sugar. As soon as the mixture comes to a boil, add the egg yolk mixture, whisking constantly to avoid scorching. Allow the mixture to return to a boil and continue to cook, whisking, until it thickens and then immediately remove it from the heat. Let stand for 2 or 3 minutes and then stir in the vanilla extract. Set the custard aside to cool and then cover with plastic wrap set directly on the surface of the custard to prevent a skin from forming. Refrigerate until ready to use. The pastry cream can be prepared ahead and kept, refrigerated in an airtight covered container, for up to 1 week. Blend well before using.

Prepare the Molds: Brush the bottoms and sides of two 6-oz. ramekins with the melted butter. Dust the molds thoroughly with the sugar, making sure it completely coats the bottom and sides, leaving no uncoated areas. Invert the molds to tap out the excess sugar and set the molds aside.

Prepare the Soufflé Base: In the clean work bowl of a stand mixer with the whisk attachment, or in a clean bowl for use with an electric handheld mixer, whip the egg whites until "sudsy." Add the salt and whip the whites to stiff peaks.

In a separate mixing bowl, whip together the pastry cream, sugar, and egg yolk until the mixture thickens and then whisk in the Grand Marnier.

Use a large rubber spatula to blend about a quarter of the whipped egg whites into the egg yolk mixture. Then fold in the remaining egg whites, gently but thoroughly, just until blended.

Spoon the soufflé mixture into the prepared molds until they are two-thirds full and place on a baking sheet. The molds can be prepared and filled ahead and kept, refrigerated and lightly covered with waxed paper, for up to 4 hours.

To Finish the Soufflés: Preheat the oven to 400°F.

Bake the soufflés until puffed up and lightly golden, about 12 to 14 minutes. Serve immediately.

le rendez-vous bistro

520 Boulevard
Kenilworth 07033
908/931-0888
www.lerendez-vousnj.com

COMPLETE WITH tiny dining room, tiny kitchen, and delicious aromas emanating from within and hand-painted artistry on its walls, chairs, and tables, Le Rendez-vous makes you feel as though you've been transported to a neighborhood bistro somewhere in France. And Le Rendez-vous is the perfect name for this tiny bistro—it's the *tres intime* collaborative effort of chef-owner Sami Elsawi, his beautiful French-born

wife, Beatrice, and their longtime friend, sous chef and manager Philippe Lievre, one of the best "get-togethers" we've ever experienced.

The food is what Sami and Philippe call French-Mediterranean, a fusion of the cuisines and ingredients of the sixteen Mediterranean countries, prepared using classic French techniques but with less than the typical abundance of cream and butter. Instead, it's the layering of flavor and Sami's artistry as a *saucier* that add the richness to his food, which is at the same time deeply satisfying and still exciting.

We think Sami's instincts coupled with his French-trained Egyptian mind is what sets his food apart. Who else would think to infuse cream with a bay leaf and then use it in a chocolate ganache? Or use Reisling in his polenta, which he pairs with foie gras and figs? But wherever it's coming from, the food (along with the delight of a French-kissed conversation with Beatrice) keeps us coming back season after season, for one great meal after another.

Braised Rabbit à la Provençale

WITH CRACKED BLACK PEPPER FETTUCCINE

We love a savory rabbit stew, and this one pairs beautifully with fresh black pepper fettuccine. It comes together surprisingly quickly with a variety of ingredients, textures, and flavors that make for interesting eating from beginning to end.

Finding the rabbit is relatively easy these days (see the chapter "Resources"), now that the baby boomer generation is more in tune with the health benefits of eating rabbit than our childhood affection for Thumper. You'll probably want your butcher to do the boning—unless you're pretty good at that sort of thing, it can be tedious and time-consuming.

Chef-owner Sami Elsawi uses candy beets here, which are like baby beets, a little lighter and sweeter than mature beets, but if you can't locate them, we had great success with small regular beets and with golden beets. Just in case you're unable to find ready-made black pepper fettuccine in specialty stores in your area, we've included our own recipe—try to cut the pasta a little on the wide side to make it easier to carry this hearty sauce.

Mise en Place:

FOR THE SHALLOT CONFIT:

1 cup peeled and trimmed shallot lobes

1 T. cold water

Pinch salt

Unsalted butter for greasing the baking dish

FOR THE CANDY BEETS:

4 candy or baby beets, trimmed, peeled, quartered

1 tsp. cold water

Pinch sugar

Unsalted butter for greasing the baking dish

FOR THE BLACK PEPPER FETTUCCINE:

$1^1/_2$ cups all-purpose unbleached flour

1 T. freshly, finely ground black pepper

$^1/_4$ tsp. finely ground sea salt

2 whole large eggs

1 large egg yolk

2 tsp. extra virgin olive oil

Kosher salt for the pasta water

FOR THE RABBIT:

1 T. extra virgin olive oil

$^1/_2$ boned rabbit, cut into $1^1/_2$-inch pieces

$^1/_2$ cup chopped shallot

1 cup quartered fresh mushrooms such as cremini, shiitake, or cepes

$^1/_2$ cup blanched and peeled fava beans

$^1/_2$ cup pitted Kalamata olives

2 tsp. grainy Dijon mustard

1 cup dry Chardonnay

1 cup chicken or vegetable stock

1/4 cup peeled, seeded, and diced fresh tomato

Salt and freshly ground black pepper, to taste

Equipment:

Food processor

Pasta machine to roll and cut pasta

Prepare the Shallot Confit: Preheat the oven to 350°F. Place the shallots in a lightly buttered baking dish just large enough to hold them in a snug single layer and add 1 tablespoon cold water and a pinch of salt to the dish.

Cover the dish tightly with aluminum foil and roast, stirring occasionally, until the shallots are soft and caramelized, about 1 hour. The shallot confit can be prepared ahead and kept, refrigerated in a covered container, for up to 4 days.

Prepare the Candy Beets: Preheat the oven to 350°F. Place the quartered beets in a buttered baking dish just large enough to hold them in a single layer and add 1 teaspoon cold water and a pinch of sugar to the dish. Cover with aluminum foil and roast the beets until they are fragrant and just tender, about 30 minutes. The roasted beets can be prepared ahead and kept, refrigerated in a covered container, for up to 4 days.

Prepare the Black Pepper Fettuccine: In the work bowl of a food processor, pulse together the flour, pepper, and salt several times until evenly mixed.

In a 2-cup liquid measuring cup, use a fork to whisk together the eggs, egg yolk, and olive oil.

With the machine running, slowly pour the egg mixture through the feed tube. Continue to process until a rough dough is formed—it will at first look dry and grainy like cornmeal, the noise will then increase and deepen, and the dough will begin to clump up. Finally the dough will pull together in one large lump and dance crazily around the work bowl, at which point it is done. Be patient—the process will take about 45 seconds to a full minute.

Remove the dough to a very lightly dusted work surface and knead it for a minute or two to smooth it out. Shape the dough into a 4-inch square, wrap in plastic wrap, and refrigerate for at least 1 hour. The pasta dough can be prepared ahead and kept, wrapped tightly in plastic wrap and refrigerated, for up to 2 days.

When you're ready to roll out the pasta, divide it into 5 equal pieces and follow the instructions for your pasta machine to achieve a fettuccine-like thickness. At this point, either use the machine to cut the pasta sheets into fettuccine or roll the sheets and use a sharp knife to make wider strips by hand. The pasta can be rolled and cut ahead and dried on parchment paper at room temperature. It can then be stored at room temperature in a sealable plastic freezer bag for up to 2 weeks.

Prepare the Rabbit: Preheat the oven to 450°F.

In a large, deep ovenproof skillet over medium-high heat, sauté the rabbit pieces in the olive oil, just until they begin to brown, about 5 minutes. Remove the rabbit to a plate.

Add the shallots and the mushrooms to the skillet and sauté until the mushroom juices have evaporated and the shallots and mushrooms are golden brown.

Return the rabbit to the skillet and add the fava beans, shallot confit, olives, and beets. Stir in the mustard and then SHUT OFF THE HEAT. Add the Chardonnay, turn the heat back on, and cook until the wine is reduced by half.

Stir in the stock and the chopped tomato and season to taste with salt and pepper. Transfer the skillet to the oven for 8 minutes.

To Finish the Dish: Cook the pasta in plenty of boiling salted water just until al dente. Drain.

To Plate: Use tongs to pick up the pasta and use a twisting motion to pile it into a high mound on each plate. Spoon the rabbit on top of the pasta along with the vegetables and all the pan juices.

the mad batter

Carroll Villa Hotel
19 Jackson Street
Cape May 08204
609/884-5970
www.madbatter.com

Breakfast is hands-down our favorite meal. The problem is, like most people who live in real time, we rarely get the opportunity to prepare it, let alone enjoy it. So our visits to Cape May, quite possibly the most amazing square mile of food in the great state of New Jersey, began every day with another fabulous breakfast at the Mad Batter. It became our mission to eat our way through the whole breakfast menu—a dirty job but someone had to do it, and it might as well be us.

And there, nestled among the intricately ginger-breaded painted ladies, the benchmark was set for us forever for every breakfast specialty we will ever encounter. From their to-die-for signature orange-almond French toast to thick pecan Belgian waffles you could take to the beach and surf with to lick-your-plate Benedict variations of eggs, not to mention the omelette artwork (we won't . . . we're embarrassed), this is breakfast heaven. Add to that the happy, good morning, "hiya-honey" wait staff with those coffeepots attached to their hands, and we can't think of a reason to begin your day elsewhere.

The other neat trick of owner Mark Kulkowitz and his wife, Pam Huber, is the attached Carroll Villa, which Pam has restored to a most comfy bed and breakfast—yeah, breakfast!

The Mad Batter also has a great lunch menu, which, if you miss your personal breakfast hour or have the creative appetite to think outside the lox, might make you decide to miss breakfast more often. And here's where we found the best crab cakes we've ever enjoyed. Yours for the reading.

Crab Cake Sandwich

WITH ROASTED PEPPER-GARLIC MAYONNAISE

We'd bet a fin that crab cakes are likely one of the most oft-ordered items on restaurant menus. We see them as appetizers and main course selections, done with high-end or exotic ingredients, with ethnic twists, for breakfast, lunch, or dinner—and certainly we order them whenever we come across them, which is probably why we've had so many overworked, mediocre, or just plain bad ones.

We've also tried more often (and more ways) to make them at home than we care to admit, but the quintessential crab cake eluded us until chef Alyn Toth shared her recipe with us. And that's when we came to the conclusion that a great crab cake is simply that, a great *crab* cake—one that's simply enhanced and minimally fooled with and really just all about the crab.

At the restaurant, the crab cake is served sandwich-style with the Mad Batter's fabulous Roasted Pepper—Garlic Mayonnaise, which is now a permanent resident of our refrigerator pantry. This recipe will leave you with a bit extra to use on anything that doesn't move when you smear it.

1 T. minced capers

1 T. freshly squeezed lemon juice

$^1/_2$ tsp. minced roasted garlic (see the chapter "Procedures and Techniques")

Salt and freshly ground black pepper, to taste

Clarified unsalted butter for frying the crab cakes (see the chapter "Procedures and Techniques")

2 hamburger rolls

2 thin slices red onion

2 slices fresh ripe beefsteak tomato

4 T. shredded iceberg lettuce

Prepare the Crab Cakes: In a mixing bowl, use a large rubber spatula to gently but thoroughly mix together the crabmeat, bell pepper, mayonnaise, 2 tablespoons fresh breadcrumbs, celery, onion, parsley, seasonings, and hot sauce.

Spread the remaining cup of fresh breadcrumbs on a piece of waxed paper.

Form the crab mixture into 2 patties and coat them with the breadcrumbs. Transfer the patties to a plate, cover lightly with waxed paper, and refrigerate. The patties should be prepared ahead and kept, refrigerated and covered with a piece of waxed paper, for up to 2 hours.

Prepare the Roasted Pepper-Garlic Mayonnaise: In a small mixing bowl, mix together the minced roasted pepper, mayonnaise, capers, lemon juice, and roasted garlic. Season to taste with salt and pepper.

To Finish the Dish: In a medium skillet over medium-high heat, melt enough clarified butter to reach a depth of about $^1/_4$ inch. Fry the crab cakes until golden, turning once, about 8 minutes total.

Meanwhile, toast the rolls.

To Plate: Spread the cut sides (top and bottom) of the rolls with roasted pepper-garlic mayonnaise and place a crab cake on the bottom half. Top the crab cakes with a slice of red onion, a slice of tomato, and shredded lettuce.

Mise en Place:

FOR THE CRAB CAKE:

$^1/_4$ lb. lump or backfin crabmeat, picked over for cartilage or shell shards

2 T. finely minced red bell pepper

2 T. good-quality mayonnaise

2 T. fresh breadcrumbs (see the chapter "Procedures and Techniques")

4 tsp. minced celery

1 T. minced red onion

$^3/_4$ tsp. chopped fresh Italian flat-leaf parsley

$^1/_4$ tsp. Old Bay Seasoning

$^1/_8$ tsp. salt

$^1/_8$ tsp. dry mustard

$^1/_8$ tsp. hot sauce, such as Tabasco

1 cup fresh breadcrumbs for coating the crab cakes

FOR THE ROASTED PEPPER–GARLIC MAYONNAISE:

$^1/_2$ roasted red bell pepper, peeled and seeded, minced (see the chapter "Procedures and Techniques")

$^1/_2$ cup good-quality mayonnaise

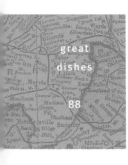

great
dishes

88

the manor

111 Prospect Avenue
West Orange 07052
973/731-2360
www.themanorrestaurant.com

*F*ESS UP—when was the last time you took someone out for a world-class dinner and dancing under the stars? If it's only a question of where you can do that anymore, the answer is—and has been for more than forty fantastic years—The Manor. And The Manor is exactly that—a palatial manor house set amid exquisitely manicured gardens, where an evening out is always a first-class event.

This DiRōNA (Distinguished Restaurants of North America) Award winner is the premier gem in the Knowles family crown jewels, New Jersey's first family of restaurateurs and owners of the Highlawn Pavilion and the Ram's Head Inn. The à la carte Terrace Lounge dining room is richly decorated and supremely comfortable, and the feeling and tone is very European—guests are seated in upholstered swivel armchairs at a table set with fine linens and tableware, and, as in their other restaurants, the service is premier. And the lavish Sunday brunch is unsurpassed.

Executive chef Jochen Voss is world-trained and world-traveled and performs consistently at the highest level of culinary artistry in his carpeted kitchens, where he sometimes shares his knowledge through cooking classes. Timeless classics such as Chateaubriand for two carved tableside and Lobster Thermidor baked in its shell still appear on the menu, updated but not adulterated. But the bulk of the menu consists of Jochen's inventive and inspirational dishes such as the foie gras-stuffed tenderloin included here, which is sure to become one of the classics of tomorrow.

The restaurant is known for its banquet facilities—we've attended more weddings here than we can count, each one quite different and each one a storybook affair.

The Manor has staying power—simply put, there's no other place like it.

Beef Tenderloin Filled with Foie Gras

ON A BED OF LIMA BEANS, POTATO GNOCCHI, AND TOMATO CONFIT WITH PORT WINE JUS

"If you love someone, let them go. If they come back, they are yours forever"—in which case executing this dish is unnecessary because you can take them to The Manor and have Chef Jochen Voss prepare it for you as you gaze into each other's eyes. (Engage a designated driver.)

However, if you love someone and they're already yours forever, let it all go—and set aside a day to prepare this absolutely and spectacularly decadent dish, serve it candlelit with a river of wine flowing and, for heaven's sake, kick off your shoes.

Mise en Place:

FOR THE TOMATO CONFIT:

4 large plum tomatoes, peeled, seeded, and halved length-wise

1 large clove garlic, peeled and smashed

2 T. olive oil

Salt and freshly ground black pepper, to taste

FOR THE PORT WINE JUS:

$^1\!/_2$ cup port wine

$^1\!/_2$ cup veal stock (see the chapter "Resources") or low-sodium, fat-free canned chicken broth

1 tsp. chopped fresh thyme leaves

$^1\!/_2$ tsp. fresh, finely chopped rosemary leaves

Salt and pepper, to taste

FOR THE POTATO GNOCCHI:

3 large Russet (baking) potatoes

1 large egg, beaten

$1^1\!/_2$ T. salt

Dash freshly ground white pepper

2 cups unbleached all-purpose flour

Cornmeal for dusting the sheet pan

1 T. olive oil for tossing the finished gnocchi

FOR THE BEEF TENDERLOIN:

2 slabs foie gras, $1^1\!/_2 \times 4$ inches each (about 3 ozs. total)

1 T. olive oil

2 trimmed 6-ozs. center-cut filet roasts of beef tenderloin (filet mignon)

Caul fat for wrapping the tenderloin roasts (see the chapter "The Tools, the Terms, the Ingredients, and When to Use Them")

$1^1\!/_2$ T. unsalted butter

2 T. finely chopped shallots

1 clove finely minced garlic

$1^1\!/_2$ cups prepared Gnocchi

$1^1\!/_2$ cups fresh shelled (or thawed frozen) lima beans

2 T. chicken stock or low-sodium, fat-free canned broth

Salt and freshly ground black pepper, to taste

FOR THE GARNISH:

2 tsp. freshly grated Parmigiano cheese

2 small sprigs fresh thyme

2 small sprigs fresh rosemary

Equipment:

Potato ricer

Bench scraper

Skimmer or slotted spoon

Boning knife

Knife-sharpening steel or long-handled wooden spoon for channeling the tenderloin

Prepare the Tomato Confit: Preheat the oven to 180°F.

In a mixing bowl, gently toss the tomatoes with the garlic clove, olive oil, salt, and pepper. Use a rubber spatula to scrape the contents of the bowl onto a sheet pan just large enough to hold everything in a snug single layer. Flip the tomatoes so they're all cut side down and roast until very fragrant and tender, about 4 hours. The tomato confit can be prepared ahead and kept, refrigerated in a covered container, for up to 1 week. Gently warm before using.

Prepare the Port Wine Jus: In a small saucepan over medium-high heat, bring the port wine to a boil and reduce to one-third of its original volume. Add the veal stock or chicken broth and reduce to sauce consistency. Stir in the thyme and rosemary and cook for about 1 minute more. Season to taste with salt and pepper. The port wine jus can be prepared ahead and kept, refrigerated in a covered container, for up to 4 days. Gently warm before using.

Prepare the Gnocchi: Place the whole unpeeled potatoes in a large pot, cover with cold water, and bring to a boil over high heat. Add 1 tablespoon of salt, reduce the heat to just maintain a boil, and cook the potatoes, until tender and easily pierced with the tip of a paring knife, about 20 to 25 minutes. Drain, transfer the potatoes to a plate, and allow to cool.

When the potatoes are cool enough to handle, peel them and pass them through a ricer onto a sheet pan, spreading to a thin layer to dry them out.

Line a clean sheet pan with parchment paper and dust lightly with a little cornmeal and set aside.

Transfer the potatoes in a mound onto a clean, dry work surface and form a well in the center. Pour the beaten egg into the well and add the $1^{1}/_{2}$ tablespoons of salt and the pepper. Work the potatoes and eggs together with both hands, gradually adding about $1^{1}/_{2}$ cups of the flour and scraping the dough up from the work surface with a bench scraper as often as necessary. Work the dough as quickly as possible—the longer it is worked, the more flour it will seem to require and the heavier the gnocchi will be.

Lightly dust the dough, your hands, and the work surface with flour and divide the dough into 6 equal parts. Continue to lightly dust the dough, your hands, and your work surface as minimally as necessary to keep the dough manageable.

Roll each piece of dough into a rope about $^{1}/_{2}$ inch thick and then cut the ropes at $^{1}/_{2}$-inch intervals. Make an indent in each gnocchi with your thumb or the tip of a butterknife, or use your thumb to roll the gnocchi down the back of the tines of a fork to create a ribbed effect. Place the finished gnocchi on the prepared sheet pan.

Bring a large pot of cold water to a boil for the gnocchi. When the water comes to a rolling boil, add 1 tablespoon of salt.

Pour 1 T. olive oil into a medium mixing bowl and swirl to coat.

Drop the gnocchi into boiling water a few at a time, stirring gently and continuously with a wooden spoon, and cook for 2 to 3 minutes, just until they rise to the surface. Remove the gnocchi from the water with a slotted spoon or skimmer, allowing them to drain for a second or two, and transfer them to the oiled bowl. Continue with the remaining gnocchi.

Measure out 1¹/₂ cups of gnocchi for the dish. The remainder can be tossed with a bit more oil and refrigerated in a covered container for up to 2 days. To use leftover gnocchi, it must be cooked further (sautéed or sauced and/or sprinkled with grated cheese and baked in a casserole).

Prepare the Beef Tenderloin: Heat a small dry black steel or other good heat-conducting pan over high heat until very hot.

Add the foie gras slabs to the hot pan and sear quickly, turning once, on both sides. Remove the foie gras from the pan immediately, place on a plate, and refrigerate. The foie gras can be prepared ahead and kept, refrigerated on a plastic-wrapped plate, for up to 1 day. The seared foie should be used directly from the refrigerator.

Place one tenderloin on a work surface—if there's a wider end, position it toward you. Using a narrow-bladed boning knife, insert the blade into the center of the wide end of tenderloin and gently work the knife through the entire length of the tenderloin and through the other end, being careful to keep the blade of the knife centered. Remove the knife. Insert a clean knife-sharpening steel or the oiled handle of a wooden spoon into the opening created by the knife, gently turning the steel or handle to create a channel through the center of the tenderloin. Repeat with the second tenderloin.

Use your thumbs to open the channel, and use your fingers to carefully stuff the seared foie gras into the open-ings, pushing and manipulating gently until the channel is fully stuffed and the foie gras is flush with the cut edges of the tenderloin.

Stretch out a length of caul fat and wrap each tenderloin until the meat is fully enclosed in 1¹/₂ to 2 thicknesses of the caul fat, twisting the ends and tucking them underneath the meat. The tenderloins can be prepared ahead to this point and kept, refrigerated on a platter covered with plastic wrap, for up to 2 hours.

Preheat the oven to 425°F.

Heat 1 tablespoon of olive oil in a large ovenproof skillet or flameproof roasting pan over medium-high heat. Add the tenderloins and brown on all sides, about 10 minutes. Transfer the pan to the preheated oven and roast the tenderloins for 12 minutes for medium rare. Remove the pan from the oven and set aside to rest, loosely tented with aluminum foil, for 10 minutes.

To Finish the Dish: In a medium skillet over medium-high heat, melt the butter and sauté the shallots and garlic just until they begin to soften. Add the lima beans and sauté, tossing occasionally, until the beans are just tender, about 3 minutes. Add the 1¹/₂ cups of gnocchi and continue to sauté, tossing occasionally, until the gnocchi just begin to color, about 3 minutes. Raise the heat to high, add the tomato confit and chicken stock, and continue to cook, tossing frequently, until everything is heated through, about 2 minutes more.

To Plate: Spoon a mound of sautéed gnocchi and lima bean mixture onto warmed plates.

Cut each tenderloin in half crosswise and place 2 halves, on end, on each plate.

Whisk the warmed port wine jus with the roasting pan drippings. Drizzle the sauce over the meat and vegetables and garnish with the thyme and rosemary sprigs.

moonstruck

517 Lake Avenue
Asbury Park 07712
732/988-0123

I F A N E I G H T E E N - Y E A R collaborative partnership doesn't produce a whole that's greater than the sum of its parts, it's been in place for too long. Not so with Moonstruck owner Luke Magliaro and chef-owner Howard Raczkiwicz. These guys just keep coming up with great ideas for their Mediterranean- and Asian-influenced menu, and now that they're in their new multilevel lakeside digs in regentrifying Asbury Park, they can really strut their stuff.

The bar is hopping, the pastas are perfect, the grill is fired up, and these guys, along with treasured sous chef Larry Akins, have a special talent for fish fare. Named for the movie, Moonstruck may be the first restaurant we've come across with its own theme song—and when the moon hits your eye like their big pizza pie, it has a crispy tortilla crust and it's to die for.

We're still diehard sun worshipers, and the Jersey shore is where we go to take the noise out of our bodies. Moonstruck is where we go when the sun goes down.

Shrimp and Scallop Seviche

This terrifically fresh-tasting, bright, and colorful appetizer should be called "Summer on a Platter"! Incorporating the best and most colorful garden goodies, most of which we grow ourselves or find in abundance at our local farmers' market, it needs only a small amount of superfresh shellfish and a few items you likely have in your pantry to complete it.

This is what we call pickup food, fabulous with drinks at a summer party or as a poolside snack or lunch. We love serving it as a "pickup" with endive leaves or scooping a spoonful of the seviche into whole Boston lettuce leaves and placing them on a platter. Guests can grip one of our legendary frozen margaritas in one hand, roll up a seviche salad with the other, and polish it off in two bites without spilling a drop.

The shrimp stock of choice here (after your own, of course) is More than Gourmet's Fruits de Mer, available at better markets and specialty stores (see the chapter "Resources"). Of course, it goes without saying that your shellfish *must* be as fresh as possible and properly handled—because rather than being traditionally cooked with heat, the method relied on here uses the acids in the fruit juices to coagulate the protein to "cook" the delicate shellfish.

Mise en Place:

FOR THE SAFFRON-SHRIMP STOCK:

$3/4$ cup reconstituted or fresh shrimp stock

1 saffron thread, crumbled

FOR THE SEVICHE:

4 large, very fresh sea scallops, tough side muscle removed

4 extra large (21–30 count) very fresh, headless peeled and deveined shrimp

1 tsp. Kosher salt for the blanching water

2 T. extra virgin olive oil, preferably Kalamata

2 T. freshly squeezed lime juice

2 T. freshly squeezed orange juice

$1/4$ cup seeded and diced yellow Jersey tomatoes

$1/4$ cup finely diced red onion

2 T. finely chopped scallions, white and light green parts

2 T. chopped fresh cilantro leaves

4 tsp. seeded, minced fresh jalapeño pepper

4 tsp. snipped fresh chives

Salt and freshly ground black pepper, to taste

Blue tortilla chips for serving

great
dishes

94

Prepare the Saffron-Shrimp Stock: Warm the shrimp stock in a medium saucepan over low heat. Measure out 3 tablespoons of the hot stock into a small bowl, crumble in the saffron thread, and set aside to infuse and cool.

Use the remaining stock for the shellfish.

Prepare the Shellfish: Cut the scallops and shrimp into ¹/₂-inch dice.

Add enough water to the warm stock to fill the saucepan three-quarters full. Stir in 1 teaspoon salt, raise the heat, and bring the mixture to a boil. Reduce the heat to a gentle simmer.

Prepare a bowl of ice and water to shock the shellfish after blanching.

Drop the shellfish into the simmering liquid and cook it,

stirring once or twice, for 60 seconds. Scoop it out and plunge it into the ice bath. Drain and pat dry with paper towels.

To Finish the Dish: Pour the olive oil into a large nonreactive mixing bowl and whisk in the lime and orange juices and the saffron-shrimp stock to form an emulsion. Add the tomatoes, onion, scallions, 1 tablespoon of the cilantro, jalapeño, and chives and mix gently. Use a large rubber spatula to gently fold in the shellfish and salt and pepper to taste.

Cover the bowl with plastic wrap and refrigerate for at least 2 hours, and up to 4, to marinate.

To Plate: Stir the seviche and transfer to a serving bowl. Sprinkle the remaining tablespoon of cilantro on top and serve with blue tortilla chips.

nicholas

160 Highway 35
Red Bank 07701
732/345-9977
www.restaurantnicholas.com

NICHOLAS (the restaurant) is what happens when brains, talent, and energetic ambition (Nicholas the entrepreneur) collide.

Owners Nicholas and Melissa Harary have created a truly class act at this amazing upscale restaurant that has to come under the heading of dinner and a show. The backdrop is modern but comfortable and subdued. At center stage is the food, which could not be better—creative New American, sophisticated and cosmopolitan but never overwrought—with a spotlight on a fluid, ever evolving wine list. No less could be expected from the man who was sommelier at Jean Georges and the woman who held the same position at Tabla. The finale is a careful selection of fine artisanal cheeses followed by fabulous desserts designed by Eric Hubert of Jean Georges and perfectly rendered in the pastry kitchen below the restaurant.

But it's the show—the entrées carved, sauced, and finished tableside, the simultaneous placement by the supporting cast of highly professional and politely attentive waitstaff, of exquisitely plated dishes that arrive *en cloche*—that sends the dining experience at Nicholas over the top.

Nicholas and Melissa were destined for success. Both are exacting and hardworking with a clear vision of exactly how to elevate every aspect and attend to every nuance of a fine European dining experience—when we left shortly before dinner service began, Melissa was ironing the tablecloths on each table—and they perform their roles as host and hostess with an amazing casual grace for a couple not yet out of their twenties.

Don't wait for a special occasion—an evening at Nicholas *is* a special occasion.

Jersey Peach Soup
WITH BLUEBERRIES AND LYCHEE NUT

We must confess—we are not usually fans of fruit soups. But the gorgeous colors and wonderful aroma of ripe Jersey peaches and a hint of the secret ingredient (lemon thyme) were the enticements to try this chilled fruit soup, and we loved it!

At Nicholas, it's sometimes served as an *amuse-bouche*, or palate teaser, and sometimes as a dessert—but it's always presented simply and exquisitely with precision-cut fruit garnish of peaches and blueberries to reflect the ingredients and a fresh lychee nut just for fun.

You can find fresh lychee nuts in Asian markets and sometimes in better supermarkets, but if not, canned lychees, rinsed and drained, work pretty well.

Mise en Place:

FOR THE SIMPLE SYRUP:

1/2 cup granulated sugar

1/2 cup cold water

A sprig of fresh lemon thyme

FOR THE SOUP:

6 ripe peaches, peeled, pitted, and diced

1/2 cup fresh orange juice

1 stalk lemongrass, tough fibrous stalk trimmed away
and discarded, remaining light interior smashed with
the back of a chef's knife

FOR THE GARNISH:

1 fresh, firm but ripe peach

24 blueberries, sliced in half

2 fresh, peeled lychee nuts or 2 canned lychee nuts,
rinsed well

Equipment:

Blender

Cheesecloth for straining the soup

Prepare the Simple Syrup: In a small saucepan over
medium heat, stir together the sugar and water until the
sugar dissolves completely. Bring the mixture to a boil,
remove the pan from the heat, and stir in the sprig of
lemon thyme. Allow the syrup to cool completely at room
temperature. Remove the lemon thyme, transfer the syrup
to a container, and refrigerate until chilled. The simple

syrup can be prepared ahead and kept, refrigerated in a covered container, for up to 2 weeks.

Prepare the Soup: Place the peaches, orange juice, simple syrup, and lemongrass in a blender and process to a completely smooth purée, about 5 minutes. Line a strainer with cheesecloth, strain the soup into a bowl, and discard the cheesecloth. Refrigerate the soup until well chilled.

Prepare the Garnish: Cut the peach in half and remove the pit as cleanly as possible. Cut one half in half again and trim away any unattractive rough edges. Use a very sharp paring knife to thinly slice the quarters.

Peel the remaining half and cut the peach into small dice.

To Plate: Ladle the soup into chilled bowls set on plates. Sprinkle the diced peaches and a few of the blueberries on top of the soup.

Fan the sliced peaches on the plate alongside the bowls and arrange a few blueberry halves and a lychee nut alongside the peaches.

old man rafferty's

106 Albany Street
New Brunswick 08901
732/846-6153

284 Route 206
Hillsborough 08844
908/904-9731

OWNER MARK JAKUBOSKI knows what he's doing, and so does executive chef Bobby Beck. Both have been in the business since their early teens, and they've been a successful team for almost fifteen years. Mark also owns SoHo on George, the upscale

New American restaurant around the corner, and together Mark and Bobby have built a great team and support structure. They take nothing for granted and use intelligent management to generate new perspectives, maintain interest, and keep things fresh, such as periodically moving their staff from one restaurant to the other. These two are so parallel that they even had their first children (two boys, of course) just a few months apart.

Size matters, and these guys aren't afraid to admit it with real grilled burgers and fries, hungry-guy sandwiches, and a river of beer to wash them down with. But you can also enjoy great wines and food for the more discerning palate like portabello mushroom napoleons, stacked with roasted eggplant, tomatoes, and goat cheese and finished with a lovely squirt of chive oil, and grilled salmon Caesar salad with roasted tomatoes and a focaccia crouton. The wine selection is the handiwork of general manager David Zelaney, and his influence is also felt in the service—he teaches tableside service at Hudson County Vo-Tech.

Another smart Mark-and-Bobby move was to assess the needs of the neighborhood and morph their insanely busy takeout service into a takeout shop attached to the restaurant. Smack in the middle of regentrified downtown New Brunswick, Old Man Rafferty's does a brisk lunch business, and they've made it easy for the business crowd to walk out with a great take-home dinner.

Old Man Rafferty's may have only been "established not too long ago," but it's clearly the grownup version of the Bennigan's-, TGI Friday's-, and Houlihan's-style eatery. And for your dining convenience, there are two—the one in New Brunswick is kept well afloat by college students (Rutgers country), and the Hillsborough location is where they go when they graduate, grow up, and buy a house.

Porterhouse Steak

WITH WEDGED POTATOES AND OVEN-ROASTED SHIITAKE MUSHROOMS

Every now and then we carnivores need to chow down on a serious chunk of protein, and this is Fred Flintstone food at its best. You know who you are, and you're not all of the male persuasion. Go for it—we're with you.

There are a few considerations to getting this roast beast to taste the way it does in the restaurant (and it usually just misses when you try to do it at home). First, spend the bucks on the meat, get it cut to order, on the bone, thick, and marbled with fat, and get the best grade you can find. Next, give it a couple of days for "dry-aging." And then flavoring—the restaurant uses McCormick's Montreal Steak Seasoning. This commercial re-creation of the famous steak seasoning of Montreal, Quebec, first blended for and distributed exclusively to restaurants, is now available in most supermarkets—it makes ALL the difference! And last, get that grill HOT!

Mise en Place:

FOR THE PORTERHOUSE STEAK:

2 Porterhouse steaks, 24 ozs. each. preferably naturally farmed (see the chapter "Resources"), well marbled and at least 1¹/₂ inches thick

Tamari soy sauce (see the chapter "The Tools, the Terms, the Ingredients, and When to Use Them")

McCormick's Montreal Steak Seasoning

¹/₂ cup veal demi-glace

FOR THE OVEN-ROASTED SHIITAKE:

1 T. unsalted butter, melted

8 ozs. shiitake mushrooms, stemmed, halved or quartered if very large

3 large cloves garlic, peeled and lightly smashed

2 T. extra virgin olive oil plus oil for brushing the sheet pan

Salt and freshly ground black pepper, to taste

Equipment:

Grill, stovetop grill, or grill pan

Prepare the Porterhouse Steak: TWO DAYS AHEAD: Clear a space in the refrigerator large enough for the steaks to be placed side by side without crowding. Use paper towels to pat the steaks as dry as possible and place them in the refrigerator, side by side on a piece of parchment paper, for 24 hours.

Remove the steaks from the refrigerator, turn bottom side up, and pat very dry with paper towels. Replace the parchment paper with a clean, dry piece and return the steaks to the refrigerator for another 24 hours.

Remove the steaks from the refrigerator and brush them generously on both sides with Tamari soy, followed by a generous sprinkling of Montreal seasoning. Return the steaks to the refrigerator for 1 hour.

Prepare the Mushrooms: Preheat the oven to 450°F.

Lightly brush with oil a sheet pan just large enough to hold the mushrooms in a snug single layer.

Toss the mushrooms and garlic cloves with the 2 tablespoons of oil and 1 tablespoon of butter and sprinkle with salt and pepper. Transfer the mushrooms and garlic to the sheet pan and roast, stirring occasionally, until the mushrooms are browned and the garlic is golden, about 20 minutes.

To Finish the Dish: Preheat an oiled grill or grill pan until it's very hot.

Place the steaks on the grill and grill to desired doneness, turning a quarter turn about halfway through on each side before flipping to the other side to create nice cross-hatched grill marks, about 7 to 9 minutes total on each side for rare.

Warm the demi-glace.

To Plate: Transfer the steaks to warm plates. Top the steaks with the roasted mushrooms and drizzle with the warm demi-glace.

panico's

103 Church Street
New Brunswick 08901
908/545-6100
www.panicosrestaurant.com

*T*HERE'S A THEME, a thread, a signature, if you will, to chef Gregg Freda's style—it's rooted in timelessness. We think it's why Panico's has been at the top of the fine Italian dining roster in New Jersey for almost as long as it's been in existence, and it may be why his uncle, owner Frank Panico, had the wisdom to sway him off his course to become a criminal lawyer.

The theme is that he takes the food he grew up with and upscales it. The thread is his penchant for doing takeoffs, like the one on *arancini*, stuffed and breaded rice balls, which permutated to the risotto cake in this dish. And classy creative takeoffs notwithstanding, Gregg's signature is that his food is straightforward and perfectly executed.

The restaurant is pretty classy, too—decorated in soft peach tones, softly lit, twinkling lights here and there, and a well-trained tuxedoed waitstaff. And it all comes together in a richly sophisticated dining experience from the moment you enter.

Panico's is one of only five New Jersey recipients of the DiRōNA (Distinguished Restaurants of North America) Award of excellence (there are only just over 550 on the continent of North America), which is bestowed by peers on restaurants committed to excellence in dining hospitality.

We'll share an insider's tip—Gregg loves one-dish meals. He also is an impresario with pasta. Pay special attention to the specials because they're going to be the kind of food Gregg loves to do. And peruse the pasta offerings—they're way beyond just another bowl of pasta.

Sformata di Aragosta e Riso
(Lobster Risotto Cake)

WITH HONEY-LEMON BEURRE BLANC

At Panico's, chef Gregg Freda serves this takeoff on *arancini* as an appetizer, but we think that, along with a crisp green salad, it also makes a great lunch.

Whatever you do with it, the dish itself is outstanding, but the technique is one you'll want to learn because risotto cakes make a great side dish, main dish, a bed for sauce or salad—the possibilities are endless. We've done this with several different variations of risotto and often make more than we know we'll eat just so we can make cakes with the extra the next day. In fact, we think the technique works best with leftover risotto.

Think about joining us outside the box, too, and go sweet on the risotto. Make it an Italian-esque rice pudding dessert, with raisins, pignoli nuts, and a drizzle of Amaretto or Frangelico and then morph THAT into cakes! (Impressive where you can go with leftover rice and a little creativity!)

Mise en Place:

FOR THE BREADCRUMB MIXTURE:

1¹/₂ cups pignoli nuts

1¹/₂ cups plain beadcrumbs

Salt and freshly ground black pepper, to taste

FOR THE BALSAMIC REDUCTION:

1 cup balsamic vinegar

1 T. chopped shallot

1 tsp. light brown sugar

4 whole black peppercorns

1 sprig fresh thyme

FOR THE RISOTTO CAKE:

2 eggs, beaten

2 cups cooked risotto, preferably left over,
   at room temperature

2 T. finely chopped scallion, light green and green parts

1 T. finely chopped red bell pepper

1 T. finely chopped yellow bell pepper

1 cup chopped cooked lobster meat

Salt and freshly ground black pepper, to taste

2 T. unsalted butter

2 T. olive oil

FOR THE HONEY-LEMON BEURRE BLANC:

2 cups dry white wine

¹/₂ cup freshly squeezed lemon juice

2 T. chopped shallots

2 T. whole black peppercorns

2 T. coriander seeds

10 fresh thyme sprigs

2 bay leaves

4 T. honey

1 cup heavy cream

4 T. (¹/₂ stick) unsalted cold butter, cut into four pieces

Pinch salt

FOR THE GARNISH:

2 whole lobster claws, shelled

1 cup baby arugula leaves

great
dishes

102

Equipment:

Food processor

Prepare the Breadcrumb Mixture: Place the pignoli nuts in the work bowl of a food processor and pulse a few times to chop coarsely. Add the breadcrumbs, salt, and pepper and pulse several times again until the nuts are finely chopped and blended with the breadcrumbs. The breadcrumb mixture can be prepared ahead and kept, in an airtight container at room temperature, for up to 1 week.

Prepare the Balsamic Reduction: In a small saucepan over medium-high heat, bring the vinegar, shallot, light brown sugar, peppercorns, and thyme sprig to a boil. Reduce the heat to maintain a gentle simmer and cook until the mixture is syrupy and thick enough to coat the back of a wooden spoon. Cool. Strain out and discard the solids. The balsamic reduction can be prepared ahead and kept, refrigerated in a covered container, for up to 1 week. Bring to room temperature before using.

Prepare the Risotto Cakes: In a large mixing bowl, gently fold the beaten eggs into the risotto until mixed. Use a large rubber spatula to fold in the scallions and bell peppers. Fold in the lobster meat, salt, and pepper.

Form the risotto mixture into 2 large or 4 smaller cakes, each about ³/₄ inch thick. Spread the breadcrumb mixture on a large piece of waxed paper and coat the risotto cakes on both sides. The risotto cake mixture can be prepared ahead and kept, refrigerated in a covered container, for up to 2 days. The formed cakes can be prepared ahead and refrigerated, covered loosely with waxed paper, for up to 2 hours. Bring either to room temperature before proceeding.

Prepare the Honey-Lemon Beurre Blanc: In a medium saucepan over medium-high heat, mix together the wine, lemon juice, shallots, peppercorns, coriander seeds, thyme springs, and bay leaves. Bring to a boil and cook until the liquid is reduced to about ¹/₂ cup.

Whisk in the honey and continue to cook until the sauce just begins to color. Whisk in the cream and continue to cook until the sauce begins to thicken. Strain the sauce and return it to the pan. Keep warm. The sauce can be prepared ahead to this point and kept, refrigerated in a covered container, for up to 2 days. Rewarm the sauce gently before proceeding.

To Finish the Dish: Preheat the oven to 350°F.

In a large ovenproof skillet over high heat, heat the 2 tablespoons butter and olive oil together until the butter is melted and bubbly. Add the risotto cakes and sauté, turning once with a spatula, until the cakes are very brown on both sides. The butter can get quite brown, but if it begins to burn, add a bit more olive oil and reduce the heat.

Transfer the skillet to the oven while you finish the Honey-Lemon Beurre Blanc.

With the saucepan set over low heat, add the 4 tablespoons butter along with a pinch of salt to the warm sauce one pat at a time, whisking constantly until the butter is incorporated and the sauce is thickened.

To Plate: Pour a pool of Honey-Lemon Beurre Blanc in the centers of individual plates and place the risotto cakes on top with a lobster claw alongside. Top with a bunch of baby arugula and drizzle the plate with the balsamic reduction.

the perryville inn

167 Perryville Road

Perryville 08827

908/730-9500

www.theperryvilleinn.com

*I*T'S ONLY out of the way if that's not where you're going. But we knew just where we were headed, and when we arrived, we understood why the Perryville Inn is a destination place for serious gastronomes and/or the betrothed. Chef-owner Paul Ingenito's classic training in French cuisine and his use of local ingredients add up to fine dining in a relaxed country

setting. And the restaurant itself is a romantic reflection of Paul and Lorraine Ingenito, a beautiful couple who met "in the business" in New York and fell in love with each other and the Perryville Inn when they wandered in by chance one day. Five years later they're married with three kids and own it.

It was a gorgeous, sunny day when we visited, and the outdoor patio gardens were in full bloom, perfect for the wedding that was to take place that afternoon and that we were tempted to crash had we not had pressing business elsewhere immediately thereafter.

But the tall to-do list didn't deter the chef and his

well-chosen staff of pros from showing off a range of specialties including Basil-Scented Jumbo Lump Crabmeat Salad in a Pool of Gazpacho Vinaigrette, Roast Breast of Griggstown Squab with Foie Gras Ravioli and Fava Beans, their famous Savory Lobster Bread Pudding and the following:

Grilled Tenderloin of American Lamb

SERVED OVER RÖSTI POTATOES
WITH ROASTED RED PEPPER COULIS AND
CRACKED BLACK OLIVE OIL

Vibrant colors and flavors and an interesting contrast of textures make this easy-to-prepare main course a guest menu winner. It's also nice to have the cracked black olive oil in your refrigerator pantry to enhance any number of things, like pizza, pasta, or salad dressings, or just spread on toasted, garlic-rubbed bruschetta along with some basil pesto or topped with a piece of mozzarella or sliced fresh Jersey tomato.

Lamb tenderloin can be difficult to find—we buy it at Wegman's or Whole Foods (see the chapter "Resources"). The boned-out and trimmed eye from a rack of lamb will work just as well, but whichever you use, we agree with chef-owner Paul Ingenito that the flavor of American lamb is much tastier (and far less gamy) than that of any of the imports. We also prefer its texture.

Mise en Place:

FOR THE CRACKED BLACK OLIVE OIL:

1 cup pitted Kalamata olives

About 1/2 cup extra virgin olive oil

Salt and freshly ground black pepper, to taste

FOR THE ROASTED RED PEPPER COULIS:

1 large roasted red bell pepper, peeled and seeded
(see the chapter "Procedures and Techniques")

1 T. chicken stock or canned low-sodium, fat-free broth

Salt and freshly ground white pepper, to taste

FOR THE RÖSTI POTATOES:

1¹/₂ cups chopped Spanish or Vidalia onion

2 T. unsalted butter

1 lb. peeled Yukon Gold potatoes

Canola oil for frying potatoes

¹/₂ tsp. fresh thyme leaves

¹/₂ tsp. snipped fresh chives

1 tsp. chopped fresh Italian flat-leaf parsley

¹/₂ cup crumbled French goat cheese

Salt and freshly ground black pepper, to taste

FOR THE LAMB TENDERLOIN:

12 ozs. American lamb tenderloin OR full rack of
American lamb, boned and trimmed

Salt and freshly ground black pepper, to taste

FOR THE HERB SALAD:

¹/₄ cup torn frisée

2 T. fresh whole Italian flat-leaf parsley leaves

1 tsp. snipped fresh chives

¹/₂ tsp. chopped fresh dill

1 T. extra virgin olive oil

Salt and freshly ground black pepper, to taste

Equipment:

Mini-processor

Food processor fitted with a shredding disk or
box grater

A 4-inch cast-iron or other heavy skillet

Grill, stovetop grill, or grill pan

Prepare the Cracked Black Olive Oil: Place the olives in the work bowl of the mini-processor and pulse a few times until the olives are coarsely chopped. Add the olive oil, 2 tablespoons at a time, pulsing in between to mix the oil with the olives until you have added all the oil and the olives are coarsely puréed. Season with salt and pepper. The black olive oil can be prepared ahead and kept, refrigerated in a covered container, for up to 1 month.

Prepare the Roasted Red Pepper Coulis: Place the skinned and seeded pepper in the work bowl of a mini-processor and pulse to chop coarsely. Add the chicken stock or broth, season with salt and white pepper, and process to a smooth purée. The coulis can be prepared ahead and kept, refrigerated in a covered container, for up to 3 days. Bring to room temperature before proceeding.

Prepare the Rösti Potatoes: Preheat the oven to 250°F. Fit a cooling rack into a sheet pan and place in the oven.

In a small skillet over medium-low heat, gently sauté the onions in the butter until soft and tender and just beginning to color, about 8 minutes.

Grate the potatoes using a food processor fitted with a grating disk or box grater and squeeze in paper towels until very dry. Transfer the potatoes to a plate and divide into 4 equal piles.

Place a 4-inch cast iron or other very heavy skillet over medium-high heat and heat the dry skillet until it is quite hot. Add oil to a depth of about $^1/_8$ inch. When the oil is hot, spoon in 1 pile of the grated potatoes and then even the potatoes out with a spatula. Sprinkle half the onion, half the herbs, and half the goat cheese on top and season with salt and pepper. Cover the pancake with another pile of grated potatoes spread out into an even layer and press down firmly with the spatula. Fry, turning once, until the pancake is well browned on both sides and cooked through. Transfer the pancake to the oven and repeat with the remaining ingredients, adding more oil as necessary, to make another pancake. Keep the pancakes warm in the oven.

To Finish the Dish: Preheat an oiled grill or grill pan until very hot.

Season the lamb with salt and pepper and brown the meat on all sides. Transfer the meat to a cutting board and loosely tent with aluminum foil.

Warm the roasted red pepper coulis in a small saucepan.

Place the frisée and herbs in a small bowl and toss with just enough extra virgin olive oil to coat the leaves. Season with salt and pepper.

To Plate: Spoon a pool of the coulis onto individual plates to cover the entire eating surface of the plate, use a small spoon to drop small dollops of the black olive oil around the edge of the sauce, and place a rösti potato cake in the center.

Carve the lamb crosswise into 1/2-inch-thin slices and fan on top of the potatoes. Top the lamb with the herb salad.

pierre's bistro restaurant

995 Mount Kemble Avenue

Morristown 07960

973/425-1212

www.pierresbistro.com

CHICKEN WITH forty cloves of garlic, country pâté, cassoulet, crusty French baguettes, brie (*real* brie, ripe and oozing), *tarte tatin*—and all digestively enhanced with the wine of your choice. Are you a Francophile? Are you hungry yet? If not, one whiff and you will be—both.

This is the quintessential country French bistro, transplanted, because it's not just about the menu or the dishes or the authentic farmhouse decor. It's about the philosophy of true French bistro food—the best of what the market offers daily, prepared simply, authentically, and traditionally. Chef de cuisine Allan Schanbacher brings not only his talent but also a social and environmental consciousness that marries perfectly with owner Michael Peters's sense of *terroire*, or the food that is local, seasonal, and organically grown. The menu changes daily—yes, daily—and is driven by what looks best and what's at its prime, paired with timeless favorites such as *lentils du puy*, soft and velvety flageolets, *pommes frites* . . .

Michael and his wife and co-owner, Marybeth, who runs the front of the house, are passionate about wines, and the list, awarded the Wine Spectator Award of Excellence, is exciting and affordable. Pierre's buffet lunch, generously served up by Michael himself, is a favorite of ours, and the restaurant regularly hosts monthly wine-tasting workshops and other interesting special events such as the annual autumn game dinner.

In a further commitment to the stuff that makes the world go round, Michael and Marybeth recently opened Artisan Bread, Wine and Cheese in Chester, where bread baker Sean Coyne is turning out some of the best bread we've ever tasted. The only thing missing is thou, and you can fix that.

Kill two birds with one meal—your bread basket at Pierre's will be filled with freshly baked breads from Artisan—but not for long.

Soft-Shell Crabs with Jersey Asparagus

WITH GRAPE TOMATO CONFIT AND BEURRE BLANC

We adore soft-shell crabs and just can't seem to get enough when they're in season. Although they're pretty tasty when grilled for a change of pace, this classic fry still remains our favorite way to enjoy them.

If you're too squeamish to kill the crabs yourself (a naturally occurring result of cutting out the gills, trimming away the apron underneath, cutting their faces off, and popping the air bubble located just behind where their eyes used to be), have the fishmonger take care of it for you—but be sure you refrigerate them right away and cook them the same day.

Mise en Place:

FOR THE GRAPE TOMATO CONFIT:

1/2 pint of fresh Jersey grape tomatoes

Salt and freshly ground black pepper, to taste

4 sprigs fresh thyme

1 cup extra virgin olive oil

FOR THE ASPARAGUS:

12 medium-thick fresh asparagus spears, trimmed to equal length

Kosher salt for the blanching water

2 T. unsalted butter

1/4 cup chicken stock or canned low-sodium, fat-free chicken or vegetable broth

Salt and freshly ground white pepper, to taste

FOR THE BEURRE BLANC:

4 T. (1/2 stick) unsalted butter

1/4 cup chopped shallots

1 sprig fresh thyme

6 black peppercorns

1/2 cup dry white wine

3 T. freshly squeezed lemon juice

1/2 cup heavy cream

Salt and freshly ground white pepper, to taste

1 T. cold unsalted butter, cut into 2 pieces

FOR THE SOFT-SHELL CRABS:

4 jumbo freshly killed, dressed soft-shell crabs (see the chapter "Procedures and Techniques")

1 cup milk

Blended oil for frying the crabs (see the chapter "The Tools, the Terms, the Ingredients, and When to Use Them")

Flour for dredging crabs

Salt and freshly ground black pepper

3 T. unsalted butter

Prepare the Grape Tomato Confit: Preheat the oven to 350°F.

Arrange the tomatoes in a baking dish just large enough to hold them in a single layer with a little room to spare. Sprinkle with salt and pepper, add the thyme sprigs, and add enough extra virgin olive oil so that the tomatoes are submerged.

Roast the tomatoes until they begin to let off small air bubbles and the skins are just slightly wrinkled, about 35 to 40 minutes. The tomato confit can be prepared ahead and kept, refrigerated in a covered container, for up to 3 days—but if you plan to store the confit, it is better to slightly undercook the tomatoes and not wait for them to wrinkle. Reheat gently before using.

Prepare the Asparagus: Bring a large pot of cold water to a boil for blanching the asparagus and add 1 tablespoon of kosher salt. Fill a bowl with ice and cold water to shock the asparagus after blanching.

Drop the asparagus into the boiling water and cook just until the color brightens. Scoop the asparagus out and immediately plunge it into the ice bath to stop the cooking and preserve the color. Drain and set the asparagus aside. The asparagus can be prepared ahead to this point and kept, refrigerated in a covered container, for up to 2 days.

Prepare the Beurre Blanc: In a medium saucepan over medium-low heat, gently sauté the shallots, thyme and peppercorns in the butter, without allowing the shallots to color, just until they become transparent. Add the wine and lemon juice and raise the heat to high. Bring the sauce to a boil and cook until it is reduced by half. Add heavy cream and continue to boil until the sauce is reduced again by half. Remove the sauce from the heat and strain. The sauce may be prepared to this point and then held in a covered container, refrigerated, for up to 2 days. Reheat gently before continuing.

Return the sauce to the pan and place over low heat. Season to taste with salt and pepper. Whisk the cold butter

into the warm sauce to thicken. Remove the pan from direct heat and keep the sauce warm.

Prepare the Soft-Shell Crabs: Place the crabs and the milk in a sealable plastic freezer bag, squeeze out as much air as possible, and refrigerate for 30 minutes.

To Finish the Dish: In a medium skillet over medium-low heat, melt the 2 tablespoons of butter with the chicken stock or broth. Add the asparagus and heat gently, basting with the butter sauce, until the asparagus is heated through, about 2 or 3 minutes. Season to taste with salt and freshly ground white pepper.

Remove the crabs from the milk bath and drain.

Pour the blended oil into a large, heavy skillet to a depth of about ⅛ inch and place the skillet over high heat.

Dredge the crabs in flour seasoned with salt and pepper and shake off the excess flour.

When the oil is very hot, add the crabs to the pan upside down and fry until they're very brown and crispy. Flip them over, add the 3 tablespoons of butter to the pan, and continue to fry until totally brown and crispy.

To Plate: Fan half of the asparagus on each plate and intersperse the spears with the grape tomatoes. Place two crabs on top and drizzle everything with the beurre blanc.

ram's head inn

9 West White Horse Pike

Absecon 08201

609/652-1700

www.ramsheadinn.com

NOT FAR FROM the not-appealing-to-everyone flash of Atlantic City is another Knowles family gem, the Ram's Head Inn, where superb food, excellent and attentive service, and quiet country elegance prevail. Not only a fine dining restaurant, the Ram's Head Inn is known for the private functions it caters, on or off

premises, from small intimate gatherings to lavish weddings or large corporate affairs. A dinner or an affair here is always lavishly beautiful and memory making.

The several dining rooms are warmly appointed, most with fireplaces. In true country style, chef Luigi Baretto works with local farmers to lard his menu with the best seasonal ingredients the area has to offer, and because his style is to keep the food classic,

he allows the ingredients to speak for themselves. Luigi's career began in the grand hotels of Europe and sailed on with stints on large cruise ships and ocean liners, where he perfected his skill at the beautiful presentations for which he's known. He was inducted by his peers into the honor society of the American Culinary Federation, the prestigious American Academy of Chefs, an honor bestowed upon those chefs who have continuously practiced the highest standards and demonstrate unerringly the highest qualities of professionalism of the organization, the society, and the hospitality industry.

The Knowles family, owners of The Manor and Highlawn Pavilion, is arguably New Jersey's premier restaurant dynasty, and although all their restaurants are elegant and sophisticated with a commitment to quality and the highest standards of hospitality, each is unique in its ambience and cuisine. The common thread, however, that runs throughout might well be summed up on the sign that is strategically placed on the kitchen wall beside the swinging doors to the dining rooms: "If you don't have the time to do it right the first time, when are you going to find the time to correct it?"

That may explain why they continue to get it right the first time, every time.

Chicken Pot Pie

Our frame of reference for chicken pot pie was a flashback to the fifties and involved a freezer, a cardboard box, and an aluminum foil pie plate over which a chicken might have flown and been the responsible party to have dropped a handful of teensy overcooked vegetables into a watery brown sauce. We don't know who applied the gluey top but they sometimes even did it before stopping to add those three microscopic pieces of chicken.

So when everyone who knew we were Ram's Head Inn-bound made us promise to try its famous Chicken Pot Pie, we lied and said we would. We didn't plan to. Chef Luigi Baretto prepared it for us anyway. We can't thank him enough.

We now know why this Chicken Pot Pie is probably the most oft-ordered dish on the menu at the Ram's Head Inn. What we have here is high-end comfort food.

Mise en Place:

FOR THE CHICKEN:

1¹/₂ lbs. chicken thighs, skin on and on the bone

1 small yellow onion, peeled and stuck with 2 cloves

1 whole peeled carrot

1 rib celery

1 bay leaf

1 sprig fresh thyme

1 T. kosher salt

4 whole black peppercorns

4 ozs. fresh or frozen peas

4 ozs. canned or thawed frozen white pearl onions

1 egg, beaten

¹/₂ lb. thawed frozen puff pastry

FOR THE DUMPLINGS:

1 cup all-purpose flour, plus extra for dusting the work surface and hands

¹/₂ tsp. baking powder

1 tsp. salt

2 T. plus 1 tsp. solid vegetable shortening

¹/₂ cup whole milk

1¹/₂ quarts chicken stock or canned, low-sodium chicken broth for cooking the dumplings

FOR THE CHICKEN SUPREME SAUCE:

4 T. unsalted butter

¹/₂ cup all-purpose flour

2 cups chicken stock (from cooking the chicken) or canned low-sodium, fat-free chicken broth

Salt and freshly ground white pepper, to taste

¹/₂ cup heavy cream

Equipment:

Mini-processor

Sieve or strainer

2 ramekins or individual casseroles, each 2-cup capacity

Prepare the Chicken: Place the chicken thighs in a medium pot with the onion, carrot, celery, bay leaf, thyme, salt, and peppercorns. Add cold water to cover and bring to a boil over high heat. Reduce the heat to maintain a gentle simmer and cook, skimming the scum and fat from the surface, until tender, about 20 minutes.

Remove the chicken and carrots from the pot and let cool. Return the pot to high heat and bring to a boil. Boil until the liquid is reduced to about 2 cups. Strain, discard the solids, and reserve the broth for the sauce.

When the chicken has cooled, remove and discard the skin, remove the meat from the bones, and cut or tear the meat into bite-sized pieces. Cut the carrot into 1/2-inch dice. The chicken, carrot, and stock can be prepared ahead and kept, refrigerated in separate covered containers, for up to 4 days. Bring to room temperature before proceeding.

Prepare the Dumplings: Place the flour, baking powder, and salt in the work bowl of a mini-processor and pulse to mix. Add the shortening and pulse until the mixture is the texture of cornmeal. Add the milk and pulse just until the dough forms a mass. Transfer the dough to a work surface lightly dusted with flour and, with lightly dusted hands, knead gently until the dough is smooth. Don't overwork the dough, and add as little flour as possible or the dumplings will be tough and heavy. The dumpling dough can be prepared ahead and kept, refrigerated in a bowl covered with plastic wrap, for up to 6 hours. Allow the dough to rest at room temperature for about 20 minutes before using.

In a medium saucepan deep enough to boil the dumplings in, bring the stock or broth to a boil. Reduce the heat to maintain a gentle boil and drop tablespoons of the dough into the boiling stock. Cook the dumplings gently until cooked through, about 5 or 6 minutes.

Prepare the Chicken Supreme Sauce: In a medium, heavy saucepan over low heat, melt the butter. Use a sieve or strainer to sprinkle the flour over the butter. Use a whisk to incorporate the flour into the butter and cook, whisking constantly, for 1 minute, taking care not to allow the roux to brown. Gradually add the stock or broth, whisking constantly to prevent lumps. Season with salt and pepper and allow the sauce to come to a boil and thicken, stirring occasionally, about 5 minutes. Add the cream and continue to cook the sauce, stirring occasionally, until thickened and fragrant, about 5 minutes more. Remove the pan from the heat and keep the sauce warm.

To Finish the Dish: Preheat the oven to 400°F.

Place an equal amount of chicken, carrots, peas, pearl onions, and dumplings into each ramekin or casserole and cover with the supreme sauce.

On a lightly floured work surface, roll out the puff pastry dough to a 1/8-inch thickness and cut out 2 squares large enough to overlap the edge of the ramekins or casseroles by at least 1/2 inch all the way around.

With the beaten egg, brush a border around the edge of the pastry where it will come in contact with the ramekin. Flip the pastry egg side down and drape it over the top of the ramekin, allowing the excess to hang over the rim. Brush the entire surface of the pastry with beaten egg and, if desired, use the pastry scraps to decorate the top.

Bake the pot pies until hot and bubbling with the crust puffed up and well browned.

rat's

Grounds for Sculpture
16 Fairgrounds Road
Hamilton 08619
609/584-7800
www.ratsrestaurant.org

DON'T LET THE NAME put you off—if you're a *Wind in the Willows* fan like Steve is, you'll recognize the name Rat as synonymous with hospitality.

From the front entrance where you pass the life-sized bronze, "strolling" couple, past the clothesline of hanging longjohns, and through the puffs of steam to enter the restaurant, whimsical would be the operative word here, and it describes the concept, the setting, the food, the owner, the chef and the pastry chef, the staff—this is a fun and happy place where the only thing taken really seriously is quality.

Rat's is a place where art meets art. Under the global palette of chef Eric Martin, the food is seasonally oriented and prepared with French technique, but his use of worldwide ingredients and his ability to pull it off with clarity and simplicity make this truly "well-traveled French cuisine." Pastry chef Peter "Max" Dierks's capricious artistry is a match for everything that is Rat's—look closely, there will always be a little bit of something tucked within or around that will make you smile.

The restaurant is situated at the edge of a lily pond and water garden, and the life and style of impressionist Claude Monet set the tone with authentic, reclaimed wood-beamed ceilings and decorative accents reminiscent of the artist's home in Giverny, France. Custom-made tables and chairs, comfortable banquette seating positioned to create the feeling of privacy, floor-to-ceiling windows in every room that overlook the fantastical grounds, fireplaces, Oriental rugs, a water's edge terrace—there's art and fascina-

tion everywhere. Even the newly renovated kitchen is a state-of-the-art work of art, with walls of hand-painted Italian tiles and a stunning blue enameled central range with ovens that sixteen chefs can easily work around simultaneously.

The 22-acre sculpture gardens showcase an eclectic collection of larger-than-life art, some of which, like that strolling 1890s couple you passed at the entrance, is the work of celebrated sculptor and owner J. Seward Johnson of J & J Johnson. A walk through Grounds for Sculpture is a transport-you-to-other-times-and-places experience.

Plan to spend the day, take the kids—if you don't have any, borrow some or behave like one. Rat's is truly a storybook place.

"There's cold chicken inside it," replied the Rat briefly; "coldtonguecoldhamcoldbeefpickled-gherkinssaladfrenchrollscresssandwichespotted-meatgingerbeerlemonadesodawater—"

"Oh stop, stop," cried the Mole in ecstasies: "This is too much!"

— FROM *WIND IN THE WILLOWS*,
BY KENNETH GRAHAME

Salad of Spicy Greens

WITH WOK-FRIED SQUID AND CHILI AIOLI

We love squid any way we can get it. Usually that's deep-fried or in tomato sauce and it's called cala-mari—but this preparation has an Asian twist and a nice spicy sauce to make it doubly interesting. The Asian twist comes from a few drops of *nam pla*, or Thai fish sauce, which is also known as *nuoc nam* in Vietnamese. You'll easily find both at Asian markets everywhere, but there are a million variations, some clear, some dense and thick, all called the same thing and all with indecipherable labels unless you read Thai or Vietnamese. We use either Squid brand or

Tiparos, both of which are the clear kind and not too pungent. The kick comes from *sambal oelek* or red chile paste, also easily found at Asian markets. This ingredient is far less confusing—choose any of the clear squeeze bottles or jars with the bright green top and you won't go wrong.

If you've never prepared squid, don't be intimidated. You're bigger than it is and it's already dead. If you're completely anxiety-ridden, buy double the amount in case you mess up the first batch—it's cheap.

Most people are put off by the warnings that if you overcook squid, it will be unpleasantly rubbery and inedible. If you make sure your wok is hot, cook the squid just until the rectangles curl up, and then get it

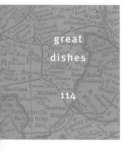

right out, it will be perfect. If it's undercooked, you can always put it back into the wok, but if it's overcooked, you can't uncook it!

Mise en Place:

FOR THE CHILI AIOLI:

1 whole peeled shallot

2 tsp. chopped fresh garlic

2 tsp. finely minced tender white interior of a stalk of lemongrass

2 tsp. chopped fresh peeled ginger root

1 large fresh hot jalapeño or 2 small serrano chilies, stemmed and seeded

1 roasted red bell pepper, peeled and seeded (see the chapter "Procedures and Techniques")

1 tsp. *sambal oelek* or red chili paste (see the chapters "The Tools, the Terms, the Ingredients, and When to Use Them" and "Resources")

4 tsp. fresh lime juice

2 tsp. *nam pla* (see the chapters "The Tools, the Terms, the Ingredients, and When to Use Them" and "Resources")

1 large egg yolk

About ¹/₂ cup extra virgin olive oil

Salt, to taste

FOR THE GARNISH:

Canola or vegetable oil for frying

2 whole peeled shallots, sliced paper-thin on a mandoline

2 lengths of whole scallion, each 4 inches, dark green tops removed, root ends trimmed

Ice water for scallion brushes

FOR THE SQUID:

6 whole cleaned, skinned squid bodies, including tentacles

1 T. peanut oil

¹/₄ cup fine julienne of carrot, cut on a mandoline

2 tsp. chili purée (reserved from the chili aioli)

FOR THE SALAD:

2 cups mixed spicy greens such as mizuna, baby red mustard, arugula, tat soi

1 T. whole fresh mint leaves

1 T. whole small fresh Thai basil leaves

1 T. whole fresh cilantro leaves

¹/₄ cup very fine slivers of fresh red bell pepper

¹/₂ cup paper-thin slices of seeded cucumber that has been halved lengthwise

2 T. minced shallots

Equipment:

Blender

Fine sieve or strainer for straining the aioli

Squeeze bottle for the aioli

Skimmer

Mandoline

Wok for stir-frying

Prepare the Chili Aioli: Place the shallot, garlic, lemongrass, ginger root, jalapeño or serrano chilies, roasted red bell pepper, and *sambal oelek* or red chili paste in a blender and pulse to chop. Add the lime juice and *nam pla* and process to a smooth purée.

Remove and reserve 2 teaspoons of this chili purée for the squid. Pass the remainder through a fine sieve and return it to the blender. Add the egg yolk and pulse a few times to blend. With the machine running, slowly add

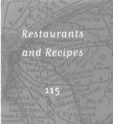

the olive oil to make a mayonnaise-like emulsion. If the emulsion is too thick, whiz in a little boiling water, 1 tablespoon at a time, until the dressing is thick but can still be squirted out of a squeeze bottle. Season with salt. Transfer the aioli to a squeeze bottle and refrigerate if not using immediately. The aioli can be prepared ahead and kept, refrigerated in a covered container, for up to 1 week.

Prepare the Garnish: Pour canola or vegetable oil into a small skillet to a depth of $1/2$ inch and place the skillet over medium-high heat. Have ready a plate lined with paper towels and a skimmer at hand to quickly remove the frizzled shallots.

When the oil is ready, a piece of shallot dropped into the oil should bubble furiously. Drop the shallots into the oil and use the skimmer to stir them around a bit so they fry evenly. Use the skimmer to remove the shallots to the lined plate as soon as they turn golden brown and crispy—work quickly, they burn easily! The frizzled shallots can be prepared ahead and kept at room temperature in an airtight container for up to 3 days (if you can keep from nibbling on them).

Use a sharp paring knife to make lots of lengthwise cuts all the way through the light green part of the scallions, leaving about $1^{1}/_{2}$ inches of the root end intact. Drop the scallions into the ice water and refrigerate until you're ready to plate the dish—the cut ends will spread out to look like brushes.

Prepare the Squid: Make a cut down the length of the squid bodies and open them up. Use the tip of a sharp paring knife to score a crosshatch pattern on the inside and then cut the flesh into even rectangles, about $3/4$ inch wide and $1^{1}/_{2}$ inches long. If the tentacles are very large, cut them in half.

To Finish the Dish: Place the salad greens, herbs, julienned bell pepper, cucumber, and minced shallots in a medium bowl. Toss with just enough chili aioli to coat the salad, and place equal portions on chilled plates.

Get a wok hot over high heat and swirl in 1 tablespoon of peanut oil. Toss in the squid with the julienned carrot and the reserved chili purée and stir-fry just until the squid rectangles curl up.

To Plate: Mound the squid and carrots on top of the salads. Squirt on a little more aioli, sprinkle the frizzled shallots on top, and garnish with a scallion brush.

royal thai

1700 Oaktree Road

Edison 08820

732/767-1263

ONE OF THE MOST intriguing flavor combos is sweet-hot, and nowhere does it show off better than in Thai food. But all too often the finesse is absent, the balance is off, and the food is just plain deadly sweet or fiery hot. Not so at Royal Thai, where, despite the fact that chef-owner Jagmohan Singh received his culinary education in his native India and went on to train in France, the food is as authentic as you'll come across outside Bangkok.

The restaurant is tucked away in a strip mall, but once you enter the pretty little dining room and are seated by Jagmohan's Thai wife, Matinee, at a lovely rosewood table with a little faux garden of orchids trapped beneath its plexiglass top, you'll know you're in the right place. Traditional sculptures, figurines, cos-

tumed dolls—the stuffed kind—bas-relief wall decorations, and other decorative goodies are everywhere, including Jagmohan's chef's jacket, which is so highly decorated with honorific paraphernalia that he looks like a culinary version of George Patton!

The menu is extensive and exotic with a considerable vegetarian selection. The food arrives in custom-made dishes usually indicative of the main ingredient—the fabulous Siamese Duck Breast included here arrives in a blue and white porcelain dish with a duck's head at the helm, and it won't take more than a quick look around to figure out who's eating pork or fish.

If you think you like Thai food, a visit to Royal Thai is a must—we're pretty sure you'll leave this BYO with the recognition that this may well be the first time you've really had Thai food.

Siamese Duck Breast

Although there might be a few unfamiliar ingredients at work here, we had no trouble locating them (see the chapter "Resources"). The dish came together quickly and easily, and the result was authentic Thai food with authentic Thai taste.

Sriracha is a bright red Southeast Asian condiment usually found in a clear squeeze bottle with a green top. It wasn't too long ago that it was a specialty item found only in Asian markets, but lately we've seen it in better supermarkets.

You probably won't be using Green Mountain Sauce or tamarind paste as often as you use Dijon mustard, but both are inexpensive and have a long shelf life, the sauce in the pantry and the paste in the refrigerator.

As for the duck breast, Magret are the ducks that are fattened to produce foie gras, and the result is a significantly meatier breast than found on other breeds. Can you do this with a Long Island or Pekin duckling? Sure. But try to find Magret—they are dis-

tributed here by D'Artagnan and available wherever its products are sold.

Mise en Place:

FOR THE DUCK:

2 Magret duck breasts

1 small fresh red chili, seeded and chopped

2 T. chopped fresh cilantro

4 cloves garlic, chopped

2 T. honey

1 tsp. finely minced fresh ginger root

1 tsp. light soy sauce

2 tsp. sriracha chili sauce

2 tsp. vegetable oil

FOR THE GARNISH:

1 tsp. vegetable oil

$^1/_4$ cup julienne-cut fresh mango

$^1/_4$ cup julienne-cut papaya

2 T. fine julienne of fresh ginger root

1 tsp. Green Mountain Sauce

FOR THE SAUCE:

2 T. honey

2 T. finely chopped ginger

1 T. tamarind paste, thinned with 1 tsp. water to sauce consistency

1 T. light soy sauce

$^1/_2$ cup water

1 tsp. cornstarch mixed with 1 T. cold water

Equipment:

Mini-processor or mortar and pestle

Grill, stovetop grill, or grill pan

Prepare the Duck: Use a sharp knife to score the skin of the duck breasts in a crosshatch pattern, making the cuts about an inch apart and deep but without cutting into the flesh.

In a mini-processor or with a mortar and pestle, process the fresh chili, cilantro, garlic, honey, ginger, light soy sauce, sriracha sauce, and vegetable oil to a rough paste.

Smear the duck breasts on both sides with the paste, place them in a sealable plastic freezer bag, squeeze out as much air as possible, and refrigerate for at least 2 hours or up to overnight.

Prepare the Sauce: In a small saucepan over medium-high heat, mix together the honey, ginger, thinned tamarind paste, and soy sauce. Whisk in the $1/2$ cup of water and bring the sauce to a boil and cook for 1 minute. Add the cornstarch mixture and continue to cook until the sauce thickens, about 30 seconds more.

To Finish the Dish: Heat an oiled grill or grill pan.

Place the duck breasts on the grill, skin side down, and grill until well browned, turning a quarter turn about halfway through on each side before flipping to the other side to create nice crosshatched grill marks, about 5 to 7 minutes total on each side. Transfer the duck to a platter and tent loosely with aluminum foil.

Place a wok or medium skillet over high heat until hot and then add the oil. Stir fry the mango, papaya, and ginger just until crisp-tender, about 1 minute. Remove the pan from the heat and add the Green Mountain sauce.

To Plate: Carve the duck breasts crosswise into $1/2$-inch-thick slices and fan on warmed plates. Arrange the stir-fried mango and papaya over the duck and spoon the sauce on top.

the ryland inn

Route 22 West

Whitehouse 08888

908/534-4011

www.rylandinn.com

DINING HERE is what's known to the cognoscenti as worshiping at the shrine. You will have either a spectacular evening dining in this two-hundred-year-old farmhouse in pastoral Whitehouse Station or a celestial one—depending on whether you understand exactly what about this food is sending you to the moon or you don't.

Chef-owner Craig Shelton is a passionate scientist first, a passionate artist next, and a genius overall whose secret weapon may be the application of his Yale degrees in molecular biophysics and biochemistry to his understanding of how to coax the most flavor and best texture from the food he prepares. He's also a gifted teacher and an amazingly nice guy who is energized, as most gifted teachers are, by sharing—his knowledge, his food, and his contagious smile.

At the Ryland Inn, perfection—Nature's perfection—begins in the garden, where fruits and vegetables, herbs and greens are organically grown just for exacting standards of the restaurant. They are harvested as dishes are prepared. Not the day of, not even hours before, but moments before the dishes are prepared.

Enter the custom-designed dream kitchen and you'll see wall-to-wall chefs. Not kids, not cooks, but real live, accomplished, experienced, educated chefs—at any given time, seventeen to twenty-three of them, all working for nothing other than the privilege of studying under the man many consider to be America's master chef. The last time we visited, we saw one friend who had been a chef-owner of an extremely successful restaurant in New Jersey and two who had been executive chefs at other great New Jersey restaurants—they were there to learn and practice perfection.

And that same careful attention and commitment to excellence and perfection are at the core of everything that is or takes place at the Ryland Inn, from the hospitality to the table settings, to the service, to the wines—every last detail of this ultimate dining experience.

The Ryland Inn's country French menu is completely driven by the seasons, not only by virtue of the garden but also by the kitchen's artistry with seasonal meats, fish, and game and the character of the wines served from its stellar cellar.

The well-deserved awards are too numerous to mention and continue to amass annually. Suffice it to say that this is the only restaurant in the country, and possibly the world, whose chef was named a "Relais

Gourmand" chef by Relais & Châteaux, making him "one of the fifty world's greatest chefs" and one of only nine so recognized in America. The DiRōNA (Distinguished Restaurants of North America) Award-winning restaurant has been named one of the world's best, and its wine list was voted The Best French Wine List of America by Restaurant Hospitality at The Eighth Annual World of Wines Festival.

We could go on and on and still be unable to truly convey what the Ryland Inn is about. We'll simply go back to the beginning and say again that dining here is worshiping at the shrine. New Jersey is privileged to be home to chef Craig Shelton and the Ryland Inn.

Warm Tart of Maine Lobster

If there's a top, this sexy springtime signature dish from chef-owner Craig Shelton goes over it—you're going to want to get dressed up and dim the lights just to eat it.

A glance at the recipe might make you want to cut to the chase and take your nap first, before you exhaust yourself preparing it, but glance again—once the ingredients are prepped (much of which can be done ahead), it really is just a series of quick steps to put it all together. Also, don't overlook obvious shortcuts—be good to yourself, most fishmongers will steam the lobster for you if you ask.

Mise en Place:

FOR THE CARAMELIZED PEARL ONIONS:

1/2 cup pearl onions

1 tsp. canola oil

1 tsp. unsalted butter

Pinch kosher salt

FOR THE POTATOES:

1 Russet potato, peeled and cut crosswise paper-thin on a mandoline

2 T. melted clarified unsalted butter (see the chapter "Procedures and Techniques")

2 T. clarified unsalted butter for sautéing

Salt and freshly ground white pepper, to taste

FOR THE LOBSTERS:

2 T. cold water

8 ozs. (2 sticks) unsalted butter, cut into 16 pieces

1 tsp. chopped fresh tarragon

2 Maine lobsters, 1 1/2 lbs. each, steamed, cooked meat carefully removed

Salt and freshly ground white pepper, to taste

FOR THE LEEK COMPOTE:

2 cups finely diced leeks, white and tender light green parts only

Kosher salt for blanching leeks

2 T. crème fraîche or heavy cream

Salt and freshly ground white pepper, to taste

FOR THE SAUCE:

1/2 cup crème fraîche or heavy cream

1/2 tsp. fresh lemon juice

10 saffron threads

Salt and freshly ground white pepper, to taste

FOR THE MUSHROOMS:

1 cup chanterelle mushrooms

2 tsp. unsalted butter

2 T. minced shallot

Caramelized pearl onions

1/2 cup blanched or thawed frozen sweet peas

Salt and freshly ground black pepper, to taste

FOR THE SWEET PEA SAUCE:

1/4 cup blanched fresh or thawed frozen sweet peas

2 tsp. hot chicken stock or canned low-sodium, fat-free chicken or vegetable broth

2 T. extra virgin olive oil

Pinch salt

FOR THE GARNISH:

Snipped fresh chives

Sprigs of fresh chervil

Chef's TRUC:

Just before service, chef Craig Shelton uses an immersion blender to whip the saffron sauce until it begins to foam to "open up" the flavors in the sauce.

Equipment:

Mandoline

Mini-processor

Handheld electric mixer or immersion blender with
cup attachment

4-inch-diameter, 3-inch-deep ring mold

Prepare the Caramelized Pearl Onions: Preheat
the oven to 350°F.

Place the unpeeled pearl onions in a small baking dish
just large enough to hold them in one snug layer. Drizzle
with the oil and add the butter, cut into a few pieces.
Sprinkle with the salt and roast, tossing occasionally,
until the onions are fragrant, tender, and just beginning

to caramelize. Cool the onions and peel them. The onions
can be prepared ahead and kept at room temperature for several
hours or refrigerated in a covered container for up to 2 days.

Prepare the Potatoes: Line a small sheet pan or platter with parchment paper.

Gently toss the potato slices in the melted clarified butter.
Use a 4-inch ring mold to arrange the potato slices in a
circle on the parchment paper, slightly overlapping the
slices. Repeat to make a second circle. Refrigerate for at
least 5 minutes before proceeding.

Prepare the Lobster Meat: Preheat the oven to
180°F. Place an empty sheet pan in the oven to hold the
various bowls of ingredients as you prepare them.

In a medium saucepan over medium heat, bring the 2 tablespoons of water to a boil. Whisk in the butter and tarragon. As soon as the butter is melted, remove the pan from the heat and gently fold in the lobster meat. Season to taste with salt and pepper and keep warm in the oven.

Prepare the Leek Compote: Bring a medium pot of cold water to a boil and add 1 tablespoon of kosher salt. Add the leeks and cook them just until they soften a bit and the color brightens, about 1 minute. Drain well and transfer the leeks to a small bowl. Stir in the crème fraîche or heavy cream, season with salt and pepper, and keep warm in the oven.

Prepare the Saffron Sauce: In a small saucepan, gently warm the crème fraîche or heavy cream and whisk in the lemon juice. Crush the saffron threads into the mixture, add 1 tablespoon of the butter-tarragon mixture from the lobster, and whisk to blend. Transfer the saucepan to the warming oven.

Prepare the Mushrooms: In a medium skillet over medium-high heat, sauté the mushrooms in 1 teaspoon of the butter, tossing occasionally, for 2 minutes. Add the shallot, caramelized pearl onions, sweet peas, and the remaining teaspoon of butter and continue to sauté, tossing occasionally, for 2 minutes more. Season with salt and pepper and transfer to the warming oven.

Prepare the Sweet Pea Sauce: In a mini-processor, whiz the peas together with the hot stock or broth to purée. Add the olive oil and continue to process to reach a very smooth purée. Pass through a fine sieve or strainer, if necessary.

To Finish the Dish: In a skillet large enough to hold the potatoes side by side, heat the clarified butter over medium-high heat. Use a spatula or simply turn over the parchment paper to transfer the potato circles to the to skillet and sauté, turning once, until golden brown and crisp, about 5 minutes.

Use a handheld electric mixer or an immersion blender fitted with the cup attachment to whip the saffron sauce until it begins to foam. (This is optional, but it does "open up" the flavors in the sauce!)

To Plate: Place a 4-inch-wide, 3-inch-deep ring mold in the center of each plate and press in a layer of the leek compote. Carefully pack the mold with the sautéed mushrooms.

Drain the lobster meat briefly on paper towels and pack it carefully into the mold on top of the mushrooms.

Add a little of the saffron sauce to the lobster and spoon the rest onto the plate, around the outside of the mold. Sprinkle the lobster with snipped chives and remove the mold.

Drizzle the pea purée around the edge of the plate. Place a crispy potato circle on top of the lobster and garnish with a sprig of fresh chervil.

scalini fedeli

63 Main Street

Chatham 07928

973/701-9200

CHEF-OWNER Michael Cetrulo is a wunderkind, or however you say it in Italian—he was only 23 years young when he opened Il Mondo Vecchio, one town up in Madison, to rave reviews, and it wasn't his first venture. It's still an outstanding favorite.

But let's talk about Scalini Fedeli. It has a real Italian feel to it—vaulted ceilings with sexy lighting and

comfy seating, cozily arranged around pillars to create a sense of privacy. Scalini Fedeli means "steps of faith," and Michael had to have it not only to open a second BYO just three miles away where jackets are required and the menu is *prix fixe* but then to open its sister of the same name in Manhattan just a few years later. Does he sound like your garden-variety type-A overachiever? Maybe—but somehow or other, he's remained an extremely nice guy, and it's all working!

If you get to know Michael, you won't be at all surprised to learn that he designed his own education. He staged a little, watched a lot, took notes on everything everywhere, and ate. A few minutes with Michael and you get the sense he's all senses. He also knew what he was looking for—his dad was a chef, and Michael grew up in restaurant kitchens.

But it doesn't matter what we think because Scalini Fedeli passed the acid test—we brought each of our kids here at one time or another, including our son-in-law Jeremy, a chef. The kids are really different, but all are real food critics and not easily impressed. Their reaction was the same—lots of eye rolling, a few "Oh, Gods" (and one "Oh, Goddess"), and not a whole lot of talking going on except for several weeks later and mainly consisting of "So . . . when are you guys going back?"

Pignoli-Crusted Salmon
IN A PINOT GRIGIO–SHALLOT REDUCTION SAUCE

We're fish freaks (just peruse the recipe index!), and this dish fast became a favorite, not only for the salmon and its deliciously healthy benefits but also because if you put pignolis on it or in it, we'll eat it.

The pinot grigio doesn't hurt, either. It works well in the dish, works well *with* the dish, and also works well for "moisturizing" the chef. Don't skip the refrigeration step—in fact, you can comfortably extend it to as much as 4 or 5 hours—or we can't guarantee the nuts will stay on board.

Mise en Place:

FOR THE SALMON:

2 pieces skinned salmon filet, cut from the wide end, 6 ozs. each

About ¹/₂ cup flour for dusting

1 T. smooth Dijon mustard

¹/₂ cup pignoli nuts

2 T. extra virgin olive oil

2 T. finely chopped shallots

4 whole fresh basil leaves

2 T. unsalted butter

Salt and freshly ground black pepper, to taste

$^1/_2$ cup peeled, seeded, and diced Roma tomato

$^1/_4$ cup pinot grigio

1 T. freshly squeezed lemon juice

$^1/_4$ cup low-sodium, fat-free chicken broth

FOR THE GARNISH

4 fresh basil leaves, cut into chiffonade

Prepare the Salmon: Dust the salmon filets with flour and shake off the excess. Apply a thin layer of Dijon mustard to the top only of each filet. Place the pignoli nuts on a plate and then press the mustard side of the fish very firmly into the pignoli nuts to coat. Place the fish on a plate, nut side up, and refrigerate for at least 20 minutes.

In a large skillet over medium-low heat, heat the oil for about 15 seconds. Place the filets nut side down into the skillet and sauté until the nuts are quite toasted, about 6 to 8 minutes.

Use a large spatula to carefully turn the fish. Add the shallots, 4 whole basil leaves, and 1 tablespoon of the butter to the pan and sauté until the shallots begin to soften, about 1 minute.

Add half the diced tomato, the pinot grigio, and the lemon juice, raise the heat to high, and reduce the liquid by half.

Add the chicken broth and continue to cook briskly until the sauce is reduced by half. Whisk in the remaining tablespoon of butter.

To Finish the Dish: Remove the fish to warm plates.

Add the remaining diced tomato to the pan and season to taste with salt and pepper. Cook for about 30 seconds more and then strain the sauce.

To Plate: Pour the sauce over the fish and garnish with chiffonade of basil.

soho on george

335 George Street

New Brunswick 08901

732/296-0533

www.sohoongeorge.net

ANOTHER WINNER by owner Mark Jakuboski and not far from his hugely successful Old Man Rafferty's is the unpretentious, comfortable, New American SoHo on George, where we were happy to find old friend, manager Pat Lytwynec, and new friend, chef Ken Hoerle.

This place has electric energy, and you can see it on the fly with a peek into the cutting-edge design of the open-theater-style kitchen. Exciting things are happening here—the restaurant often has an interesting happening on the horizon from charitable events to focused wine tastings and theme menus that attract a lively crowd.

Evocative of a downtown hot spot, the restaurant is aptly named. SoHo on George is all about fine dining in a relaxed atmosphere, refreshing because getting Steve into a jacket and tie is like getting most guys into a cocktail dress—neither easy nor enjoyable—for the guy or the dress.

Ken has an eye for seeing old things in a new way, which is as refreshing as the cutting-edge decor and Pat's fantastic wine list or her martini menu. The chef's lobster BLT is a customer favorite, the paella is a sculptured piece of artwork on a plate, and the bar menu, which they call "Easy Food," is interesting enough to put a couple of dishes together and call it dinner and a date.

You may have to struggle to leave room for a treat from the equally whimsical dessert menu and one of the creative coffee concoctions, but they've anticipated that—both the cookies to go and the famous breadsticks that match up with the generous cheese plate are available boxed and ready for the ride home.

Salmon Gravlax Crab Roll

WITH AVOCADO, DAIKON RADISH SPROUTS, AND A SESAME VINAIGRETTE

For this gorgeous appetizer, we're including chef Ken Hoerle's cure for his house-made gravlax, but be absolutely sure that the fish you buy is top quality, that you handle it properly and keep it well chilled because it will not be cooked! Plan ahead—the cure takes three days. Once you know the method, you can cure salmon into gravlax using lots of different flavor variations—but that's another whole book! And if you're not the adventurous sort, you can use ready-made gravlax, which is available in most better supermarkets.

The avocado you choose needs to be ripe—make sure it's a Hass avocado (the one with the bumpy alligator skin) and that it gives when pressed with your thumb. If the stem pops out readily when flicked with your thumbnail, it's ripe. The daikon radish sprouts are easy to find at Asian markets (yes, those teeny little sprouts are the same plant that will eventually grow into those humongous daikon radishes!)—and they're also delicious in sandwiches and tossed into mixed salads.

Mise en Place:

FOR THE SALMON GRAVLAX:

$^1/_2$ cup granulated sugar

6 T. kosher salt

1 tsp. fennel seeds

1 tsp. red pepper flakes

$^1/_4$-inch piece of peeled fresh ginger, chopped

1 clove garlic, minced

A 2-inch piece from the tender heart of lemongrass, sliced thin

Small bunch of cilantro, including stems, left whole but crushed a bit with the back of a knife

Small bunch of dill, including stems, left whole but crushed a bit with the back of a knife

1 filet of salmon, 2 lbs., skin on

FOR THE CILANTRO OIL:

1 cup cleaned cilantro leaves, spun very dry

$^1/_4$ cup canola oil

FOR THE CRAB SALAD:

2 T. extra virgin olive oil

Salt and freshly ground black pepper, to taste

2 tsp. fresh lemon juice

8 ozs. jumbo lump crab meat

1 T. snipped fresh chives

FOR THE SESAME VINAIGRETTE:

$^1/_4$ cup dark (toasted) sesame oil

Salt and freshly ground black pepper, to taste

1 tsp. white sesame seeds

1 tsp. black sesame seeds

2 T. rice wine vinegar

1 T. fresh orange juice

FOR THE SEASONED AVOCADO:

1 ripe Hass avocado, peeled, pitted, and finely diced (see the chapter "Procedures and Techniques")

1 ripe plum tomato, seeded and finely diced

1 T. minced red onion

$1^1/_2$ tsp. chopped fresh cilantro leaves

1 T. extra virgin olive oil

1 T. fresh lemon juice

Salt and freshly ground black pepper, to taste

FOR THE GARNISH:

Daikon radish sprouts

2 Belgian endive leaves, cut into fine julienne

2 chives

1 T. extra virgin olive oil

1 tsp. fresh lemon juice

Salt and freshly ground black pepper, to taste

1 ripe plum tomato, seeded and diced

Equipment:

Mini-processor or mortar and pestle

Carving knife, sharp, with a narrow blade

Prepare the Gravlax: In a small bowl, mix together the sugar, salt, fennel seed, and red pepper flakes.

Line a sheet pan with parchment paper. Arrange half of the ginger, garlic, lemongrass, cilantro, and dill on the parchment in a pile approximately the size and shape of the salmon.

Rub the flesh side of the salmon with half of the spice mixture and place it, skin side up, on top of the herbs. Apply the remainder of the spice mixture followed by the remaining ginger, garlic, lemongrass, and herbs to the skin side of the salmon. Cover the salmon tightly with plastic wrap and refrigerate to cure for 3 days.

At the end of the curing time, remove the salmon and wipe off all the cure mixture with paper towels. The salmon gravlax can be prepared ahead and kept, tightly wrapped in plastic and refrigerated, for up to 1 week.

Prepare the Cilantro Oil: Place the cilantro leaves in the work bowl of a mini-processor (or chop them and use a mortar and pestle to pound them to a paste) and process, scraping down the sides of the bowl as necessary, until very finely chopped. Add the canola oil, salt and pepper to taste, and process to a purée. Transfer to a small squeeze bottle and store in the refrigerator between uses. The cilantro oil can be prepared ahead and kept, refrigerated in the squeeze bottle, for up to 2 weeks.

Prepare the Crab Salad: In a small mixing bowl, whisk together the olive oil, salt, and pepper. Gradually whisk in the lemon juice to form an emulsion.

Place the crab in a separate mixing bowl and use a large rubber spatula to gently fold in the dressing, being careful not to break up the crabmeat more than necessary. Fold in the snipped chives. The crab salad can be prepared ahead and kept, refrigerated in a covered container, for up to 4 hours.

Prepare the Sesame Vinaigrette: In a small bowl, whisk together the sesame oil, salt, pepper, and white and black sesame seeds. Whisking constantly, gradually add the rice wine vinegar and the orange juice to form an emulsion. The sesame vinaigrette can be prepared ahead and kept, covered, at room temperature for up to 4 hours.

Prepare the Seasoned Avocado: Place the diced avocado in a mixing bowl and use a rubber spatula to gently fold in the tomato, red onion, and cilantro.

In a separate bowl, whisk together the olive oil, lemon juice, salt, and pepper. Gently fold the dressing into the avocado mixture.

To Finish the Dish: Use a very sharp narrow-bladed carving knife to carve the gravlax crosswise and at a sharp diagonal into very thin slices.

Place a length of plastic wrap about the size of a piece of copy paper on a clean work surface. Arrange the salmon slices, overlapping by about one-third, on the plastic wrap to form a sheet about 6 inches long—this will be the outside "shell" of the roll.

Spread a 3/4-inch-high line of the crab mixture lengthwise down the center of the "sheet" of salmon.

Using the plastic wrap to facilitate rolling, roll the bottom edge of the salmon "sheet" up and over the filling and press firmly with the plastic wrap to form a tight log. Lift the edge of the plastic wrap and, holding the plastic wrap with your fingers, roll forward until you've formed a tight log, stopping as necessary to pull the plastic wrap out from within the log and to shape the log evenly.

Unwrap the salmon log, remove the plastic wrap and cut the log into 3 equal pieces. Repeat to form a second log and cut in the same manner. Trim off unsightly edges. You should now have 6 rolls.

Use two soup spoons to form 6 football-shaped quenelles with the avocado mixture—holding one spoon in each hand, scoop up a heaping spoonful and transfer the mixture back and forth between the two spoons.

Make 2 equal bunches of the daikon radish sprouts and the julienned endive, using a chive as a "belt" to tie them.

Whisk together the olive oil, lemon juice, salt, and pepper for the garnish.

To Plate: Place 3 salmon rolls on end on each chilled plate with 3 avocado quenelles surrounding them and stuff the sprout bundle in the center. Drizzle the sprout bundle with the olive oil-lemon mixture.

Squirt the sesame vinaigrette over the rolls and avocado quenelles.

Surround the rolls and quenelles with drizzles of cilantro oil and sprinkle the plates with the diced tomatoes.

stage house inn

366 Park Avenue

Scotch Plains 07076

908/322-4224

www.stagehouseinn.com

THE ONE CONSTANT at the Stage House Inn is that you can expect the unexpected. The cozy colonial building with its intimate dining rooms with fireplaces, planked floors, and simple furnishings sets the expectation for an early American meal, but the modern French cuisine you're about to be stunned by is nothing short of cutting edge.

Chef-owner David Drake is a master in the art of presentation. He has an eye for color, texture, and balance that is likely a result of his early interest in film and photography, and he knows exactly when to let go and let the dish speak for itself. The plates are a photographer's dream—in fact, Steve's shot of David's circle of translucent, paper-thin sliced salmon ringed with a fine line of caviar pearls garnered accolades from more than a few of his peers at a recent international food photographers exhibit.

Ditto on the food that adorns his beautifully presented plates. There's an elusive quality to David's food, and its lightness of being is likely a result of his inventive use of vegetables, which often take the place of heavier stocks as the base of his cuisine. By definition, the menu is driven by the seasons and showcases David's skill with vegetables and game meats and in constructing the tasting menus the Stage House Inn is known for.

The Stage House Inn, consistently a frontrunner in New Jersey and recognized as one of America's Top Tables by *Gourmet* magazine, manages to be a complete fine-dining experience in part because this is not a one-person show. Despite his personal brilliance, David Drake has recognized the value of an exceptional support system. Manager Lee Chasalow subtly sets the stage to provide graciously efficient but unobtrusive service, and in every corner of the kitchen we saw skill and attention to detail with perfection as the goal.

They know what they're doing at the Stage House Inn, every day and in every way—our advice is to let them do it. This is a place for serious food lovers. Go with one of the prix fixe tasting menus or the seven-course dégustation and let the sommelier pair your selections with the restaurant's exceptional wines for an experience you will likely never forget.

Savoy Cabbage-Wrapped Pekin Duck

WITH A WARM SALAD OF LENTILS, SMOKED BACON, AND GARLIC CONFIT

We chose this unique appetizer not only because it's representative of chef-owner David Drake's cuisine but also because the technique is a springboard for all kinds of "sausages." Although the duck roll is not classically a sausage, the technique used to create and cook it is one that can be used with any number of ingredients (think layers of thinly sliced and blanched vegetables, stuffed sheets of pasta, finely chopped or ground meats or fish. . .) and in any number of permutations (wrapped, not wrapped, thin, thick, appetizer, main course . . .).

This dish is also exciting in its use of ingredients you don't see every day such as the D'Artagnan duck prosciutto, which you can get wherever you get D'Artagnan products (see the chapter "Resources"). Try to find it, it's really special. But if you can't, a substitute with prosciutto di Parma or di San Daniele (our preference) is perfectly acceptable.

And last, the lentil salad alone would have been enough for this one to make the cut!

Mise en Place:

FOR THE HERB MIXTURE:

1 tsp. finely chopped fresh Italian flat-leaf parsley

1 tsp. finely chopped fresh tarragon

1 tsp. finely chopped fresh chervil

1 tsp. finely chopped fresh cilantro leaves

1 tsp. finely chopped fresh mint

1 tsp. finely chopped fresh dill

FOR THE SAVOY CABBAGE:

6 whole outer leaves of Savoy cabbage, preferably dark green

1 T. kosher salt for blanching the cabbage

FOR THE LENTILS:

$1/2$ cup French green *du puy* lentils (see the chapter "Resources")

1 bay leaf

1 sprig fresh thyme

2 sprigs Italian flat-leaf parsley

1 small peeled carrot

Salt and freshly ground black pepper, to taste

FOR THE WRAPPED DUCK:

4 slices D'Artagnan duck prosciutto (see the chapter "Resources") OR 4 whole slices prosciutto di San Daniele or prosciutto di Parma

1 whole D'Artagnan duck breast, skinned, trimmed of all fat, halved lengthwise

Salt and freshly ground black pepper, to taste

2 cups chicken stock or canned low-sodium, fat-free chicken broth

2 cups vegetable stock or canned low-sodium, fat-free vegetable broth

1 cup water

FOR THE LENTIL SALAD:

2 slices applewood-smoked bacon, cut crosswise into $1/4$-inch strips (see the chapter "Resources")

1 large clove garlic, smashed with the side of a chef's knife

2 T. extra virgin olive oil

2 T. minced shallots

1 ripe plum tomato, peeled, seeded, and cut into small dice

Salt and freshly ground black pepper, to taste

FOR THE SAUCE:

$1/2$ cup veal demi-glace

1 T. port wine

2 T. water

2 tsp. unsalted butter

Salt and freshly ground black pepper, to taste

FOR THE GARNISH:

2 cups microgreens or chiffonade of mesclun

Salt and freshly ground black pepper, to taste

2 T. extra virgin olive oil

1 tsp. fresh lemon juice

Prepare the Herb Mixture: In a small bowl, mix together the parsley, tarragon, chervil, cilantro leaves, mint, and dill.

Prepare the Savoy Cabbage: Bring a large pot of cold water to a boil to blanch the cabbage leaves. Prepare an ice bath of ice and cold water to shock the cabbage leaves after blanching.

When the water comes to a boil, add 1 tablespoon of kosher salt. Drop the cabbage leaves into the boiling water and cook until they brighten or darken in color and are limp, about 3 to 4 minutes. Scoop the leaves out and plunge them into the ice bath to stop the cooking and preserve the color. Drain the leaves well and pat dry with paper towels.

Spread half the leaves out on a clean work surface, overlapping them to create a "sheet." Use a sharp paring knife to trim the sheet to a rectangle about 4 inches wide and 8 inches long. Repeat with the remaining leaves to create a second rectangular sheet.

Prepare the Lentils: In a small saucepan over medium heat, place the lentils, bay leaf, thyme sprig, parsley, and carrot. Add cold water to cover by 1 inch and bring to a boil. Reduce the heat to maintain a simmer, partially cover the pot, and cook until the lentils are tender, about 20 to 30 minutes.

Drain the lentils and remove and discard the herbs and carrot. Transfer the lentils to a mixing bowl and season to taste with salt and pepper.

Prepare the Wrapped Duck: Place a length of plastic wrap about 14 inches long on a clean work surface and place the blanched cabbage rectangle at the lower bottom edge.

Position a single layer of duck prosciutto across the bottom of the cabbage about ¹/₂ inch from the bottom edge. Sprinkle with salt and pepper and place a half duck breast on top.

Using the plastic wrap to facilitate rolling, roll the bottom edge of the cabbage up and over the duck and press firmly with the plastic wrap to form a tight log. Lift the

edge of the plastic wrap and, holding the plastic wrap with your fingers, roll forward until you've formed a tight log, stopping as necessary to pull the plastic wrap out from within the log and to shape the log evenly. Then completely roll up and encase the cabbage roll in the plastic wrap, twisting the ends very tightly and manipulating and condensing the contents to create an even, uniform log. Knot the ends.

In a saucepan large enough to hold the duck rolls side by side, bring the chicken and vegetable stocks or broths and an additional cup of water to a boil. Add the duck rolls, reduce the heat to maintain a gentle boil, and poach the rolls for exactly 10 minutes. Remove the rolls from the pan and set aside to rest for 5 minutes.

Prepare the Lentil Salad: Line a plate with paper towels to drain the bacon.

In a small skillet, sauté the bacon strips until the fat is rendered and the bacon is golden brown. Transfer the bacon to the lined plate to drain.

Place the garlic and 1 tablespoon of the olive oil in a medium saucepan over medium heat and sauté gently until the garlic begins to brown. Remove the garlic and discard.

Add the shallots to the pan and sauté just until tender and fragrant, about 1 minute. Add the lentils to the pan along with the diced tomato and cook until heated through, about 1 minute. Remove the pan from the heat and fold in the bacon, 2 teaspoons of the herb mixture, and 1 tablespoon of extra virgin olive oil. Season to taste with salt and pepper.

Prepare the Sauce: In a small saucepan over medium heat, bring the demi-glace, port wine, and an additional 2 tablespoons of water to a boil. Shut off the heat and whisk in the butter. Season with salt and pepper and keep warm.

To Finish the Dish: Place the microgreens or mesclun in a medium bowl and season with salt and pepper. Drizzle the olive oil down the sides of the bowl and toss to coat the greens. Add the lemon juice and toss again.

Unwrap the duck rolls, remove the plastic wrap, and trim the edges. Cut each crosswise roll into 5 equal pieces.

To Plate: Place a mound of lentil salad in the center of each plate. Arrange the duck rolls around the lentil salad, top the salad with the dressed greens, and surround with a generous drizzle of sauce.

a taste of asia

245 Main Street

Chatham 07928

973/701-8821

W HEN A CHEF BECOMES a protégé of the renowned restaurateur and mentor Gloria Chu Feng, he or she joins a legion of the best Asian culinarians in the Northeast, and restaurant-goers can be assured an outstanding experience. Such is the case with Malaysian-born chef-owner Steven Chia of A Taste of Asia.

I first met Gloria on Sunday visits to the Dragon Restaurant, where Gloria was hostess-manager. I was eight years old and hopelessly in love with the owner's twenty-something drop-dead-gorgeous son, Harold Li Suey. As the traditional Sunday Chinese restaurant visits migrated closer to home and I aged, Gloria didn't. She did, however, resurface as an exceptionally savvy and successful restaurant owner, and it was a lively game of Jewish geography that ensued (complete with her scarily accurate Yiddish) when Gloria greeted us at A Taste of Asia.

If you haven't yet experienced Malaysian food, you're in for a special and unusual treat. Many of the flavor-base ingredients are reflections of Chinese, Indian, and Thai influences—garlic, kaffir lime, shallots, ginger, galanga, lemongrass, Thai basil, and chili sauces—but their interaction is purely classic provincial Malaysian.

Although he had no formal culinary training to speak of, Steven apparently received all the education he needed from his caterer mom, because if you fly to Malaysia tomorrow, you will taste the same foods and flavors he serves at his restaurant. The menu doesn't change much—classic cuisine doesn't, after all—but specials change seasonally and get Malaysian-ized in Chia's kitchen.

The restaurant is a BYO—we suggest something bubbly, Thai beer, gewürztraminer, or all of the above. Chilled.

Malaysian Seafood Bouillabaise

Hot, spicy, and fabulously aromatic, you'll love trolling through this one-pot treasure chest of goodies from the sea. We had no trouble finding the Knorr's Tamarind Soup Base recommended or the Squid brand fish sauce at the Asian markets (see the chapter "Resources").

Chef-owner Steven Chia serves the bouillabaisse with a delicious mixture of long grain and jasmine rice. We dropped a cube of Knorr's Shrimp Bouillon Mix into a pot of boiling water, and when it dissolved, we stirred in rice noodles, covered the pot, and shut off the heat. When the bouillabaisse was ready, so were our noodles. We also used the Knorr's Shrimp Bouillon Mix for the shrimp stock.

We left the shells and heads on the shrimp and although this is optional, we think it's important to make eye contact whenever possible. We've also found that heads-on enormously enhances the flavor of the shrimp and the soup—after all, it's the shells that are used to make shrimp stock!

Mise en Place:

FOR THE CARAMELIZED SHALLOTS:

2 whole shallots, peeled and thinly sliced

3 T. canola oil

FOR THE BOUILLABAISE:

1 T. canola or corn oil

1 T. finely minced garlic

1 tsp. finely minced fresh ginger root

$1/2$ cup thinly sliced red onion

3 cups shrimp stock

1 T. Knorr's Tamarind Soup Base (see the chapter "Resources")

2 tsp. Squid brand fish sauce

1 T. drained canned crushed pineapple

$^{1}/_{2}$ tsp. chili powder

1 T. granulated sugar

1 cup $^{1}/_{2}$-inch wedges of fresh tomato

$^{1}/_{4}$ cup drained straw mushrooms

2 scallions, roots trimmed, green and white parts cut into $^{1}/_{2}$-inch pieces

3 or 4 small sprigs of fresh Thai basil

4 scallops (10–12 count), tough side muscle removed

4 shrimp (16–20 count), shells on, heads on (optional)

6 large mussels, shells scrubbed, debearded

4 chunks of white fish, such as turbot, sea bass, or snapper, 1 inch each

1 T. chopped fresh cilantro

Equipment:

Mandoline

Prepare the Caramelized Shallots: Line a plate with paper towels to drain the shallots.

In a small skillet over medium-high heat, sauté the shallots in the canola oil until they are golden brown. Use a slotted spoon or skimmer to remove the shallots as soon as they reach the desired color—they burn in an instant!—and set them on the lined plate to drain.

Prepare the Bouillabaise: In a Dutch oven or large, low-sided soup pot over medium-high heat, sauté the garlic and ginger in oil until fragrant and beginning to color.

Stir in the red onion and then add the shrimp stock, tamarind soup base, fish sauce, pineapple, chili powder, sugar, tomato, mushrooms, scallions, and Thai basil and bring to a boil.

Reduce the heat to a gentle boil, add the scallops, and cook for 1 minute. Add the rest of the seafood, cover, and cook for 1 to 2 minutes more, until the mussels open.

Shut off the heat and add the cilantro, replace the cover and let stand for 3 minutes more.

To Plate: Spoon the soup into large bowls, dividing the ingredients equally, and garnish with the caramelized shallots.

tre figlio

500 West White Horse Pike
Egg Harbor City 08215
609/965-3303
www.trefiglio.com

*T*RE FIGLIO is just off the beaten path from Atlantic City, but that doesn't stop those who know and love great Italian food from taking a little side trip. It's hard to believe that only fifteen years ago, this building housed a genuine redneck bar! Owners Jack and Toni Cordivari, seasoned restaurateurs, rebuilt and redesigned the building, and the warmly decorated intimate space resembles a private dining room in someone's home.

Whether you're in the mood for a mountain of arugula draped in sweet prosciutto di Parma with house-roasted red peppers and shards of pecorino cheese, a plate of the tender homemade pasta the restaurant is known for, its signature gargantuan breaded veal chop, or one of the delicate seafood dishes the restaurant built its reputation on, you'd have to travel many miles to find comparable authentic Italian food. Served up generously by talented chef Frank Mulino and accompanied by great wines from the award-winning list, the food at Tre Figlio is freshly authentic.

Make a point to try out a few of Frank's originals—there are usually at least six on the menu and they're easy to find because they're named after Jack and Toni's six grandchildren. Your cravings and expectations will be satisfied at Tre Figlio. If the question is what's a hidden gem, the answer is Tre Figlio.

Lobster Venetian

A rich hybrid of francese and Alfredo, this dish is a killer! (We mean that in only the most complimentary way, although we do advise postponement of any cholesterol testing for at least a week after enjoying it.)

It's a great showcase for those sweet little baby lobster tails and the gi-normous shrimp that can pass as them. And if you want to make it even "more better," think about serving it on a bed of angel hair pasta. Yes, it breaks the rule of no cheese on seafood pasta dishes, but go ahead and report us to the Italian pasta police, we don't care—if it tastes good, do it.

Mise en Place:

FOR THE "ALFREDO" SAUCE:

$1/2$ cup chicken stock or low-sodium, fat-free chicken broth

3 T. heavy cream

3 T. grated Parmesan cheese

Salt, to taste

FOR THE FRANCESE BATTER:

4 whole eggs

2 T. grated Parmesan cheese

2 tsp. finely chopped fresh Italian flat-leaf parsley

FOR THE SHELLFISH:

4 lobster tails, 4 ozs. each

4 shrimp (12–15 count), shelled and deveined

Blended oil as needed to sauté the shellfish (see the chapter "The Tools, the Terms, the Ingredients, and When to Use Them")

Flour for coating shellfish

Salt and freshly ground white pepper, to taste

2 tsp. minced shallots

6 T. fresh lemon juice

$1/4$ cup dry white wine

2 T. unsalted butter

Prepare the "Alfredo" Sauce: In a small saucepan over low heat, warm the chicken stock or broth together with the heavy cream. Gradually add the cheese, whisking continuously until it's melted. Set aside. The "Alfredo" sauce can be prepared ahead and kept, refrigerated in a covered container, for up to 3 days. Bring the sauce to room temperature or gently warm before using.

Prepare the Francese Batter: In a medium shallow or wide bowl, whisk together the eggs and Parmesan cheese. Add the parsley and stir to blend.

Prepare the Shellfish: Use a sharp knife or scissors to cut through the lobster shells (down the center of the back and the underside). Remove the lobster flesh from the shell, leaving the "tail feathers," if possible. Position the lobster tail belly side up and use the tip of a knife to make two parallel shallow lengthwise cuts into the belly meat. Turn the meat over and pound/smack it with the flat side of a chef's knife to flatten the meat to an even thickness of about $1/2$ inch.

Shell and butterfly the shrimp, leaving the "tail feathers" intact; smack the meat with the flat side of a chef's knife to flatten it.

To Finish the Dish: Heat about $1/4$ inch of blended oil in a large skillet over high heat.

Dredge the lobster in the flour, then drag it through the francese batter to coat it, and place in the hot skillet. Turn the lobster when it moves easily and is lightly browned on one side.

Dredge the shrimp in the flour and then coat them with the francese batter. Add the shrimp to the hot skillet and turn when the shrimp move easily and are lightly browned.

Immediately pour off the oil and return the pan to the heat. Season with salt and pepper and add the shallots, lemon juice, and wine to the pan. Add the "Alfredo" sauce and the butter and cook until the shellfish is cooked through. Remove the shellfish and cook the sauce until it is slightly thickened. Season to taste with salt and pepper.

To Plate: Spoon some of the sauce into the center of warm plates. Arrange equal portions of the lobster and shrimp on the plates and spoon the remaining sauce on top.

Chef's TRUC:

To assure that the shellfish is cooked through and the egg-based batter doesn't overcook, Chef Frank Mulino makes a few shallow lengthwise cuts in the lobster tail and butterflies the shrimp and then uses the flat side of his chef's knife to smack and flatten each one to a thin, even piece—much the same way you'd pound scalloppini of veal!

Restaurants and Recipes

tre piani

120 Rockingham Row

Princeton 08540

609/452-1515

www.trepiani.com

W<small>E'RE LONGTIME FANS</small> of executive chef and part-owner Jim Weaver and his fresh and fabulous Italian-Mediterranean cuisine, so it was with great expectations, happy anticipation, and hearty appetites that we visited Tre Piani, where he's doing what he does best—and that's what he calls taking the rough edge off fine dining. Our kind of place.

Jim is a great proponent of organic and locally grown food, which he chooses and uses with care and respect to allow the food to speak for itself. He's deeply committed and connected to the state of New Jersey and its farming community and to the philosophies of the Slow Food Movement, the international organization whose manifesto is to promote efforts to rebuild and revive our increasingly endangered biodiversity

through the support of local growers, products, and artisans. But he not only talks the talk, he walks the walk—he started and continues to lead the first New Jersey convivium of Slow Food USA.

The restaurant's design is almost as exciting as the food—Tre Piani means three floors. The vaulted ceiling at the ground-floor level and the sweeping staircase leading up to the second floor and then the third set the feeling of airy spaciousness, and the ability to see the nooks and crannies and into each level from the other is captivating—it's fun just looking around. The well-stocked ground-floor bar is comfortable and beautiful, as is the smaller one on the second level. The restaurant has great bistro and lunch menus with outdoor dining when the weather is friendly and also maintains a humidor with a great inventory of hand-picked cigars.

Speaking of looking around, one of the value-added benefits of a visit to Tre Piani is that it's located in the outlet "city" of Forrestal Village in Princeton. So make it a day—go for the food, stay for the shopping. Shopping is hard work. You may have to go back for more food.

Cape May Salt Oysters on the Half Shell

SERVED WITH SPICY CILANTRO-SCENTED HARISSA SAUCE

New Jersey is home to Cape May salt oysters, considered such a local treasure that they have been inducted into Slow Food's Ark USA, whose mission is to preserve endangered tastes historically, socioe-conomically, or culturally tied to a precise region or locality, which are at risk of extinction by the forces of agricultural or industrial standardization—and to celebrate them, by introducing them to the world, through media, public relations, and Slow Food member events.

The Ark seeks, first and foremost, to save an economic, social, and cultural heritage—a universe of animal breeds, fruit and vegetables, cured meats, cheese, cereals, pastas, cakes and confectionery. It works to rediscover, catalog, describe, and publicize foods and flavors that have disappeared or are in danger of disappearing from our tables. It also strives to protect biodiversity and to acknowledge and promote sustainable practices in agriculture and food production. And not least of its goals is to champion the art of taste and the right to pleasure.

Cape May salt oysters, also known as Delaware Bay oysters, are prized for their fine flavor and plump, firm meat. Their distinct character—size, color, texture, and taste—is directly related to their habitat. The Delaware Bay produces oysters with two distinct flavors, one from the inner bay and the other from the Cape Shore. The Cape Shore oysters are briny, with a sweet, nutty astringency, while the inner bay oysters have a milder flavor.

This simple dish by chef-owner Jim Weaver recognizes and celebrates the fact that Cape May salt oysters need only the most minimal enhancement for maximum enjoyment.

Mise en Place:

FOR THE OVEN ROASTED TOMATOES:

2 ripe beefsteak tomatoes, halved

3 T. extra virgin olive oil

2 cloves garlic, peeled and smashed

1 tsp. chopped fresh basil leaves

1 tsp. chopped fresh Italian flat-leaf parsley

$^1/_2$ tsp. fresh thyme leaves

Salt and freshly ground black pepper, to taste

FOR THE SPICY CILANTRO-SCENTED HARISSA:

2 roasted red bell peppers, peeled and seeded (see the chapter "Procedures and Techniques")

6 cloves roasted garlic (see the chapter "Procedures and Techniques")

$^1/_2$ tsp. ground cumin

1 ancho chile, soaked in hot water to cover for 10 minutes and then drained, stemmed, seeded, and torn into small pieces

$^1/_2$ cup fresh chopped cilantro leaves

$^1/_2$ cup extra virgin olive oil

1 tsp. salt

10 freshly shucked Cape May salt oysters, meat loosened from the shell and put back in place on the most stable half of the shell for serving

FOR THE SALAD:

2 cups mesclun greens

$^1/_4$ cup fresh stemmed cilantro leaves

2 T. extra virgin olive oil

Salt and freshly ground black pepper, to taste

2 tsp. balsamic vinegar

$^1/_2$ roasted red bell pepper, peeled and seeded, cut in thin julienne strips

FOR THE GARNISH:

Fresh stemmed cilantro leaves

Equipment:

Food processor or blender

Prepare the Oven Roasted Tomatoes: Preheat the oven to 350°F.

In a medium bowl, gently toss the tomatoes with the olive oil, garlic, herbs, salt, and pepper and place them, cut side down, on a sheet pan. Roast the tomatoes for 1 hour, until somewhat softened and very fragrant.

Prepare the Spicy Cilantro-Scented Harissa: Place the oven roasted tomatoes, peeled and seeded roasted red bell peppers, roasted garlic, cumin, ancho chile, cilantro leaves, olive oil, and salt in the work bowl of a food processor or blender and process until smooth. Strain through a sieve or strainer.

To Finish the Dish: Place the mesclun greens and cilantro leaves in a medium bowl and drizzle with the 2 tablespoons of olive oil. Sprinkle with salt and pepper to taste and toss until the leaves are coated. Drizzle in the balsamic vinegar and toss again.

To Plate: Place a mound of dressed salad in the center of each chilled plate and garnish the salad with the julienne of roasted pepper.

Arrange an equal number of shucked oysters around the salad and spoon sauce onto each oyster. Garnish the plate with cilantro leaves.

the washington inn

801 Washington Street

Cape May 08204

609/884-5697

www.washingtoninn.com

THE WASHINGTON INN is a Cape May icon. If there's one restaurant that is the queen of the scene, it's this converted 1840s-era plantation-style home owned by the Craig family, where civility, grace, and charm have reigned supreme for the past twenty-five years.

We were ecstatic to discover that the kitchens at the Washington Inn are presided over by a female, executive chef Mimi Wood, the queen whose treasures include her ability to deftly tweak classic and traditional dishes with her light personal touch. Equally happy was our discovery of the artist who is the pastry chef, Kathy Cressman, also a traditionalist who likes to put her own twist on the classics.

Passionate oenophiles, general manager Michael Craig and his brother David have developed one of the best wine lists in the state of New Jersey. They are known and respected throughout New Jersey and well beyond for their knowledge and skill and, in fact, have created the Cape May Wine School, where they teach a comprehensive course of study in wine appreciation.

It's a well-integrated team at the Washington Inn. In addition to a formidable list of other skills, Mike also cooks, and together he and Mimi wrote the terrific *Washington Inn Cookbook*, filled with great recipes from their menus and their home kitchens.

The Craigs also own the Pelican Club, the outstanding penthouse restaurant at the top of the Marquis de Lafayette Hotel where we enjoyed fabulous food and the breathtaking view of the Cape May coastline and the colorful skyline of the painted ladies' rooftops with a bunch of professional (rug) "hooker"

friends during their annual week down there (more on that some other time . . .). Also theirs at the Marquis de Lafayette are the Fin Bar, a laid-back beachfront barefoot bar that serves lunch and early dinner, and the Savannah Room. And, just in case there might have been a few hours with nothing to do, they opened Love the Cook, for gourmet kitchen and gadget shop junkies like us to wander through between meals.

We don't think there was a person we spoke with who, when we mentioned the Washington Inn, hadn't dined there. Nor was there a person we spoke with who, when we mentioned Cape May, didn't mention the Washington Inn. If you haven't been there, make it a priority. If you have, consider the even more special experience of one of their intimate private dinners, which they will prepare and serve you in their beautiful wine cellar.

But whichever you do, remember that life is uncertain. So maybe eat dessert first.

Chocolate Mousse Tower

We all know you can never have too much chocolate, and how spectacular is this dessert by pastry chef Kathy Cressman?? Trust us—you can do it! We did, and it was as easy as Kathy promised.

We subbed a few trucs (see sidebar) from our bag of, but if you're OK making your own chocolate sauce and a classic crème anglaise (vanilla sauce) like the big kids, go for it.

Kathy uses custom-cut PVC pipe, $2^1/_4$ inches in diameter and $2^1/_2$ inches high, for the mousse molds. If you can't get this done for you at your local hardware store (or don't have a handy-dandy tool guy to do it for you), think about using tomato paste cans, tops and bottoms removed (tomato paste frozen for later use)!

For the chocolate trellis, you'll need food-safe acetate sheets, which you'll cut to size, depending on the mold you choose for your mousse. We found them—cheap and reusable—at our local art supply shop.

One word of caution—this recipe calls for uncooked egg white, which requires careful handling and involves some decision making on your part. We buy the freshest organic eggs we can find and make sure they're refrigerated properly. However, this is no guarantee that the risks associated with salmonella are eliminated! If you have concerns, this may not be the recipe to prepare for pregnant ladies, babies, or immune-compromised or elderly folks.

Mise en Place:

FOR THE RASPBERRY SAUCE:

1 package frozen sweetened raspberries, thawed

3 to 4 T. superfine sugar, to taste

FOR THE CHOCOLATE MOUSSE:

$3^1/_2$ ozs. good-quality semisweet or bittersweet chocolate, chopped into small pieces

1 large egg white

Pinch salt

1 T. plus 2 tsp. superfine sugar (see the chapter "The Tools, the Terms, the Ingredients, and When to Use Them")

$^3/_4$ cup plus 1 T. heavy cream

FOR THE CHOCOLATE TRELLIS:

8 ozs. good-quality semisweet or bittersweet chocolate, chopped into small pieces

FOR THE WHIPPED CREAM TOPPING:

$^1/_2$ cup heavy cream

1 to 2 T. superfine sugar, to taste

FOR THE GARNISH:

Hershey's syrup in a squeeze bottle

$^1/_2$ cup melted good-quality French vanilla ice cream

Equipment:

Food processor or blender

Squeeze bottles for raspberry sauce, vanilla sauce, and chocolate for the Trellis

Immersion blender with cup and whisk attachment or electric handheld mixer

Parchment paper

2 ring molds, each $2^1/_4$ inches in diameter and $2^1/_2$ inches high

Two squares of food-safe acetate, cut to wrap completely around the ring molds and to exceed the height of the molds by 2 inches

Prepare the Raspberry Sauce: Use a food processor or blender to whiz the defrosted berries and sauce to a smooth purée. Pass the purée through a sieve or strainer to capture pulp and seeds. Transfer the sauce into a squeeze bottle and refrigerate until ready to use. The sauce can be prepared ahead and kept, refrigerated in the squeeze bottle, for up to 4 days.

Prepare the Chocolate Mousse: Line the ring molds with parchment paper cut to size to line the inside of the ring molds and extend about 1 inch above the top edge. Place the lined ring molds on a sheet pan or in a shallow flat dish for freezing.

Our TRUC:

Instead of making a full recipe of classic crème anglaise when we needed only about half a cup, we defrosted high-quality French vanilla ice cream for the vanilla sauce—after all, ice cream base, before freezing, is vanilla custard! And for the chocolate sauce, our shortcut use of Hershey's syrup, already conveniently packaged in a squeeze bottle, worked out just fine.

Melt the chocolate using the microwave or double-boiler method (see the chapter "Procedures and Techniques"). Set aside to cool slightly but keep warm.

Place the egg white in the cup attachment for an immersion blender fitted with the whisk attachment or in a small bowl and use an electric handheld mixer to whip the egg white until foamy like soapsuds. Add a pinch of salt and continue to whip, adding the sugar gradually, until the meringue holds a soft peak. It should look like shaving cream, and the peak should flop over but not fully collapse.

Place the heavy cream in a small bowl and whip with the immersion blender fitted with a whisk or an electric handheld mixer just until it thickens to the consistency of sour cream.

Use a large rubber spatula to fold half of the whipped cream into the chocolate until blended. Fold in and blend the remainder of the whipped cream.

Fold in the meringue in two additions, blending until smooth.

Carefully spoon the mousse into the lined ring molds, just to the level of the top edge of the mold. The parchment should extend above the level of the mousse. Freeze the mousses until very solid, about 6 to 8 hours, depending on the effectiveness of your freezer.

Prepare the Whipped Cream Topping: Place the heavy cream and superfine sugar in a small bowl and whip with the immersion blender fitted with a whisk or an electric handheld mixer until it thickens to a consistency just a bit firmer than shaving cream.

To Finish the Dish: Melt the chocolate using the microwave or double-boiler method. Set aside to cool slightly and then transfer the chocolate to a squeeze bottle.

Remove the mousses from the freezer and, grasping the parchment paper, ease the mousses from the molds. Remove the parchment paper.

Place the acetate squares on a work surface and cover each square from top to bottom with thick lines of drizzled melted chocolate about ¹/₂ inch apart. Make sure the lines are not too thin—the trellis will break if the chocolate lines are fragile.

Next, cover each square with sturdy diagonal lines about ¹/₂ inch apart and then repeat in the opposite direction to create a lacy pattern.

Carefully wrap a decorated acetate square around each mousse, making sure the bottom edge of the trellis is flush with the bottom of the mouse and place the mousses seam side down on the sheet pan and back into the freezer for the chocolate to firm up and set, about 15 minutes. If some of the lines of chocolate extend beyond the bottom of the mousse, break them off so the mousse will stand straight when positioned upright on the plate.

Pour the melted vanilla ice cream into a third squeeze bottle.

To Plate: Drizzle a ring of chocolate sauce around the edge of each chilled plate. Drizzle a ring of vanilla sauce next to and inside the ring of chocolate sauce and a ring of raspberry sauce inside the ring of vanilla sauce. Use a toothpick or skewer to drag decorative lines through all three sauces.

Place a frozen mousse in the center of the plate and carefully unwrap the acetate. Spoon or pipe the whipped cream topping into the trellis on top of the mousse and sprinkle with a few berries.

the waters edge

1317 Beach Drive

Cape May 08204

609/884-1717

www.watersedgerestaurant.com

IT SEEMED THAT everyone we spoke with in Cape May had accolades for chef-owner Neil Elsohn of the Waters Edge. Admittedly, that included Neil himself, but the majority really *were* from fellow restaurateurs. On the cusp of his second decade there, he's an old-timer by Cape May standards, and by all accounts he was a pioneer in what many critics recognize as the restaurant capital of New Jersey.

But despite the pregame hype, we were still unprepared for his intriguingly esoteric food combining. He's a one-of-a-kind, this guy—his food is highly stylized and bold, laced with global accents and Asian and Caribbean zingers.

While many of the area's eateries close for the winter months, the Waters Edge remains open, likely because of the steady stream of devotees year round. And

with the artistic contributions of longtime chef Glenn Turner, Neil knows exactly what to do with the changing seasons as they meld seamlessly from summer to fall to spring and back again without losing a beat.

Go for the food, enjoy the extensive single-malt Scotch collection or sip from the super selection of wines, fall in love with (or over) the view, and plan your next visit over one of the deliciously decadent dessert wines.

Cracked Black Pepper-Studded Seared Aged Ribeye Steak

ROASTED ONION GRAVY WITH CRISPY ONION FRITTER AND MASHED POTATOES

Meat on the bone is exponentially more flavorful than boneless. Think about it—the way to make a great stock is with bones, so doesn't it stand to reason that the bones carry a significant amount of flavor? But even more important, a great steak is one that's really well marbled, so if you're fat phobic, don't even bother. You'll be wasting your time and money and missing the whole point.

The treat that sends this dish over the top, however, is the crispy onion fritter. It's a cross between a lacy potato pancake and crispy French-fried onion rings.

Add some mashed potatoes and drown it all with a caloric river of roasted onion gravy and this is comfort food raised to new heights!

Mise en Place:

FOR THE ROASTED ONION GRAVY:

2 white onions, sliced into ¹/₂-inch-thick rounds

3 T. vegetable oil

Kosher salt for sprinkling

1 cup demi-glace (see the chapters "The Tools, the Terms, the Ingredients, and When to Use Them" and "Resources")

1¹/₂ tsp. soy sauce

![steak image — no prose]

Chef's TRUC:

The addition of ginger ale to the cripsy onion fritter batter serves two purposes—the carbonation enhances the batter's ability to puff, and the sugar in the soda turns the fritter to a gorgeous golden brown.

FOR THE MASHED POTATOES:

³/₄ lb. red bliss or Yukon Gold potatoes, scrubbed, peeled, and cut into 1¹/₂-inch chunks

1 T. kosher salt

4 T. unsalted butter

¹/₂ cup half-and-half

Salt and freshly ground white pepper, to taste

FOR THE CRISPY ONION FRITTER:

1 cup all-purpose flour

¹/₄ tsp. baking soda

1 cup plus 2 T. ginger ale (NOT diet!)

2 Vidalia or other sweet onions, cut in half from top to bottom and then into thin ¹/₄- to ¹/₈-inch wedges

Canola or vegetable oil for deep frying

FOR THE STEAKS:

2 aged ribeye steaks on the bone, each 12 to 16 ozs.

Kosher salt

Freshly cracked black pepper

Equipment:

Grill, stovetop grill, or grill pan

Food processor or blender

Ricer or food mill

Deep-fry thermometer

Prepare the Roasted Onion Gravy: Preheat the oven to 350°F.

Place the onions on a sheet pan and drizzle with the vegetable oil. Sprinkle lightly with kosher salt and roast the onions, turning occasionally, until well browned, about 30 minutes.

Warm the demi-glace.

Transfer the roasted onions to a food processor or blender and process to a coarse purée. Drizzle in the demi-glace and continue to process to an almost smooth purée. Stir in the soy sauce and keep the sauce warm. The sauce can be prepared ahead and kept, refrigerated in a covered container, for up to 5 days. Reheat gently when ready to use.

Prepare the Mashed Potatoes: Place the potatoes in a saucepan and cover by 2 inches with cold water. Add the kosher salt and bring to a boil over high heat. Reduce the heat to a gentle boil, partially cover the pot, and cook until the potatoes are tender when pierced with the tip of a paring knife, about 12 to 15 minutes.

Drain the cooked potatoes and return the empty pan to the stovetop over low heat. Add the butter, and when it's melted, whisk in the half-and-half until blended.

Use a ricer or food mill to rice the potatoes into the pan and add salt and pepper to taste. Stir vigorously with a spatula or wooden paddle to blend the potatoes and butter mixture. Keep warm.

Prepare the Crispy Onion Fritter: Preheat the oven to 200°F. Line a sheet pan with paper towels and position a cooling rack on top.

In a medium mixing bowl, whisk together the flour and baking soda and then whisk in the ginger ale, a little bit at a time, until the mixture is smooth. Fold the sliced onions into the batter.

Pour canola or vegetable oil into a large, deep, heavy skillet to a depth of 1¹/₂ inches. Place the skillet over high heat, and heat until the oil reaches 375°F on a deep-fry thermometer.

When the oil is ready, use a slotted spoon to scoop out half of the batter-onion mixture. Carefully lower it into the hot oil on one side of the pan and flatten a bit, repeat with the remaining mixture, and fry the fritters, turning once, until they're golden brown and cooked through, about 2 minutes per side. Transfer the fritters to the rack and keep warm in the oven.

To Finish the Dish: Preheat an oiled grill or grill pan until it's very hot.

Sprinkle the steaks with kosher salt and press a heavy coating of cracked black pepper onto each side.

Place the steaks on the grill and grill to desired doneness, turning a quarter turn about halfway through on each side before flipping to the other side to create nice cross-hatched grill marks, about 7 to 9 minutes total on each side for rare, depending on the thickness of the steaks.

To Plate: Mound the potatoes just off center on each plate and top with an onion fritter. Lean the steak against the potato-fritter pile and pour the onion gravy over all.

lagniappe

(n., lan-YAP) — A Cajun idiom that means "an unexpected little something extra," or a bonus, like the thirteenth donut in a baker's dozen.

P OSSIBLY THE HARDEST THING we had to do in the writing of this book was to choose which recipes to include and which had to be left out. Each chef prepared at least three outstanding dishes, and we would have loved to include them all! But in the interests of time, space, consideration to the type of cuisine, and the goal to achieve balance, we could choose only one representative dish from each restaurant.

That said, there were many recipes that did not make it into this book that have become personal favorites like these three that, in the spirit of *lagniappe,* follow.

Giumarello's Spicy Shrimp and Calamari Salad

Mise en Place:

FOR THE WARM SPICY VINAIGRETTE:

2 tsp. pure olive oil

1 T. minced garlic

2 T. chopped scallions

2 T. finely chopped hot and/or sweet cherry peppers in vinegar

2 T. freshly squeezed lemon juice

Salt and a pinch of freshly ground black pepper

FOR THE BALSAMIC VINAIGRETTE:

$1/4$ cup extra virgin olive oil

Salt and freshly ground black pepper, to taste

4 tsp. balsamic vinegar

FOR THE SALAD:

4 cups chiffonade of packaged Italian salad mix or assortment of mixed greens

FOR THE SHRIMP AND CALAMARI:

12 shrimp, 16–20 count, peeled cleaned and halved lengthwise

6 ozs. cleaned squid bodies and tentacles, cut into rings

1 cup buttermilk

$2^{1}/_{2}$ cups all-purpose flour

$1/_{2}$ cup cornstarch

1 T. salt

1 tsp. freshly ground black pepper

Canola or vegetable oil for deep-frying

GARNISH:

Snipped chives

Equipment:

Large mesh strainer

Prepare the Shrimp and Calamari: In a nonreactive bowl, toss the shrimp and calamari with the buttermilk and refrigerate for at least 30 minutes and up to 2 hours.

Prepare the Balsamic Vinaigrette: In a small bowl, whisk together the olive oil, salt, and pepper. Slowly add the vinegar, whisking constantly to form an emulsion. Set aside at room temperature.

Prepare the Warm Vinaigrette: In a small skillet over medium heat, sauté the garlic in the olive oil until the garlic is soft and just beginning to color. Remove the skillet from the heat and let it cool for about 5 minutes. Whisk in the scallions, vinegar peppers, and lemon juice and season to taste with salt and pepper.

To Finish the Dish: In a large bowl, mix together the flour, cornstarch, salt, and pepper.

Line a sheet pan with paper towels for draining.

Fill a large, deep pot with 4 inches of canola or vegetable oil for deep-frying, making sure the pot is deep enough so that the oil reaches a level of no more than one-third of the total depth of the pot. Place the pot over high heat and heat until the oil reaches 375°F.

When the oil is ready, toss the shrimp and calamari in the flour mixture. Scoop half of the floured shellfish into the strainer and shake off the excess flour.

Fry until lightly golden, no longer than 2 minutes. Scoop them out onto the paper towel-lined pan. Repeat with the remaining shellfish.

To Plate: In a medium bowl, toss the salad greens with just enough balsamic vinaigrette to coat the leaves and place a mounds of dressed greens on each plate.

Toss the fried shrimp and calamari with the warm vinaigrette (you can do this right in the vinaigrette pan) and mound the shellfish on top of the greens. Garnish with snipped chives.

The Hilton at Short Hills's Warm Banana Chocolate Financiers

Mise en Place:

FOR THE ALMOND FLOUR:

1 cup blanched skinned almonds
1 T. all-purpose flour

FOR THE BANANA FINANCIER BATTER:

2 large egg whites
Pinch salt
2 T. superfine sugar
$1^1/_2$ T. almond flour
3 T. 10-X (confectioners') sugar
3 T. all-purpose flour
3 T. melted unsalted butter
$1^1/_2$ tsp. whiskey

3 ozs. (about 1 cup) semisweet chocolate mini-chips
1 ripe banana, peeled and cut into $^1/_4$-inch dice

Butter for greasing the ring molds

Equipment:

2 ovenproof 3-inch-diameter x 2-inch-high metal ring molds
Parchment paper
Standing or hand-held electric mixer

Prepare the Almond Flour: In a food processor, process the almonds and 1 tablespoon of flour to a fine powder. You will have more than you need for this recipe, but almond flour may be frozen for up to 6 months.

Prepare the Banana Financier Batter: Preheat the oven to 350°F. Line a sheet pan with parchment paper. Lightly butter the insides of the ring molds and place them on the sheet pan.

Whip the egg whites until sudsy and then add a pinch of salt. Whipping continually, gradually add the superfine sugar to form a soft meringue.

In a large mixing bowl, whisk together 1¹/₂ tablespoons of the almond flour, confectioners' sugar, all-purpose flour, and salt.

Quickly whisk the melted butter into the dry ingredients and then fold in the whiskey and the meringue. Fold in the chocolate chips and the diced bananas.

Spoon the mixture into the buttered ring molds and bake until the financiers are golden brown and the top springs back when pushed with a finger, about 35 to 45 minutes.

Allow to cool for 5 minutes and the cakes will release from the rings.

Serve warm!

Tre Piani's Tagliatelle
WITH SMOKED CHICKEN AND ASPARAGUS SAUCE

Mise en Place:

FOR THE ASPARAGUS SAUCE:

1 lb. asparagus, trimmed of woody stem ends, tips cut off and reserved, stems cut into ¹/₂-inch pieces

1 T. salt

1 cup chopped yellow onion

4 cloves garlic, sliced paper-thin on a mandoline

3 cups chicken stock or canned low-sodium, fat-free broth

Pinch crushed red pepper flakes

¹/₂ lb. skinless, boneless smoked chicken, preferably leg or thigh meat,

cut into 1¹/₂ × ¹/₂ inch strips

4 basil leaves, coarsely chopped

¹/₄ cup heavy cream

¹/₄ to ¹/₂ cup freshly grated Parmigiano-Reggiano cheese

Salt and freshly ground black pepper

FOR THE PASTA:

8 ozs. fresh or dried tagliatelle or fettuccine
Kosher salt for the pasta water

FOR THE GARNISH:

2 small basil sprigs

4-oz. block of Parmigiano-Reggiano cheese

Equipment:

Traditional or immersion blender

Prepare the Garnish: Use a vegetable peeler to shave shards from the block of Parmgiano-Reggiano cheese. Set aside.

Prepare the Asparagus Sauce: Prepare an ice bath by filling a small bowl with ice and cold water.

Bring 4 quarts of cold water to a boil and add a table-spoon of salt. Add the asparagus tips and let the water come back to a boil. Cook just until the tips are bright green and just beginning to feel tender, about 1 to 2 minutes, depending on their thickness. Scoop the asparagus tips out with a slotted spoon and plunge them into the ice bath to stop the cooking and preserve the color. Drain and set the tips aside.

In a wide, shallow pot over medium-low heat, sauté the garlic and onions together in the olive oil until they begin to soften. Add the asparagus stems and continue to cook, stirring occasionally, until the asparagus is fairly tender, about 5 to 7 minutes. Add the chicken stock or broth and a pinch of crushed red pepper flakes, raise the heat to medium-high, and cook until the liquid comes to a boil.

Transfer the contents of the pan to a traditional blender (or use an immersion blender) and process to a slightly coarse purée.

Return the purée to the pan and add the smoked chicken and basil and cook over medium heat until bubbling. Add the cream and heat through. Shut off the heat while you prepare the pasta.

Prepare the Pasta: Bring a large pot of cold water to a boil for pasta.

When the pasta water has reached a full, rolling boil, add 2 tablespoons of kosher salt. When the water returns to a boil, add the pasta all at once and cook, stirring frequently, until the pasta is almost al dente but still quite firm in the center.

Finish the Dish: Drain the pasta, reserving about a $1/2$ cup of the pasta water to add to the sauce if needed. Add the pasta to the pan with the sauce and toss. Add the reserved asparagus tips, the grated Parmigiano-Reggiano, and season with salt and pepper, tossing until the pasta is coated and well mixed with the sauce.

Transfer the pasta to individual serving plates and garnish each plate with the Parmigiano shavings and a basil sprig.

procedures and techniques

- Thaw everything that needs to be thawed in the refrigerator, preferably overnight.

- Keep knives SHARP—a dull knife might well be the most dangerous thing in a kitchen because you know it's dull and therefore you put more force behind your efforts, so when it slips, the damage usually is as bad as it can be. When your knives are kept optimally sharp, you can relax your grip and tension and cause less damage to your food and to yourself. Use a steel or similar sharpening tool *every time* you begin a cooking session, and once every one or two years, depending on use, have your knives professionally sharpened.

- When in doubt, throw it out! Don't take chances with food you're not sure about—it's just not worth making yourself or someone else sick.

- *Sanitize* at the end of every prep session. At the sink we keep a small condiment-style squirt bottle filled with a mixture of one part bleach and three parts water. After we wash our cutting boards, work surfaces, knives, and utensils, we then squirt them with the sanitizing solution, wait a few seconds, and rinse them with hot water. You'll not only prevent cross contamination from raw foods, which can often carry nasty bacteria, you'll be surprised how brand-new your cutting boards look if you keep up with it. Also, most acrylic and plastic cutting boards are dishwasher-safe—every so often, run them through a cycle with your dishes.

- Don't refrigerate garlic, onions, and shallots! Take your cue from nature—these alliums come ready-wrapped in papery shells because they do best when kept cool and dry. Refrigeration creates dampness and accelerates the development of sugars, which also help to shorten their useful life. If you're lucky, the worst that will occur is sprouting; if you're not, it will be molding and rotting. If onions and shallots sprout, we throw them out. When our garlic sprouts, we plant it, any time of year, sprout end up, paper removed or not, about 1 inch below ground level and then forget about them. They're bulbs, just like tulips are—they go forth and multiply. And about six months later we can dig up a cute baby head of our very own garlic. When we really need to use the sprouted cloves, we cut them in half, discard the green sprout, and use $1^1/_2$ to 2 times as much because the clove (bulb) will have lost its energy and flavor to the creation and nurturing of the sprout.

- Work BIG. Prepping food on a Lilliputian-sized cutting board is an exercise in frustration and assures that your muscles will absolutely ache when you're done from the effort of crunching your action into a too-small area.

- Don't get lazy and try to chop things in huge piles—it's an accident waiting to happen. Your knife action will be awkward and unnatural, your rhythm will be arrythmatic, and you will miss your mark and have to stop in order to bandage yourself before long. Silly when you consider that you probably attempted to take care of that giant pile all at once to be efficient and save time.

Balsamic Reduction In a small pan over high heat, bring 2 cups of balsamic vinegar to a boil. Reduce immediately to a simmer. Depending on intended use and taste, 2 teaspoons or more of sugar can be added to the vinegar. Gently simmer until the liquid is reduced by about two-thirds (leaving about 2/3 cup) and is thick and syrupy. The vinegar must be very gently boiled or simmered—if the heat is too high and the vinegar is boiled too vigorously, it will burn to a charcoaled, gummy mess with a nasty burned flavor. The reduction can be stored at room temperature in a covered container or squeeze bottle almost indefinitely.

Blanching (and Shocking) Blanching is plunging food into boiling, usually salted, water for a short period to take the raw edge off and to enhance or brighten the color. Shocking is immediately plunging the blanched food into an ice bath (a mix of ice and ice water) to stop the cooking process and preserve the color. Certain vegetables when brightened by blanching and shocking, such as asparagus and broccoli, can often even sustain their attractive color after a second cooking process, such as when used in pasta sauce or risotto.

Chive Oil Purée chives with a pinch of salt in the work bowl of a mini-processor. Add just enough oil, pulsing several times to blend, until the mixture reaches a pourable consistency. Transfer the mixture to a fine sieve set over a glass measuring cup and strain (this may take up to an hour). Discard the residue in the sieve and pour the strained chive oil into a small squeeze bottle. The chive oil may be refrigerated for up to four weeks. Bring to room temperature to use.

Clarifying Butter Butter is clarified to remove the water added during processing and to remove the milk solids, which, because they contain lactose (a form of sugar), burn easily. By clarifying butter, the smoking point or flash point of the resultant purified fat is raised, which means you can cook with clarified butter at higher temperatures for longer periods of time without burning the fat.

Butter is clarified by melting it and then setting it aside to rest for several minutes so that the three entities (fat, water, and milk solids) clearly separate. The foam at the top is then skimmed off, and the clear butter, which constitutes the middle layer, is then poured off and saved. The white milky residue remaining at the bottom is discarded. The clear middle layer, the fat, is the clarified butter.

The butter can be gently melted in a Pyrex liquid measure in the microwave, which is our preferred method because it's then easiest to skim off the foamy top. Pour off the clarified butter, and leave the milk solids behind. Or it can be accomplished in a small saucepan on the stovetop. Whichever method you choose, bear in mind that the butter must be melted gently and not allowed to boil or bubble up or it will reblend itself and emulsify, making it almost impossible for it to separate into distinct layers.

Cleaning and Storing Greens and Herbs   Herewith is a dissertation on one of our pet peeves!

To assure that salads are crisp, greens to be sautéed don't end up a soggy mess, and herbs don't turn black and unrecognizable and taste like something that died in the vegetable bin, proper selection and handling of fresh greens and herbs are essential.

First, select the best greens and herbs you can find and avoid those waterlogged supermarket lettuces and other greens whenever possible. Certainly, if you have no other options, shake out as much water as possible before bagging them for the trip to the checkout counter. And then complain—or don't, and pay for the water weight.

When you get your greens and herbs home, carefully pick through and remove any rotted or imperfect leaves. Rot begets rot, sort of on the order of one bad apple destroys the whole bunch. A rotted leaf that attaches itself to a healthy leaf is contagious—it will rot everything around it.

Most heads of lettuce or bunches of greens can be stored for up to ten days by simply shaking out any excess water, wrapping the heads in a couple of layers of damp paper toweling, and bagging them in plastic. We then take the extra step of blowing a little air in the bag and knotting it "ballooned out" so that the delicate leaves are protected from being crushed by a crowded refrigerator or falling condiments. This great method does NOT work with arugula, spinach, or watercress. For some reason, these greens turn yellow when wrapped in paper toweling for any extended period of time, so we eliminate that step.

We usually clean our greens and herbs as we use them, but many can be prepared a few hours to a few days ahead, and in some cases, such as with romaine for a Caesar salad, the result is exceptionally icy cold and crispy greens.

To clean greens and herbs, fill a clean sink with lukewarm (not cold) water—don't worry, they won't wilt, but you don't get clean in cold water and neither do your greens. As the sink fills, drop the leaves, cut or whole, into the sink and swish them around with your hands. When the sink is completely full, shut the water off and swish the leaves around again—the leaves will float to the top, and the heavier dirt and sand will sink to the bottom. Scoop the leaves out into a salad spinner and spin them as dry as possible, occasionally stopping the spinning to dump out the accumulated water from the spinner.

Sprinkle a length of paper toweling lightly with water, lay the clean leaves out in a single layer on the damp paper toweling (bypass this step for spinach, arugula, and watercress), roll them up, and place the roll in a plastic bag. Blow a little air in the bag for protection against crushing, knot or seal the bag, and refrigerate for up to two days before use.

What makes herbs turn black, unappealing, and often even bitter is excess moisture and bruising, usually by bashing them to death with a dull knife. To be able to create a fine chiffonade or finely chopped herbs that can be sprinkled or broadcast attractively, the herbs must be perfectly clean and dry. To minimize damage to delicate leaves such as those of basil or arugula, we stack and then roll them before cutting them with a very sharp knife. Or in the cases of parsley and cilantro, which can't be stacked or rolled, we bunch them up on a dry, clean cutting board before chopping. Either way, the number of times the leaves are attacked by the knife before the end result is reached minimizes bruising.

One last tip—after going to all the trouble of assuring that your greens and herbs are clean and dry before processing, don't then place them on a wet cutting board or use a wet knife on them!

Cutting a Mango The approach to cutting a mango is sort of opposite that of cutting an avocado. Rather than removing the pit from the fruit, you remove the fruit from the pit. The pit of a mango is a flat oval that echoes the shape of the whole fruit. The mango flesh clings to it somewhat like cling peach flesh clings to its pit.

Stand the mango on end on a cutting board and position the blade of a sharp knife just off center at the top. Cut downward all the way, removing as big a section as possible, working around, but as close to the pit as you can. Repeat with the remaining half, again dodging the pit and removing as large a section of the fruit as possible.

With the skin on, use a sharp paring knife to score the flesh to, but not through the shell, either in slices or in a grid pattern. Now, turn the shell inside out and cut the fruit away from it.

Debearding Mussels The "beard" of a mussel is actually shreds of rope that the mussel, whether in a natural or farmed environment, attaches itself to as its "home base." When the mussel is harvested, it often takes a little piece of home along for the journey.

To debeard, or remove this shredded rope from the clutches of the mussel's clamped-tight shells, grasp the beard with your fingers or a fish tweezer (which looks like a regulation-type tweezer with broad flat ends) and pull out and discard the beard.

Killing and Dressing Soft-Shell Crabs Use a sharp kitchen scissor to cut about $1/4$ inch from the front of the crab, removing the eyes and face; then poke the sharp ends of the scissor into the opening to pop the air bubbles located just under the carapace and behind the eyes. Turn the crab over and cut off the triangular apron flap. Lift the carapace on each side and cut away the feathery gills.

Knife Cuts

JULIENNE A julienne cut is a matchstick cut. Regardless of the shape of whatever you're cutting, if you can slice it evenly and then stack a few slices at a time, you can then cut it (usually lengthwise) into thin strips. This is julienne.

CHIFFONADE A chiffonade is a julienne or matchstick cut when done on leaves and is used either for garnishing or to create volume, such as when you order an expensive lobster salad and it looks like a gi-normous serving until you begin to eat it and discover it's all shredded greens holding up a single layer of bite-sized lobster chunks.

To get a fine chiffonade that fluffs up nicely, make sure the leaves are stemmed, clean, and *dry*—it won't happen if they're wet. Then stack the leaves and roll them like a cigar (or whatever it was you last rolled). Use a very sharp knife to cut the rolled leaves crosswise, as thin as you like.

CHOP For our purposes, we define a chop as pieces that have been cut, usually by working a chef's knife back and forth across food on a cutting board. But it is also possible to accomplish a chop with a food processor, which cuts uniformly sized (not necessarily shaped) pieces, usually about $1/4$ to $1/2$ inch. However, size is a variable, and we respectfully request that you use common sense. A chop on a tomato is rather larger than a chop on, say, garlic or parsley. (Then, of course, there's a fine chop . . .)

DICE We define a dice, which is usually preceded by a defining word or fraction such as "small" or "$1/2$-inch," as pieces that are uniformly sized and shaped into squares.

MINCE Keep going on the chop until the pieces are really small and uniformly sized and you have a mince. (And then there's finely minced . . .)

Making Fresh or Dried Breadcrumbs Our preferred way to make fresh breadcrumbs is simply to remove the crust from any good-quality bread (Italian, whole wheat, coarse white bread, rye, pumpernickel, multigrain, etc.), tear it into small chunks, and process it to crumbs in a food processor.

You can also use this technique with dried-out stale bread or "grate" very dried out stale bread on a box grater.

Both fresh breadcrumbs and dried breadcrumbs can be seasoned with herbs, spices, and/or cheese, and both can be "toasted" on a sheet pan in a 300°F oven.

Freshly made breadcrumbs can be stored in an airtight container at room temperature for up to three days or frozen for up to three months for long-term storage.

Measuring Flour There are two generally accepted ways to measure flour, and both dictate that it be done into a dry measure (see the chapter "The Tools, the Terms, the Ingredients, and When to Use Them"). One method is the "spoon-and-level," and the other is the "dip-and-sweep."

Since in baked goods the more flour used, the denser the end product, and also because you can always add more flour but it's usually impossible to remove it from a mixture, we like to err on the side of less and therefore prefer the spoon-and-level method.

To spoon and level flour (or any dry ingredient), use a large serving spoon to lightly drop the dry flour into the measuring vessel (nesting cups or spoons) to point overfill. Then swipe a straight edge across the top of the measuring vessel to level off the mound. You should now have an accurate measurement.

Melting Chocolate The temperature you want to achieve for properly melted or tempered, satiny smooth chocolate is between 88°F and 92°F. Think about it—you are 98.6°F; properly tempered chocolate should be slightly cooler than your body temperature. The chocolate will retain its shape even after it's reached the proper temperature, so stop often to whisk it and you will find that, regardless of its shape, it will whisk smooth long before you expect it to. Be sure to use gentle heat—too hot and it will be grainy. And take precautions to assure that no moisture gets into the chocolate or it will seize!

MICROWAVE METHOD   Place chocolate in microwave-safe bowl. Microwave on medium (50 percent power) for 1 minute. Stir. Microwave 30 seconds more or until chocolate is softened. Stir until smooth and let cool.

DOUBLE-BOILER METHOD   Set a bowl over a pot of barely simmering water, making sure the water is well below the bottom of the bowl. Allow the chocolate to just begin to melt around the edges of the bowl and then stir constantly until it is fully melted and smooth.

Pitting and Cutting an Avocado   Use your fingernail to flick the out stem and position a sharp knife at the top (narrow end) of the avocado with the blade bisecting the depression where the stem was. Slice down carefully until the knife comes in contact with the pit. Then, keeping the knife in contact with the pit at all times, roll the avocado against the knife until you have made a cut all the way around the avocado and the knife is back at the original position.

Remove the knife and hold the avocado with one hand on either side of the cut and twist in opposite directions. The avocado will come apart in two sections, one containing the pit.

Place the avocado skin side down on a work surface and, using the knife as you would a hatchet, hit the pit to embed the sharp edge of the knife firmly into it. Hold the avocado steady and twist the knife—the pit will loosen and come out, attached to the knife. Knock the pit against the side of a bowl to remove it from the knife edge.

To cut the avocado with the shell intact, use a sharp paring knife to score the flesh to the shell but not through it, either in slices or in a grid pattern. Run the tip of the paring knife around the inside edge of the shell and ease out the avocado flesh or, if perfect slices or squares are not crucial, squeeze the flesh out into a bowl.

Pressing versus Mincing Garlic   Garlic is high in starches and naturally occurring sugars, which is why, when your fingers get covered with garlic juice, all the papery covering within a one-mile radius will stick to them. When garlic is pressed through one of those gizmos, it gets mangled to a degree and lots of that juice is released so when it comes in contact with a hot surface, it browns as fast as it can. But when garlic is cleanly minced with a sharp knife, less juice is released; the garlic is easier to work with and burns less readily, and the flavor is fresher, cleaner, and more pronounced. We do have and use one of those gizmos, but we use it only when the garlic is not going to come into direct contact with a hot surface and is instead getting mixed into something such as oil to be brushed on vegetables or meat before cooking.

Reducing Liquids   If the recipe instruction is to reduce a liquid to $1/2$ cup, begin by pouring $1/2$ cup of water into the pan. Measure the water level with a stick, such as a bamboo skewer or the handle of a wooden spoon, mark the water level on the stick, and dump out the water. You can then use the marked stick to determine when the liquid has been reduced to $1/2$ cup.

If a recipe says to reduce the liquid by half, use a stick to measure the level of the liquid before you begin to heat it, mark the stick at the halfway point, and then use the marked stick to determine when the liquid has been reduced by half.

For both, shut off the heat before trying to determine the level if you're using a bamboo skewer because the fibrous nature of the bamboo will cause intense bubbling, making it impossible to see the mark you've made.

Removing the Side Muscle from Scallops There is a side muscle that is positioned at the side of the scallop and attaches the part you want to eat to its shell. You want to remove it. It's not always there—but if it is, when raw it's the same color and texture of the rest of the scallop, so you may not be nuts if you can't find it.

If it's noticeable, it's because it interrupts the smooth line of the exterior of the scallop. The muscle is small, often not more than $1/4$ inch in width and 1 inch in length, and it sits as a belt or an epaulet would, on the side of the scallop and parallel to the top and bottom edges.

To remove the muscle, flick it away from the scallop with your thumbnail. If it's really the attaching muscle, it will come away easily and cleanly. If it's not, you'll know after the first few passes, in which case chop up the scallop and pretend it came that way.

Roasted Garlic Roasted garlic is ubiquitous—and that may be a good thing. We find it delicious and tremendously useful. But we also think it's obnoxious when presented still wrapped in its paper as part of a bread basket or appetizer. Who wants to be seated at a restaurant table or at a party, dressed like a grownup, and have to figure out how to gracefully detach the gummy paper (not to mention get rid of the distinctive odor) from your fingers and fingernails?

So we roast garlic in this way, which provides us with a sort of "confit," or garlic cloves preserved in the tasty fat in which they were roasted, storable for months in the refrigerator and readily available for the plucking as needed. The treasure of the delicious garlic-infused oil and butter mixture in which the cloves were roasted is just value-added benefit—we smear it on fish or other steaks before grilling, add it to salad dressings, toss pasta with it, add it to the sauté pan, or just spread it on bread—whatever!

Here's the recipe:

1 cup whole peeled garlic cloves

2 T. butter

2 T. olive oil

3 or 4 branches of fresh thyme

$1/4$ tsp. kosher salt

Preheat the oven to 350°F.

Place the whole garlic cloves in a small baking dish or ovenproof bowl—the bowl should be small enough so that the garlic is crowded and about $1^1/_2$ to 2 layers deep.

Add the butter, oil, thyme branches, and salt, cover with foil, and bake for about 1 to 1¹/₂ hours just until the cloves are lightly golden—the cloves will continue to darken after the dish is removed from the oven. Remove the dish from the oven, discard the thyme branches, and allow the roasted garlic to cool.

The roasted garlic can be stored, refrigerated in the oil and butter and covered tightly, for up to 2 months.

Roasting Peppers: The idea is to char and blacken the skin as fast as possible so that the flesh inside, which is what you want, doesn't cook away before the skin is charred. For this you need to get the peppers as close to a flame as you can, and don't turn them until the flame-exposed side is fully charred—turning constantly just allows the partially cooked side to cool off, and then it takes that much longer to get it back to the point where it will blacken.

If you can get a high enough flame or heat on a gas grill, it's very convenient for roasting peppers, especially if you're doing several. We also like to use our stovetop, which has a bonfire for a front burner.

Char the skin of the bell pepper on all sides by placing it either directly on the flame of a gas burner or under the broiler, turning the pepper only when the skin is completely blackened. Transfer the pepper to a bowl and cover with plastic wrap. When the pepper is cool, the charred skin will easily slip off. Gently rinse off any residual bits of skin and remove and discard the stem and seeds.

Saffron Oil Warm a small pan over medium heat and crumble in 1 teaspoon saffron threads. Add 1 teaspoon water and swirl over medium heat until the water evaporates. Add 1 cup of rapeseed oil and stir until the oil turns a bright orange-yellow. Remove the pan from the heat, and when the oil is cool, transfer it to an airtight container. The saffron oil may be kept refrigerated for up to 4 weeks. Bring to room temperature to use.

Seeding Tomatoes Tomatoes are often seeded to keep them from getting "sloshy" as the gel surrounding the seeds melts. The easiest way to do this is to cut the tomato in half at its waistline or equator, which exposes all the seed pods. Then, holding the tomato cut side down over a bowl, gently manipulate the shell until the seeds and their gel spill out. Use your fingertip, a small spoon, or the tip of a butterknife to get any seeds that don't readily squeeze out.

Shucking Oysters The object is to cut the incredibly strong muscle that holds the top and bottom shells together and the oyster , which you should only be dealing with if it's alive, doesn't want you to do this. You'll need an oyster knife, which is a short, somewhat narrow knife with a handle and a collar between the handle and the blade that acts as a guard (we're not sure whether to protect you or the oyster). Be smart and wrap a kitchen towel around your hand in case you slip and attempt to stab yourself. Insert the pointy end of the knife between the top and bottom shells at the pointy end of the oyster, and if you're lucky and get it in there, twist it and hope you hear it click. Then work the knife around the edge of the shells so that it severs the muscle connecting them. Discard the top shell and work your knife carefully under the oyster to separate it from the bottom shell.

the tools, the terms, the ingredients, and when to use them

Bench scraper: A flat, spatula-like rectangular tool, usually about 4 inches by 3 inches, used to maneuver or cut dough. It is also called a pastry knife and can be constructed of plastic or metal with a wood or rubber grip.

Blenders: Two types we have and love:

TRADITIONAL: This is like the one we all grew up with. It's the one we reach for to whiz up a frozen drink and makes the smoothest purées.

IMMERSION: These new "stick" blenders aren't really new—they've been around in professional kitchens for decades, and we're thrilled that they've been redesigned for home use. The convenience of being able to purée a soup or thicken it with a few pulses without transferring the hot liquid to another container and back again is priceless. Ours can be operated with or without the cord and has adjustable speeds. It came with several attachments including a whisk and a cup so we can whip up just one egg white or a small amount of cream without hauling out the heavy equipment.

Broth: See "Stock."

Butter: Unsalted! Salt, as magical and wonderful as it is, is a preservative and also can mask "off" flavors. Consequently the cream of the cream crop is usually reserved for unsalted butter, and the less than terrific gets salted and can often be older. You can always add salt—you can't take it out. And why not have the option?

BYO: A very New Jersey kind of thing is Bring Your Own, and it means to bring your own (alcoholic) beverage! We love it because it means that we're not paying an additional markup and overhead for wines and spirits and the licenses and insurance that come along with a restaurant's permission to serve alcohol. It means our choice of beverage is limitless and usually means a lower tab with a single focus—on the food.

Caul fat: A lacy, weblike membrane that lines the stomachs of hogs and sheep and is sometimes used to wrap forcemeat-filled or skinless meats such as rabbit for roasting or braising because it melts down quickly, basting as it goes.

Chiffonade: Shredded or finely cut strips of leafy vegetables or herbs.

Cooking oils:

BLENDED OIL: Many chefs choose to use blends of two or more cooking oils, usually canola or vegetable oil and olive oil based on taste and smoking-point or flash-point characteristics. A few brands of blended oil are commonly found in supermarkets.

CANOLA OIL: See "Rapeseed Oil."

GRAPESEED OIL: An oil that is extracted from grapeseeds, light in color with a neutral flavor and a high smoking point.

OLIVE OIL: Olive oil is oil pressed from tree-ripened olives, and the best is cold-pressed (extracted simply by pressure). It is graded based on its acidity, and the taste and quality are largely based on growing conditions such as location and weather. It is used for cooking and for flavoring. All grades of olive oil have the same caloric value, and its fat profile is considered to be among the most healthful because olive oil is high in beneficial monounsaturated fat.

▸ EXTRA VIRGIN OLIVE OIL: Extra virgin olive oil is the oil obtained from the first pressing and considered to be the finest grade of olive oil with the lowest percentage of acidity, not to exceed 1 percent. Its flavor can range from quite fruity to peppery, and its color can range from vibrant green to gold, depending on its regional origin. Its distinctive flavors determine its use—whether for cooking or just for flavoring. Some chefs feel that extra virgin olive oil should not be used for cooking, as its flavor is distinct and noticeable, which is exactly why other chefs will choose to use it for cooking. It is rarely used for deep-frying, and the higher-end brands are best saved for salad dressings because the distinct yet delicate flavor can change when cooked.

▸ VIRGIN OLIVE OIL: Virgin olive oil has an acidity range of around 2 percent and is used for cooking and flavoring.

▸ LIGHT OLIVE OIL: Light olive oil has the same fat and calorie profile as other olive oils but is termed "light" because of its flavor—or lack thereof. It is olive oil that has been refined with its color and flavor filtered out, making it useful for baking and certain cooking in which the presence of a distinct flavor might not be desired. The acidity of light olive oil ranges around 3 percent.

RAPESEED OIL: Also known and marketed as canola oil, rapeseed oil is a product of Canada and is made from the seeds of the rape, a vegetable similar to a turnip. It is considered to be one of the more healthful choices for its high percentage of beneficial monounsaturated fat and omega-3 fatty acids. It has a neutral flavor and one of the higher smoking points, making it a good choice for cooking and deep-frying.

SESAME OIL: Extracted from sesame seeds, sesame oil comes in two basic varieties. The lighter has a nutty flavor and relatively high smoking point and is used in cooking, salads, and other dressings. The darker is toasted and has a much more intense flavor and fragrance and is used more often as a condiment, although it is sometimes used in addition to other oils for stir-frying. The difference in flavor is similar to the difference in flavor between an untoasted and a toasted nut.

Cooking wines: Don't use them! Cooking wine is the stuff found on supermarket shelves and is usually a poor grade of wine to which salt has been added. It is not for drinking, either. The rule of thumb is if a wine is unsuitable for drinking, it is also unsuitable for cooking. For cooking, use only wines that are palatable for drinking.

Eggs: We use organic only. We find the shells stronger, the yolks deeper in color and more flavorful, and prefer to take our hormones, antibiotics, and other like chemicals only when it's a case of live or die (we mean us, not the chicken), although usually not at all.

When a recipe calls for eggs, unless it originated prior to the mid-sixties or the recipe specifies otherwise, it's looking for large eggs.

Emulsion: For everyday kitchen purposes, an emulsion is the suspension of one liquid in another and is created by vigorously whisking two liquids that normally don't mix (e.g., oil and vinegar) so that the lighter one (the vinegar) is broken up into tiny droplets and suspended in the heavier one (the oil). In the case of a vinaigrette, certain ingredients enhance the mixture's ability to achieve this suspended state, such as mustard or egg, which is one of the reasons you sometimes see either or both included in a recipe.

Farci: French for stuffing or forcemeat. See "Forcemeat."

Filo: See "Phyllo."

Foodmill: It looks like a pot with holes in the bottom, a handle on the side, and a crank in the center for mobilizing the blade inside to mash food through the holes. In a word, it purées stuff. It works a little harder than a potato ricer, but a ricer can sub for a foodmill in many cases and is a lot cheaper. What a foodmill can do but a ricer can't is extract skin and seeds when processing things like tomatoes for canning or sauce.

Food processors: We have two types and use them equally as often.

CLASSIC FOOD PROCESSOR: The most common brand is Cuisinart and, in fact, the use of the word to describe this indispensable piece of equipment is to a food processor what Kleenex is to tissues. There are many food processors on the market today, but not all can handle an intense workout. If you're going to buy one, we suggest you invest the bucks and buy one of the top brands such as KitchenAid or Cuisinart. Fitted with the proper attachments, it chops, pulverizes, slices, grates, and kneads and can sometimes produce an acceptable purée. It does not, however, replace a blender, especially when the result you're trying to achieve is a totally or ultrasmooth purée.

MINI-PROCESSOR: These little workhorses are terrific for processing small amounts of things (too small for a full-size processor) and for emulsifying things like certain vinaigrettes. They're very inexpensive, and some of the classic large food processors, such as the terrific ones made by KitchenAid, come with a mini-bowl attachment that fits right inside the full-size work bowl—excellent for storage-impaired kitchens like ours.

Forcemeat: This term refers to a mixture of ground meats, fish, poultry, or vegetables that is seasoned and held together with a binding ingredient such as eggs or fat and is used as the filling for sausage or meats, poultry, or fish or for pâté. It is often puréed but can also be textured or even chunky.

Frenched: When bones on chops are exposed and scraped clean of all meat, fat, and adhering tissue, they are frenched.

Graters and zesters: Although technically these terms refer to two different types of utensils, in most home kitchens, a box grater generally provides all the capability the cook needs. Having said that, however (and having a lifelong aversion to knuckle and fingernail in our food), we are very much enjoying the new generation of grater-zesters (actually rasps) now on the market. They come in various sizes and designs for different purposes (cheese, nutmeg, chocolate, citrus zest), seem to be available everywhere cookware is sold, and when carefully and properly used, leave unscathed all the usual body parts. Be aware when grating hard cheeses such as Parmigiano, as the results are quite fluffy and need to be packed down to get an accurate measurement.

Julienne: To cut food, usually vegetables, into very thin strips or matchstick shape.

Knives: This is a huge enough subject for another book complete with video and a hands-on course on skills, care, and use. The most salient points, however, are that you want to buy and use the best-quality knives you can afford, in sizes most comfortable for you and your size and which can be sharpened and hold an edge at least throughout a cooking session. You do not need dozens of knives to be a good cook. You can do just about anything with the essential three: a good chef's knife (or, if you're so inclined, a cleaver), a paring knife, and a serrated bread knife. It's delightful to have an assortment of carving, boning, filet, and other knives, but they aren't essential.

You will want to make sure that whatever knives you buy are of sturdy construction and that, especially in the case of chef's knives (those elongated triangular workhorses with straight edges that can slice, chop, and bash), the knife has a full tang, meaning it is of one-piece construction with the metal running the full length and solidly bolted to the handle. And never put your knives in the dishwasher.

But most important, keep your knives as sharp as possible! A dull knife is one of the most dangerous things in a kitchen, far more deadly than a sharp one. Because you know it's dull and so you put your whole body torque behind it, and when it slips, it creates major damage. If your knife is well sharpened, you can relax your grip and slice through foods easily, and if you happen to cut yourself, it's usually just as clean and shallow as a paper cut. Enough said (for now).

Mandoline: A hand-operated slicing tool with an adjustable blade for uniformly slicing food. It is an invaluable tool and can be used to create thick to impossibly thin slices, especially of vegetables, and it is used throughout this book, as well as in just about every restaurant kitchen we visited. Most mandolines come with either capability or attachment blades to julienne foods, and some have the ability to produce waffle cuts. We greatly prefer and recommend the inexpensive Asian mandoline made by Benriner (see the chapter "Resources"). The Benriner is lightweight and easier to handle and to store. It can do everything the traditional expensive, heavyweight French mandolines can PLUS it's sharper and stays that way for years and years. We have traveled with one for ten years and despite its almost constant use by us, other teachers, several hundred students, and assistants, it is as sharp as the day we took it out of the box and far sharper than our French mandoline. At home, we use it daily—literally. The Benriner mandoline has the distinction of twice being the tool of the month at the CIA (Culinary Institute of America), also at the CCA (California Culinary Academy) and number one in the list of favorite chef's tools in a *Food & Wine* magazine survey. Get one. They're cheap. Get several and give them to all your friends and relatives.

Measuring cups and spoons: Liquid and dry measures are NOT interchangeable if accuracy is your goal!

   LIQUID MEASURE: You can tell that it's made for liquid measure because it's transparent (or should be). And because liquids seek their own level, you can place the measuring cup on a level surface and pour liquid into it, and when the (level) liquid reaches the right line—which you'll know because you can see through it!—you have an accurate measurement. Liquid measures also usually have a pouring lip and a handle. We do NOT use these for dry or semisolid (mayonnaise, sour cream) ingredients because it's impossible to perfectly level these in liquid measures.

   DRY MEASURE: Dry measures are usually found in the form of nesting cups or spoons and are meant to be overfilled with dry or semisolid ingredients; the ingredient is then leveled with a straight edge, such as a knife, so that it is even with the side edges of the dry measure. It is conceivable that liquids can be measured in dry measuring cups; however, since the measurement is accurate only when the contents are flush to the top, getting the contents from one place to another without a spill is highly unlikely and much more anxiety producing than using the proper equipment to begin with.

Mirepoix: A French term (meer-uh-PWAH) that refers to a mixture of onions, carrots, and celery (classically a 2:1:1 ratio) used in the bases of soups, stews, sauces, and braises for its sweetening and caramelizing properties. In Latin-based languages, it is sometimes called a *soffrito* (spelled in various but similar ways) and can consist of additions or replacements such as herbs, peppers, and other flavorful goodies, including smoked meats. The three-ingredient base is so ubiquitous and shows up in one form or another in so many cuisines that it is fondly referred to in the culinary world as the holy trinity.

Mise en place: A French term (pronounced meez-on-PLAHS) that, loosely translated, means to "put in place" and refers to the measurement and preparation of ingredients, as well as the gathering of tools and equipment, necessary to prepare a recipe before beginning the cooking process. It is essential!

Montreal Steak Seasoning: A wonderful seasoning blend by the McCormick or Schilling company, once available only for professional or restaurant use but now readily available in supermarkets. We also use it when grilling strong-flavored fish such as bluefish, mackerel, and sardines.

Nam pla: Thai fish sauce; it's also called *nuoc nam* in Vietnamese.

Nonreactive: Of a composition or material that does not react to acids such as citrus juices, wine, milk (lactic acid), tomato, etc. The use of reactive equipment in the presence of high acid content can result in "tinny" or metallic flavor distortions or discoloration (milk turns bluish) of the food or the equipment. Glass, stainless steel, and enamel-coated equipment (without chips!) is nonreactive. Cast iron, aluminum, carbon steel, and copper cause reactions. Manufacturers of "anodized aluminum" claim that it is nonreactive—our jury is still out on that one.

Onions: Not all onions are the same, not even remotely so! Onions have vastly varying degrees of sweetness (and therefore inherent sugar), sulphur, pungency, and water content, all of which factor into how they will taste as well as how they will behave when processed. An onion high in sugar is likely to burn in far less time even with the application of less heat than one that is not. Onions with high water content behave differently when sautéed or sweated. Unless specifically stated otherwise, presume that an "onion" refers to a yellow storage onion that you purchase in bulk in those net begs. In addition, a "large" onion, unless specifically called a Spanish onion, means grab one of the largest ones in the bag. They are NOT interchangeable, and (well-written) recipes are developed with that in mind. (And while we're on the subject, a scallion is also not a chive.)

Panko: An unflavored, large-flaked type of Japanese breadcrumb, made from soft, fluffy white bread that, when fried or deep-fried, makes for a wonderfully crunchy crust. Panko comes toasted or plain and sometimes has honey added, presumably to enhance the color when fried—we prefer the plain.

Parchment paper: Good-quality parchment paper is a heavy heat-, moisture-, and grease-resistant paper with multiple uses, and we cannot imagine managing a kitchen without it. It is used for everything from lining baking pans and pizza stones, making disposable piping bags for small jobs, and baking *en papillote* (in a bag) to the initial wrapping of foods to be frozen. Invest in the good stuff (see the chapter "Resources")—the flimsy supermarket stuff that comes on a roll is usually worthless and will burn in a heartbeat.

Peelers: One of our pet peeves is dull peelers. We are stunned by the number of kitchens we've tried to work in where the peeler is a hand-me-down antique from a long-dead ancestor and that cannot even cut butter. Go to a cookware store and play with the traditional as well as the Y-shaped ones. Buy the one you like. Buy several. They're cheap. And when they are no longer sharp, replace them. Dull blades are not only worthless, they're dangerous.

Pentola: An insert with a handle for a stockpot or pasta pot that looks like a pail with holes in it. Once you own one, you'll wonder what you ever did without it. A pentola is extremely useful for quickly removing and draining pasta and blanched foods from boiling water and is invaluable for refreshing cooked pasta just before saucing, especially if the water will continue to be used.

Phyllo: Also spelled "filo," this is a Middle Eastern tissue-thin pastry dough made with flour and water, used for both sweet and savory pastries. It is usually used in multiple layers that are brushed with a moisturizing fat such as butter, as it dries out quickly, becoming brittle and flaky and unmanageable. Phyllo is readily available frozen in supermarkets and is also available fresh in Middle Eastern markets. Frozen phyllo should be defrosted overnight in the refrigerator and, despite the package assurances, probably should not be refrozen, as it adds to its tendency to be brittle.

Ponzu: A tart Japanese citrus and vinegar dipping sauce. Authentic ponzu contains yuzu juice, which can be approximated with a mixture of lime, lemon, and orange juices.

Puff pastry: A rich, delicate multilayered pastry or pastry dough that, when baked, puffs and separates into hundreds of thin, flaky, buttery layers. The French name for puff pastry is *pâte feuilletée*. It is available frozen in most supermarkets, although most brands are made with hydrogenated fats and contain numerous unpronounceable chemicals. There are a few brands that contain only the classic ingredients of flour, butter, and maybe a touch of lemon juice. These are definitely worth seeking out (see the chapter "Resources"). Always thaw puff pastry overnight in the refrigerator—it needs to be consistently chilled all the way through in order to puff properly when baked.

Ricer: The tool of choice for creating the fluffiest mashed potatoes and also great for cooked root vegetables, a ricer (aka potato ricer) resembles a giant garlic press. It is a device into which cooked food is placed and pushed through tiny holes about the size of grains of rice. Ricers are quite inexpensive and are available in cookware shops and some supermarkets. A foodmill is a perfect substitute.

Ring molds: These are the essential equipment for constructing "towering" food, as well as for shaping and forming just about anything into a circle, disk, or muffin/biscuit shape. They vary in both diameter and depth as well as in grade—they can be as simple and flimsy as an English muffin ring or heavy duty and expensive, ranging around $8 to $10 in professional cookware outlets. Ring molds can be made of metal, which is suitable for baking, or cut from PVC pipe, which, although not for use with heat, are perfect for frozen concoctions. You can also sometimes substitute with a can, both ends removed with a can opener, if you can find the old-fashioned type of can without the new user-friendly rounded bottom designed to facilitate stacking. Beware, if you go the converted can route, of dangerous sharp edges!

Salt: We could write a book on salt. Actually, someone has. We'll cut to the chase:

KOSHER SALT: It is the cleanest, purest land salt and is also referred to as coarse salt. It's the salt we most often cook with, as it broadcasts easily, has no "off" or distinctive flavors, and allows room for error because it takes less kosher salt to fill a measure than finely ground salt and therefore one tends to err on the side of under- rather than over-salting. And it melts the ice off our porch. We do not use kosher salt for baking.

SEA SALT: This is, as its generic name implies, salt harvested from the sea, and it is available finely ground and coarse as well as in damp flakes known as *fleur du sel* and gray, damp flakes known as *sel gris* (or gray salt). Depending on its regional origin, sea salt has a variety of flavors that are often herbaceous. It is usually perceived to be saltier than land salt; however, we suspect this is really due to the fact that it is briny. We do not use sea salt for baking.

TABLE SALT: Right. This is the stuff in the cardboard canister and comes plain or fortified with iodine (iodized), which our government lovingly determined we need to prevent certain thyroid disorders and therefore made available to everyone in a product we all use and use often. Your call. We bake with table salt.

Sambal oelek A specific type of red chile paste available in Asian markets.

Sheet pan: Also known and referred to as baking sheets, these are usually aluminum trays with rolled 1-inch-high sides. They are also available with coated nonstick interiors, dark or light. We prefer the inexpensive garden-variety plain aluminum, and when we're looking for nonstick, we line them with parchment paper. For home purposes, a standard sheet pan is about 12 inches by 18 inches, although this is actually referred to in professional kitchens as a half-sheet. Probably more than you wanted to know.

Spaetzle maker: A nonessential but nifty piece of equipment with colanderlike holes used to make (you guessed it) spaetzle, yummy little German or Austrian noodle dumplings traditionally made with flour, eggs, and milk or water and briefly boiled before sauceing. If you don't plan to prepare spaetzle on a weekly basis, consider using a large-holed colander—it works pretty well.

Sriracha: This fiery Southeast Asian chili sauce has become ubiquitous. It's available everywhere Asian food products are sold and the most common brand comes in clear plastic bottles with green squirt tops and is called Tuong Ot. We use it to make spicy tuna by mixing it to taste (hot!) with mayonnaise, chopped sashimi-grade raw tuna, and chopped scallions.

Stock: If you have the time, space, and inclination to make your own stock, we admire you. We don't. If you don't either, buy it frozen, in cardboard cartons, or in dehydrated hockey-puck form. Herewith, we briefly define the differences between stock, demi-glace, and broth.

BROTH: An extraction similar to stock but is often lighter in strength and flavor and is seasoned with salt. It is also sometimes referred to as bouillon. A good-quality canned low-sodium, fat-free broth such as Swanson's Natural Goodness can often stand in for stock as long as care is taken to reduce or eliminate the salt called for in the recipe.

STOCK: A strained liquid extraction usually with the addition of a mirepoix and made by gently simmering poultry, meat, or fish bones and scraps and/or cartilaginous parts. A brown stock differs from a white stock in that the bones of a brown stock are first roasted to enhance and strengthen its flavor. Stock can also be made with only vegetables or mushrooms and is traditionally unsalted.

DEMI-GLACE: French for "half-glaze." It is a thick reduction by half of a blend of Madeira- or sherry-enhanced brown sauce and brown stock.

Sugar: As all salts are not alike, neither certainly are sugars. A short primer prepared only for our purposes here:

GRANULATED: Everyday table sugar found in five-pound bags. It is white and refined from cane or beet sugar. It is used when the type of sugar in a recipe is unspecified.

SUPERFINE: This is granulated sugar that is finely ground and dissolves almost instantly, making it very useful for cold drinks and meringue-based desserts.

LIGHT BROWN SUGAR: A sweet refined sugar with a light coating of molasses and used when brown sugar is called for but the type is not specified.

DARK BROWN SUGAR: A strong-tasting, extremely sweet refined sugar with a heavier coating of molasses.

CONFECTIONERS' SUGAR: Also called powdered sugar or 10-X, this sugar not only is powdered but also contains cornstarch. It is NOT interchangeable with other sugars and is used primarily for dusting and icings.

Tamari soy: Made from soybeans but aged, slightly thicker, less pungent, and more mellow than regular soy, tamari is soy sauce with a college degree. It is used mostly as a condiment, in sauces, and for marinating and basting.

Thermometers:

INSTANT-READ: A small thermometer with a narrow stem used to measure the internal temperature of foods by inserting the probe about two inches into the food and holding it for just a few moments until a stable reading is obtained and then removing it.

MEAT: A slight larger thermometer than an instant-read, ovenproof, and of sturdier construction that is inserted into meat and left in place during roasting. Meat thermometers are usually marked with indications for doneness of various types of meat (beef, lamb, pork).

OVEN: An invaluable tool that is unfortunately not used as often as it should be, an oven thermometer is used to determine the ambient temperature of the oven. When properly used— that is, once an oven has been allowed the necessary thirty to forty minutes to fully preheat—it determines the accuracy of the oven's temperature. Buy one. They're cheap. And your oven's probably off temp. They do that.

Tongs: We like tongs. Tongs are most useful, and we found them used more often than not in the restaurants we visited. They work better than forks for lifting and repositioning things and don't leaves holes in the food. We especially like the OXO brand, which are heavyweight and have rubber grips on the handles and a locking mechanism with a hook for hanging.

Truc: This is French for kitchen trick (pronounced trewk), usually referring to a neat method, technique, or shortcut used by chefs or other culinary pros.

Vermouth: Many wines are used for cooking, depending on the application and the desired outcome, but most recipes, unless for a specific defined use such as in a chardonnay sauce, simply call for dry white wine. Unless the preparation is a sweet dessert such as poached pears, we almost invariably substitute white or dry vermouth. Vermouth is dry white wine that has been enhanced with herbs and spices, the combinations of which vary with regional origin and winery. To us, that defines it as already food-friendly, and we take advantage of that. We even go so far as to use Italian vermouth in Italian dishes and French vermouth in French cooking, surmising that the herbs and spices used are likely those that best enhance that cuisine. Even within the same provenance of country or region, vermouths can vary greatly in flavor—we suggest you do as we did and sample all the various brands before settling on the one that best suits your tastes. It's a dirty job, but you'll be rewarded in the end.

Wooden spoons and paddles: We don't completely get the wooden spoon thing. We generally reach for paddles or wooden forks. Wooden spoons have rounded edges. Pans, skillets, and the like are flat. Trying to do anything other than draw lines on the bottom of the pan is nearly impossible with a wooden spoon. Paddles, on the other hand, do a very efficient job of deglazing a pan or nudging food where you want it to go. And trying to taste something from a shallow wooden spoon is an exercise in frustration—if you're lucky enough to actually get something up on it, it's likely you'll be wearing it before it ever gets to your mouth.

A LAST WORD ON EQUIPMENT:

Make the investment. Your time in the kitchen should be efficiently spent and enjoyable, and struggling with poor or insufficient equipment takes away from that.

resources

Beauty and the Feast, Inc.
320 South Street
Morristown, NJ 07960
(973) 292-0904
www.beautyandthefeast.com

Benriner Asian Mandolines

Chile Today—Hot Tamale
31 Richboynton Road
Dover, NJ 07801
(800) Hot-Pepper—(800) 468-7377
www.chiletoday.com

Dried whole and ground chiles, hot sauces, salsa mixes, etc.

D'Artagnan
280 Wilson Avenue
Newark, NJ 07105
(800) 327-8246
www.dartagnan.com

Duck (fresh, smoked, and confit), demi-glace, duck fat, foie gras, game, game birds, pâtés, truffle butter, wild mushrooms, variety of duck and game sausages, etc.

Delicious Orchards
36 Highway 34 South
Colts Neck, NJ 07722
(732) 462-1989

Baked goods, imported cheeses, fresh produce, specialty items, truffle oil, etc.

East Brunswick Fish Market
328 State Route 18
East Brunswick, NJ 08816
(732) 238-6161

Fresh fish, shellfish, seafood, prepared fish specialties, etc.

Fossil Farms Ostrich
294 West Oakland Avenue
Oakland, NJ 07436
(201) 651-1190
www.fossilfarmsostrich.com

Ostrich, alligator, buffalo, caribou, frog, pheasant, rabbit, turtle, wild boar, wild game meats, etc.

Freeman Fish Market
155 Maplewood Avenue
Maplewood, NJ 07040
(973) 763-9363

Fresh fish, seafood.

Garden of Eden Gourmet
162 West Twenty-third Street
New York, NY 10010
(212) 675-6300
www.gardenofedengourmet.com

Fresh produce, imported cheeses, imported specialty items, Looza fruit nectars, etc.

Griggstown Quail Farm
986 Canal Road
Princeton, NJ 08540
(908) 359-5375
www.griggstownquailfarm.com

Natural game birds: pheasants, poussins, quail, quail eggs, turkeys, etc.

Hong Kong Supermarkets
275 Route 18
East Brunswick, NJ 08816
(908) 238-2384

3600 Park Avenue
South Plainfield, NJ 07080
(908) 668-8862

Asian products and ingredients, Asian condiments, fresh produce, fresh seafood and shellfish, cookware, etc.

Kam Man Supermarkets
200 Route 10 West
East Hanover, NJ 07934
(973) 503-1770

828 Route 46
Parsippany, NJ 07054
(973) 299-1881

Asian products and ingredients, Asian condiments, fresh produce, fresh seafood and shellfish, cookware, etc.

King Arthur Flour and
King Arthur Baker's Catalogue
Route 5 South
Norwich, VT
(800) 827-6836
www.kingarthurflour.com

Flour and specialty flours, baking equipment and supplies, parchment paper, spices, etc.

Klein's Fish Market
708 River Road
Belmar, NJ 07719
(732) 681-1177
www.kleinsfish.com

Fresh fish, shellfish, seafood, prepared foods, etc.

More Than Gourmet
929 Home Avenue
Akron, Ohio 44310
(800) 860-9385
www.morethangourmet.com

Classically made concentrated meat, shellfish, and vegetable stocks, demi-glace, etc.

Sugar Ranch
P.O. BOX 608
Goshen, CA 93227
(800) 821-5989
www.fennelpollen.com

Fennel pollen

Summit Cheese Shop
75 Union Place
Summit, NJ 07901
(908) 273-7700

Imported cheeses, jams, etc.

The Greek Store
612 Boulevard
Kenilworth, NJ 07033
(908) 272-2550

Phyllo, Greek cheeses and olives, specialty foods, halvah, kataiffi, prepared foods, etc.

Wegman's Markets
724 Route 202 South
Bridgewater, NJ 08807
(908) 243-9600

55 U.S. Route 9 South
Manalapan, NJ 07726
(732) 625-4100

240 Nassau Park Boulevard
Princeton, NJ 08540
(609) 919-9300
www.wegmans.com

Artisanal breads and baked goods, D'Artagnan products, French green du puy lentils, fresh produce, fresh meats, fish and shellfish, imported cheeses, Niman ranch natural meats and applewood-smoked bacon, specialty items, truffle oils, wild mushrooms, etc.

what you eat

Would you put soda in the gas tank or engine of your car? Why not? Because you know it's bad for the car and will cause it to break down.

But although you'd destroy the workings of the car and have to replace it, your car is replaceable.

When you put bad, unhealthy, or inappropriate stuff into your body, the result's the same—you eventually ruin the workings and the "vehicle" breaks down. The problem is rather more serious, though, because you can't go out and buy a new one. You only get one body and it's therefore crucial that you take the very best care of it that you can.

We're not exclusionary eaters or fanatic dieters. We're feet-on-the-ground homo sapien omnivores. We eat happily from every food group and try to do it with variety and as often as possible. But we draw the line at processed foods, chemically engineered foods, protein that's been frozen, genetically manipulated food, and produce out of its natural season.

Why? That's also another book! But suffice to say that in the simplest sense, it tastes better, it's nutritionally better for us, we can almost instantly see and feel the difference when we don't observe these facts or fail to respect the exquisitely designed machines our bodies are. And we won't even get into the politics or life-threatening cost in health and the financial costs of health care we all bear from giving in to the convenience of the megabusiness of bad food.

Don't compromise what goes into your body. Ever. You only get the one you have and you need and want to take the very best care of it that you can. Here are a couple of resources to help educate ourselves and our children and make the healthiest choices—and to send a grassroots message to the food suppliers of America that we are reeducating ourselves and our children to spend our money on healthy choices:

WHOLE FOODS MARKETS

905 River Road
Edgewater, NJ 07020
(201) 941-4000
www.wholefoods.com

222 Main Street
Madison, NJ 07940
(973) 822-0192

Greentree Square Shopping Circle
940 Route 73 North
Marlton, NJ 08053
(856) 797-1115

187 Millburn Avenue
Millburn, NJ 07041
(973) 376-4668

701 Bloomfield Avenue
Montclair, NJ 07042
(973) 746-5110

Ridgewood Plaza
44 Godwin Place
Ridgewood, NJ 07450
(201) 670-0383

Large selection of organic and conventional produce; fresh fish and seafood; all-natural hormone-free meat and poultry; high-quality traditional grocery items from baby foods and paper products to pasta sauces, salsa, and chips; bulk foods such as specialty flours, granolas, sulfite-free dried fruits and nuts, beans and grains; skin and hair care products; supplements and herbs that are naturally made, free of artificial preservatives and dyes and cruelty free; books and gift items; classic, organic, and artisan cheeses; patés, olives, homemade pastas, sauces and spreads, handcrafted, sustainably grown coffees; large selection of international teas and coffee alternatives; artisan breads and baked goods free of preservatives, artificial additives, and colors' gluten-, wheat-, dairy-, and sugar-free products; prepared foods; as well as sushi, tofu and grain-based dishes, etc.

Whole Foods Market is the world's largest retailer of natural and organic foods, uniquely mission-driven and highly selective about what it sells, dedicated to stringent quality goals and committed to sustainable agriculture.

Products are obtained locally and from all over the world, often from small, uniquely dedicated food artisans, and consist of the highest-quality, least-processed, most flavorful and naturally preserved foods—unadulterated by artificial additives, sweeteners, colorings, and preservatives.

For information on joining your local chapter of Slow Food USA:

Slow Food U.S.A. National Office
434 Broadway, 7th Floor
New York, NY 10013
Tel: 212-965-5640
Fax: 212-226-0672
Email: info@slowfoodusa.org

Soon after you have joined Slow Food, you will begin receiving invitations from your local convivium.

. . . and don't neglect to patronize local New Jersey's farmer's markets!
For schedules and information on Jersey Fresh, send a self-addressed, stamped envelope to:

The New Jersey Council of
Farmers & Communities
PO Box 1114
Madison, NJ 07940

a word on awards

THERE ARE TOO MANY AWARDS to define in these pages, and therefore, for fear of leaving some out, we've chosen to forgo listing all the many well-deserved awards the restaurants have earned.

However, some awards do stand out more than others, especially those from peer organizations. We think these are restaurants you'll want to pay attention to when you come across them. So for purposes of definition, we've listed a couple of the more outstanding awards.

DIRŌNA

Distinguished Restaurants of North America, founded in 1990, is a nonprofit organization governed by an independent board of directors. Its mission is to preserve and promote the ultimate in distinguished dining throughout Canada, Mexico, and the United States.

The DiRōNA award program was launched in 1992, and "The Award Of Excellence" is given to restaurants exemplifying the highest-quality standards in all aspects of the dining experience.

The Award Inspection Program is the ONLY independent and anonymous restaurant inspection program in North America.

Award qualification requires a restaurant to be in business under the same ownership for three years and pass a seventy-five-point evaluation conducted by trained industry professionals. The recipient retains the award for three years by maintaining all requirements and standards of excellence and is then reinspected.

The inspection team is composed of forty inspectors specially trained and qualified to evaluate restaurants throughout North America. All inspections are conducted anonymously, and the inspectors analyze all aspects of the dining experience from reservations through departure.

WINE SPECTATOR AWARDS OF EXCELLENCE

The basic award is the Award of Excellence. This award recognizes a commitment to a fine wine list, with a selection of better producers along with a thematic match to the menu in both price and style. There are no rules regarding the minimum number of selections a wine list must have, but most of the Award of Excellence lists generally have at least seventy-five selections.

The intermediate award, the Best of Award of Excellence, was created to give special recognition to those restaurants who exceed the basic category. These lists must display vintage depth, including vertical offerings of several top wines, as well as excellent breadth from several major wine-growing regions. A Best of Award of Excellence wine list generally provides 350 or more offerings.

The highest award is the Grand Award, which is given to those restaurants that show an uncompromising, passionate devotion to quality. These lists show serious depth of mature vintages, outstanding breadth in vertical offerings, excellent harmony with the menu, and superior organization and presentation. Most Grand Award wine lists have one thousand or more selections.

GOURMET MAGAZINE'S LIST OF AMERICA'S 50 TOP TABLES

This annual list, which includes only restaurants more than two years old, is a roster of valedictorians, the finest restaurants in the United States.

RELAIS & CHÂTEAUX

Relais & Châteaux is a unique association of restaurants, hotels, and inns, often called the "finest association in the world" by its clients. These properties of exceptional character offer a personalized welcome and varied services in a peaceful setting.

The Relais Gourmands are the award-winning restaurants of Relais & Châteaux. They are renowned for their excellent cuisine and feature some of the world's best contemporary chefs. Atmosphere, décor, service, wine cellar, and cuisine come together in these restaurants to embody the highest culinary standards in the world to provide their patrons with the very best in fine and elegant dining.

There are 460 Relais & Chateau "properties" in fifty-one countries throughout the world. Of these, 154 restaurants in twenty countries have been awarded their prestigious Relais Gourmand designation. They are ambassadors of French *art de vivre*. Fifteen Relais Gourmand restaurants are located in the United States.

AMERICAN ACADEMY OF HOSPITALITY SCIENCES FIVE-STAR DIAMOND AWARD

Each year the American Academy of Hospitality selects outstanding establishments for their unsurpassed commitment to the hospitality industry and acknowledges these "crown jewels" of the hospitality industry.

recipe index

*Savoy Cabbage-Wrapped Pekin Duck
with a Warm Salad of Lentils, Smoked Bacon
and Garlic Confit,*
Stage House Inn, 130

*Arugula Salad with Crispy Duck Confit and Lemon-
Garlic Vinaigrette,*
The Harvest Moon Inn, 56

SEAFOOD

*PEI Mussels and Linguine with Chorizo,
Tomatoes, and Scallions and Pernod,*
Doris & Ed's, 35

Soft-Shell Crab BLT,
Anton's at the Swan, 6

Malaysian Seafood Bouillabaise,
A Taste of Asia, 134

*Filo-Wrapped Shrimp with Thai Slaw
and Soy Vinaigrette,*
Amanda's, 2

*Pan-Roasted Pork Chop with
Littleneck Clams, Wild Mushrooms,
and Tomatoes in a Sherry Wine Sauce,*
Joe & Maggie's Bistro on Broadway, 76

*Pan-Seared Red Snapper with Roasted Jersey Corn Hash
and Smoked Yellow Tomato Coulis,*
Arthur's Landing, 8

*Salmon Filet in Filo with Maine Lobster Claws
on Chive Beurre Blanc,*
Black Forest Inn, 15

*Dusted and Glazed Scallops with
Potato Pancake, Seared Foie Gras,
and Vanilla-Almond Vinaigrette,*
Café Matisse, 18

Fiery Garlic Shrimp Quesadillas,
Casa Comida, 23

*Lobster, Leek, and Mascarpone Dumplings
with Lobster-Brandy Sauce,*
Daniel's on Broadway, 28

Fromagerie Lobster Sausage,
Fromagerie, 47

*Fried Chesapeake Bay Oysters with
Sun-Dried Tomato Aioli,*
Giumarello's, 50

*Branzino al Sale alla Erbe Aromatiche
(Sea Bass in a Salt Crust with Herbs),*
Il Capriccio, 62

*Lobster Salad with Mango-Basil Quenelle
and Truffled Vanilla Aioli with Microgreens
in Champagne Vinaigrette,*
Jocelyne's, 73

Tuna Tataki
Kuishimbo, 79

*Crab Cake Sandwich with
Roasted Pepper-Garlic Mayonnaise,*
Mad Batter, 87

Shrimp and Scallop Seviche,
Moonstruck, 93

*Sformata di Aragosta e Riso
(Lobster Risotto Cake with
Honey-Lemon Beurre Blanc),*
Panico's, 101

*Soft-Shell Crabs with Jersey Asparagus with Grape
Tomato Confit and Beurre Blanc,*
Pierre's Bistro Restaurant, 107

*Salad of Spicy Greens with Wok-Fried Squid
and Chili Aioli,*
Rat's, 113

*Pignoli-Crusted Salmon in a
Pinot Grigio-Shallot Reduction Sauce,*
Scalini Fedeli, 124